I0793068

IMAGES
of Modern America

LAWRENCE PARK AND WESLEYVILLE

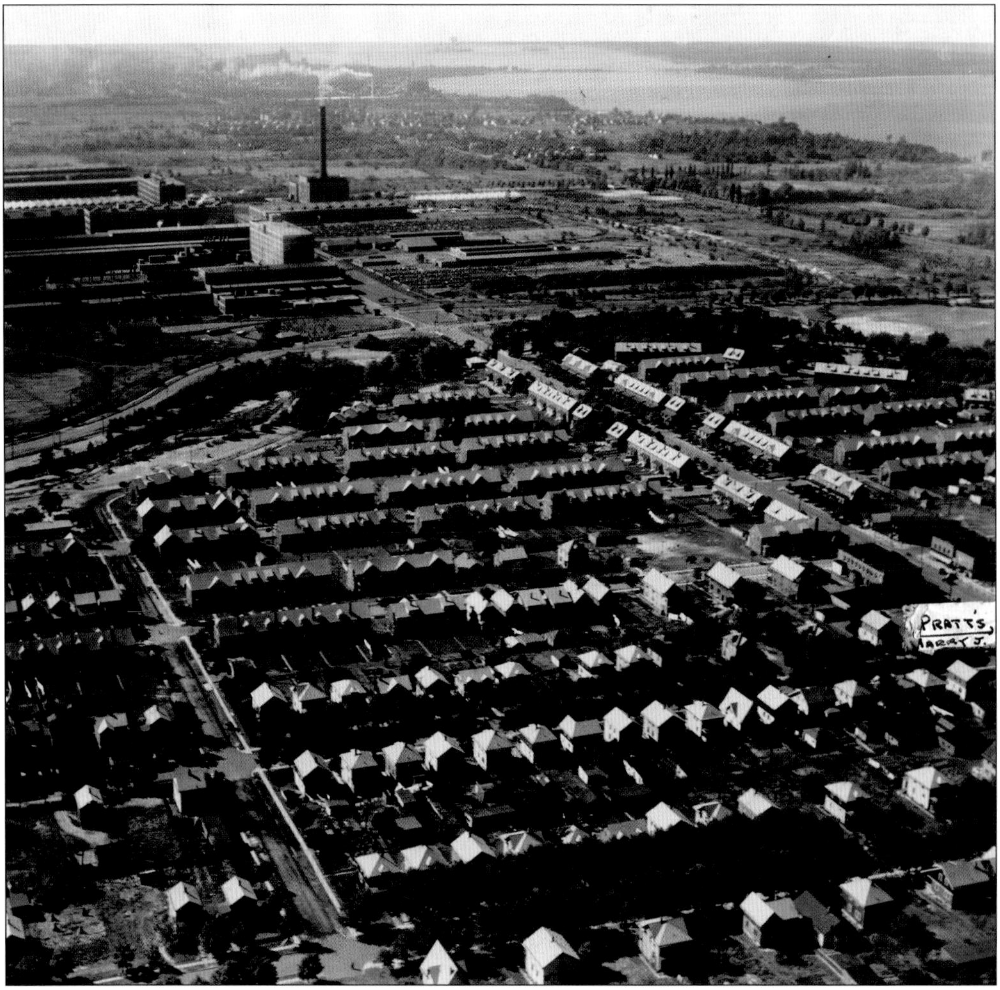

The above photograph is an aerial view of Lawrence Park and the General Electric Company Erie Works from the 1950s. Lawrence Park, with its neat rows of single-family homes and row houses, is shown at the center of the photograph. The diagonal street is Main Street, which leads to the east gate of the General Electric Company buildings. A view of Lake Erie is at the top right of the photograph. (Courtesy of the Lawrence Park Historical Society.)

ON THE FRONT COVER: Clockwise from top left:
Emory "Red" Hinkler Park (see page 34), Beute Park gazebo (see page 26), Four Mile Creek (see page 36), the Stone House (see page 14), Mary Ripley Park (see page 27)

ON THE BACK COVER: Clockwise from top left:
Veterans Memorial Park (see page 30), Iroquois High School Cadets Fourth of July parade (Courtesy of Howard Luthey), Iroquois Elementary School kindergarten field trip (Author's collection)

IMAGES
of Modern America

Lawrence Park and Wesleyville

Marjorie D. McLean

ARCADIA
PUBLISHING

ISBN 978-1-4671-3410-1

Published by Arcadia Publishing
Charleston, South Carolina

Printed in the United States of America

Library of Congress Control Number: 2015938948

For all general information, please contact Arcadia Publishing:
Telephone 843-853-2070
Fax 843-853-0044
E-mail sales@arcadiapublishing.com
For customer service and orders:
Toll-Free 1-888-313-2665

Visit us on the Internet at www.arcadiapublishing.com

To my 25-member extended family from Lawrence Park and Wesleyville who have shared their many stories during Sunday dinners

Contents

ACKNOWLEDGMENTS

In the words of Richard Cheney, Wesleyville historian, "We realize that were it not for the past and the people in it, we would have no present with which to contend." The history of Wesleyville has been chronicled in great detail by Richard Cheney and Debbi Lyon and some of it preserved in the Wesleyville Borough Hall. I relied heavily on the archives of the Lawrence Park Historical Society and wish to thank all those members who have preserved its history in words and photographs, especially Howard Luthey, Dick Chilcott, and Art Bennett.

Many thanks to the team of Jim and Rachel Van Dyne, whose computer knowledge and willingness to devote hours to scanning photographs was invaluable. They also offered constant help and encouragement when problems arose. Thanks also to Dale Sweet. My appreciation goes to Tom Crozier, former Social Studies teacher, whose efforts enabled this book to be built on the work he had done. Many thanks to Gerard Drozdowski, yearbook advisor, who supplied a multitude of photographs. Unless otherwise noted, images are courtesy of the author. I also wish to thank my editor at Arcadia Publishing, Lily Watkins, who has guided me through the complexities of bringing this book to fruition. Also, many thanks to my daughter Sue Johnson for her proofreading skills.

Recognition and gratitude are also given to the many administrators, teachers, coaches, school-board members, volunteers, and all other school personnel who have contributed, during the past 50 years, their time and expertise to the schools of these communities. The merger of the Wesleyville and Lawrence Park School Districts to become the Iroquois School District has bound our two communities together with pride in our young people as they journey through school and expectations for a bright future for them as they graduate and go forth into the world.

Introduction

Wesleyville and Lawrence Park, suburbs of Erie, Pennsylvania, had very different beginnings. One began as a farming community while the other was planned as a company town. However, 50 years ago, they joined forces in the most important aspect of any community, the education of their young people.

The area that Wesleyville now occupies was a wilderness when Thomas Rees acquired a large tract of land in 1795 in the area that became Harborcreek. In 1797, William Saltsman joined him, and many families soon settled on farms scattered around the area. Wesleyville had its start in 1810, when an itinerant preacher, the Reverend Joshua Monroe, held services near Buffalo Road, on the banks of Four Mile Creek. This area was recognized as an ideal location for a town, and families soon began to settle there.

The naming of Wesleyville is shrouded in mystery, but we do know it was named in honor of John Wesley, the founder of Methodism. In 1820, Capt. James Flower bought 193 acres, and in time he sold off a large tract to John Shadduck. Shadduck built a gristmill and a sawmill on the west bank of Four Mile Creek, which provided lumber for housing. In 1828, Shadduck laid out plans for the village of Wesleyville that would include buildings on both sides of Buffalo Road, with two roads to run parallel to Buffalo Road, North Street, and South Street, crossed by Center Street and Market Street.

Also, in 1828, John Shadduck deeded land for a fine redbrick Methodist church on the north side of Buffalo Road and land for a public burying ground. The cemetery contains the graves of Nancy and John Shadduck and Reverend Monroe and his wife and is still lovingly cared for by volunteers. Although families moved into Wesleyville and shops and taverns were established, there were only about 100 people living in Wesleyville by 1850. However, in 1852, the Erie & North East Railroad Company began regular service, and Wesleyville was designated as a depot.

In 1846, the Reverend John and Laura McLean were sent to the church in Wesleyville. After a series of revival meetings that preached against demon rum, Laura McLean organized a group of women who, armed with axes, marched into the saloons and quickly freed the evil spirits from their barrels.

Wesleyville was a part of Harborcreek and Millcreek until on May 31, 1912, the borough of Wesleyville was incorporated, and the seven-member borough council began to administer the affairs of Wesleyville.

Four Mile Creek, so named as it is four miles from downtown Erie, passes on the east side of Wesleyville then continues through the area that became Lawrence Park. Near the mouth of Four Mile Creek where it empties into Lake Erie, in 1797 Thomas Rees built a sawmill that provided the lumber to build the 30-ton sloop, the *Washington*, the first ship built on the south shore of Lake Erie.

In the early 1800s, Michael Crowley, an Irish immigrant, acquired a large tract of land along Four Mile Creek from the lakeshore south to what is now Wesleyville. In 1832, on East Lake Road, he built the sturdy Stone House that is still occupied. The road from East Lake Road south to Buffalo Road was known as Crowley Road. It was later named Lawrence Parkway, and today we know it as Water Street.

On the bank of Lake Erie near Four Mile Creek in 1888, Jacob Lang and Christian Rabe built a beautiful three-story hotel called the Grove House Park Hotel. The hotel could be accessed by boat from Erie to the hotel's 200-foot dock. The remains of the steps to the dock are still visible. The completion of the trolley line in 1901 gave patrons another way to arrive and enjoy the amenities of this hotel. Sadly, this elegant hotel was destroyed by fire in 1902. The hotel was not rebuilt, but Jacob Lang's son Alfred Lang began building the Four Mile Creek Amusement Park at this location. This lively entertainment spot had a dance hall, theater, midway, and rides, including a roller coaster.

In 1901, the East Sixth Street trolley traveled out East Lake Road, past Reed's Driving Park where horse races were held, and continued across what is now the Lawrence Park Golf Course. The trolley crossed Four Mile Creek on the steel bridge that still stands, and brought pleasure seekers to the Four Mile Creek Amusement Park. The park provided entertainment for many years until it burned to the ground in 1919. Today, the General Electric Company picnic grounds are located on this beautiful site on the bank of Lake Erie.

When the General Electric Company decided to build a "monster" plant at the Erie location, attorney James Sherwin was given the task of quietly buying up about 800 acres of land in the area east of Erie in what was then Harborcreek and Millcreek. There were only a few homes along East Lake Road. In 1907, the *Erie Daily Times* carried the headlines "General Electric Plant Will Come to Erie For a Certainty." This was great news for Wesleyville residents, and it was the beginning of Lawrence Park.

In addition to the plant, General Electric Company personnel designed a planned community for its employees and others. After much discussion, Matthew Griswold and James Sherwin named this town Lawrence Park in honor of Capt. James Lawrence, a courageous naval officer whose dying words were, "Don't give up the ship." The following streets were laid out: Field, Main, Iroquois, Spencer, Smithson, Silliman, and Rankine, and on May 29, 1911, the first building lots were offered for sale. Four Mile Creek played a part in the location of this new town, as the tree-lined creek banks provided a green barrier between the factory and the community.

By 1915, the town of Lawrence Park had, in addition to homes, several stores, a school building, and two churches. During World War I, the Erie Plant produced war materials and required many more employees who needed additional housing. In 1917–1918, two firms built the brick row-type homes that eventually accommodated 494 families. Traffic was beginning to increase, and in 1920, the dangerous railroad crossing on Water Street was eliminated by building a subway under the tracks. This necessitated lowering Four Mile Creek in that area.

Lawrence Park was a part of Harborcreek and Millcreek until February 8, 1926, when it became a first-class township administered by five commissioners. The Erie Plant of the General Electric Company built refrigerators in addition to locomotives, but World War II caused civilian production to cease while General Electric concentrated on the needs of war. Again, more housing was needed, so a trailer park was set up across from the main entrance of the General Electric plant. Also, White City, a concrete-block housing development that was painted white, was constructed. Wesleyville also felt the need for additional housing and so began to develop mobile-home parks.

In the years following World War II, production of refrigerators resumed in Erie until in the 1950s, when the company moved this operation to Appliance Park in Louisville, Kentucky. Many families in Lawrence Park and Wesleyville followed their jobs to this new location. In Lawrence Park, the new residential area of Lake Cliff in the late 1940s and Crotty Subdivision in the 1950s and in Wesleyville the area of College Heights increased the population of both communities.

In the early 1960s, it was mandated that small school districts must be merged, and a study of both Lawrence Park and Wesleyville schools indicated that a merger of the two school districts would be beneficial to both. This new district was named the Iroquois School District. It was decided that a new high school would be built on the vacant property that had previously been occupied by White City. The story of the history of these two communities and their school district continues as the Iroquois School District celebrates 50 years of educating its youth, so "Roll on Big I."

One

Communities

The communities of Wesleyville and Lawrence Park have developed in different ways. Wesleyville grew from a small pretty village that was located on both sides of Buffalo Road. It was part of Harborcreek until 1912 when it became a borough, governed by a seven-member council and a mayor. With the annexation of College Heights, Wesleyville expanded its area. The nearby General Electric Company provided employment to many individuals. The advent of malls on Buffalo Road in Harborcreek changed the nature of the Wesleyville business district; however, the district still maintains many basic services. Wesleyville was named for John Wesley, the founder of Methodism, so it is only natural for the Wesley United Methodist Church to be located here. The community also supports Lutheran, Baptist, and Catholic churches. The volunteer fire departments of Wesleyville and Lawrence Park offer mutual aid in times of need.

Lawrence Park had its beginnings in 1910 when the General Electric Company built a large factory and began a planned community that it named Lawrence Park. During World War I, the need for more housing was answered by the building of row houses in groups of 2, 6, 8, and even 10 that would accommodate 494 families. During World War II, temporary housing was provided by Hunt's Trailer Camp across from the General Electric factory and in White City that accommodated about 300 families. White City was razed when the housing crisis passed. In 1947, the residential area of Lake Cliff was begun and soon expanded to the lakefront, including Halley and Harvey Streets, which had been known as New Colony. In the early 1950s, David Crotty developed the Crotty Subdivision, which included the area from Smithson Avenue to Nagle Road and from East Lake Road to Iroquois Avenue. In the 1960s, the area that had been the site of White City became the prime location for the new high school when the two communities merged their school districts to become the Iroquois School District. Although the two communities had different beginnings, the people and organizations of both communities have always cared for the needs of others and have supported their schools in providing educational opportunities for all students.

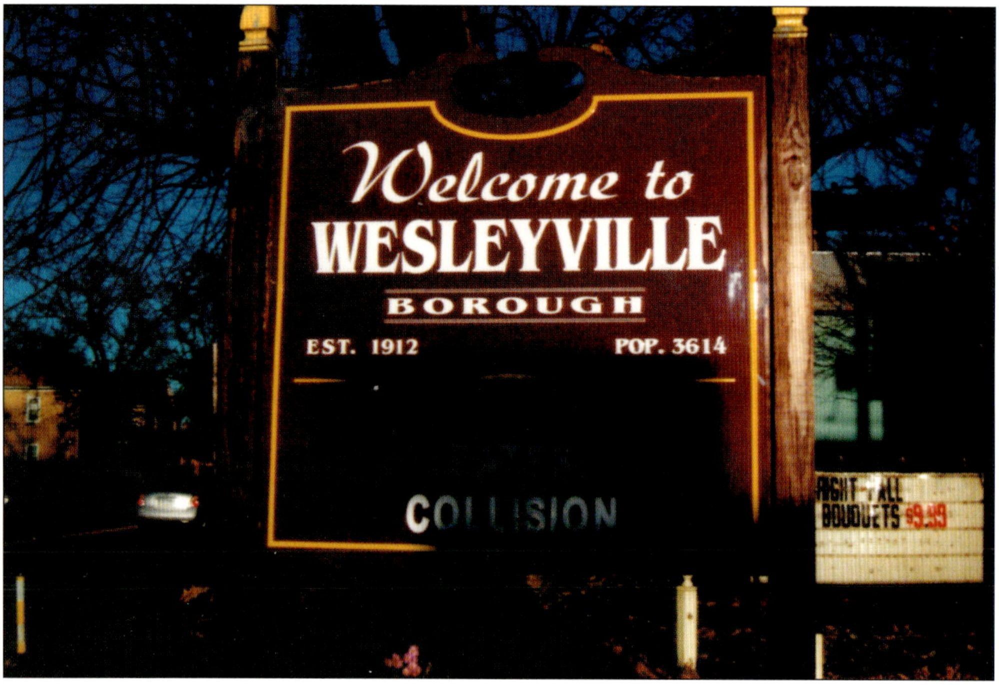

The Welcome to Wesleyville sign not only extends a welcome, but also gives the date that Wesleyville became a borough (1912) and the current population (3,614). Signs like this, provided by Bates Collision, identify the boundaries of Wesleyville. These signs are on the eastern and western boundaries of Wesleyville on Buffalo Road, the northern boundary on Water Street, and the southern boundary on Shannon Road.

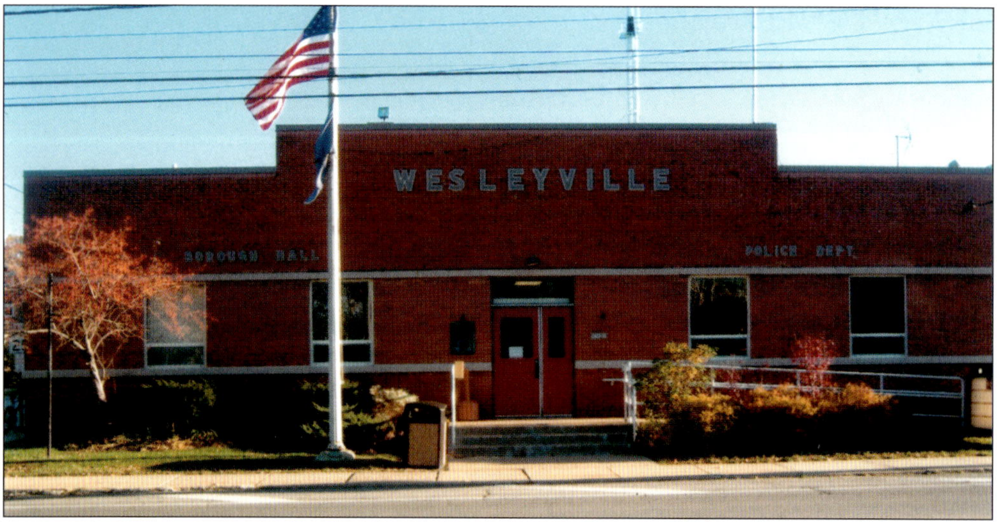

The Wesleyville Borough Hall was built on Buffalo Road and Market Street in 1954 and provides borough offices and police headquarters. The plaque on the front of the hall lists the seven councilmen who held office at the time the borough hall was built. Wesleyville was incorporated as the Borough of Wesleyville on May 31, 1912, when the borough council met at Chaffee Hall.

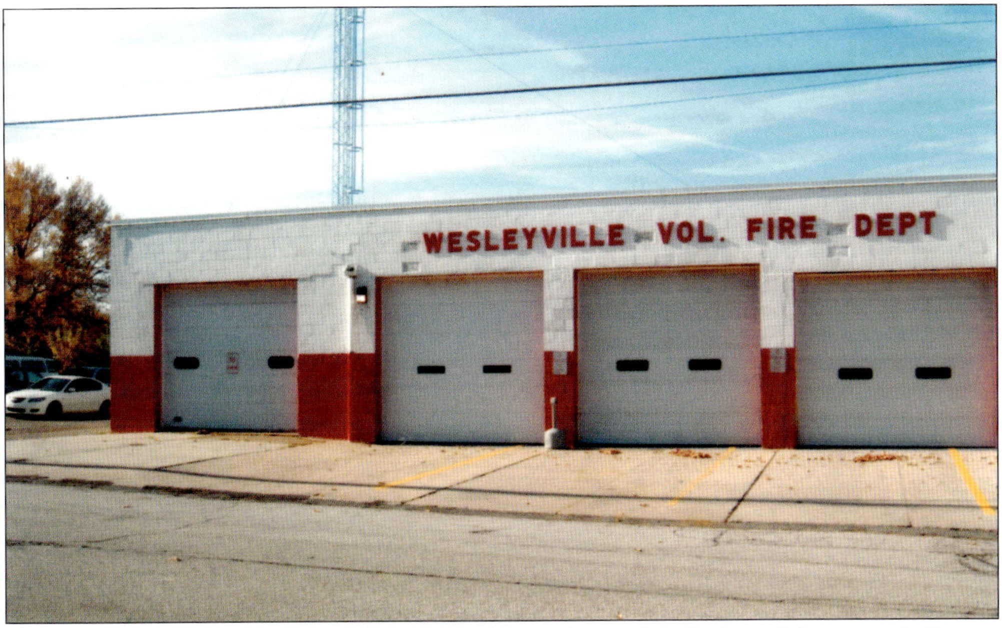

The Wesleyville Volunteer Fire Hall is attached to the borough hall. One of the many challenges that the volunteers have faced was fighting the Nickel Plate Mills fire on October 30, 1956. At the time of the fire, the mill had hay and feed stored inside. This feed mill on Buffalo Road had a platform across the whole front that was a popular gathering place to sit and watch the world go by.

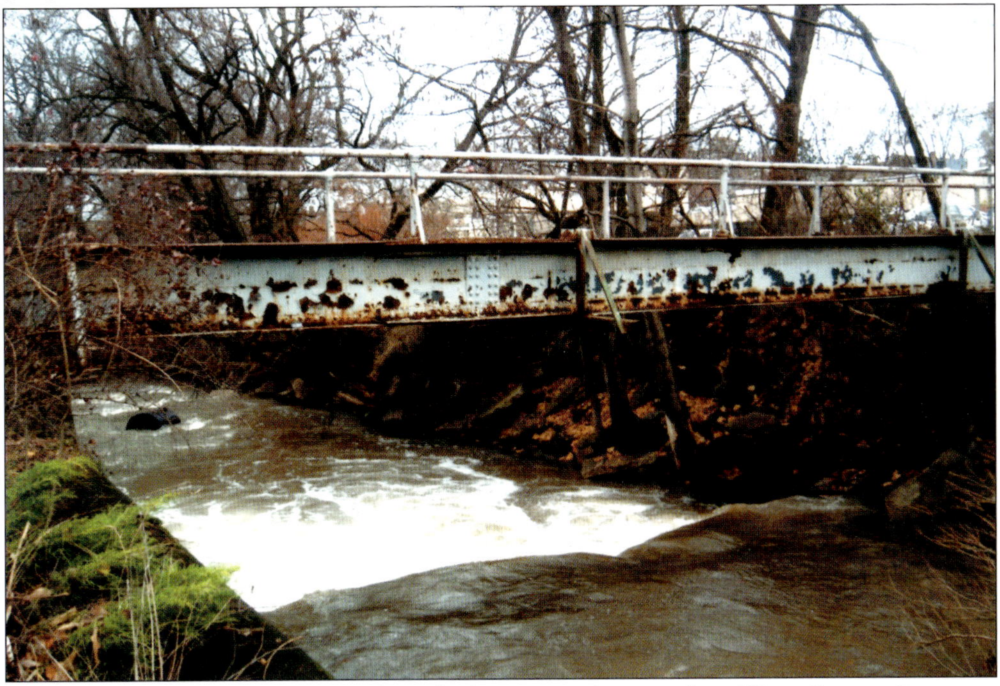

Four Mile Creek flows under this bridge, which carries pedestrians from Water Street to Lawrence Park. Since 1923, the bridge has been a shortcut for students and other walkers going to and from Wesleyville and Lawrence Park. It is another connecting link between the two communities.

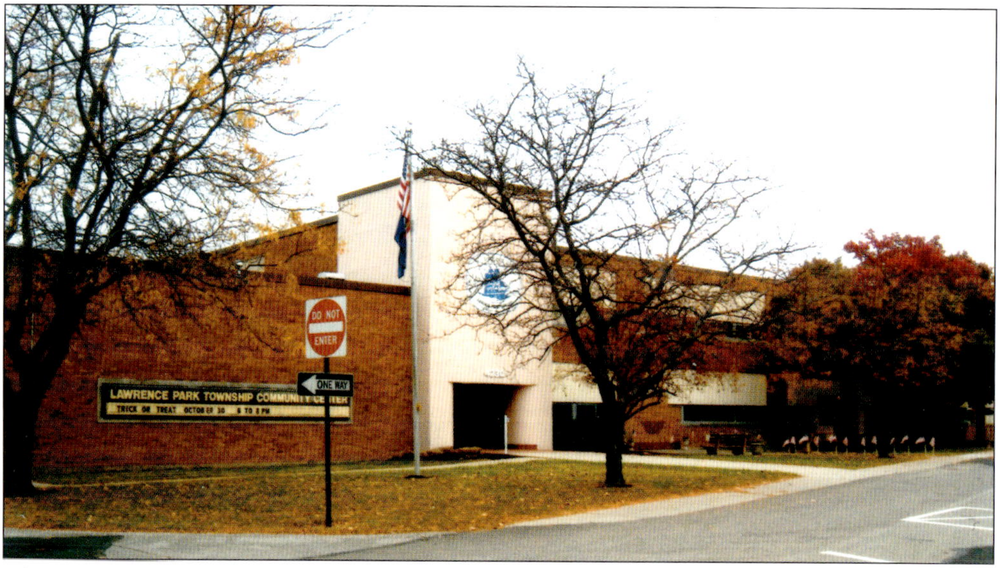

The Lawrence Park Township Community Center was constructed in 1952 and originally built to serve as Primary School. Some time after Iroquois High School was finished in 1966 and there was no longer a need for the Primary School Building, it was sold. Eventually, this building was acquired by the Lawrence Park Township and dedicated on December 6, 1987, as the Lawrence Park Township Community Center.

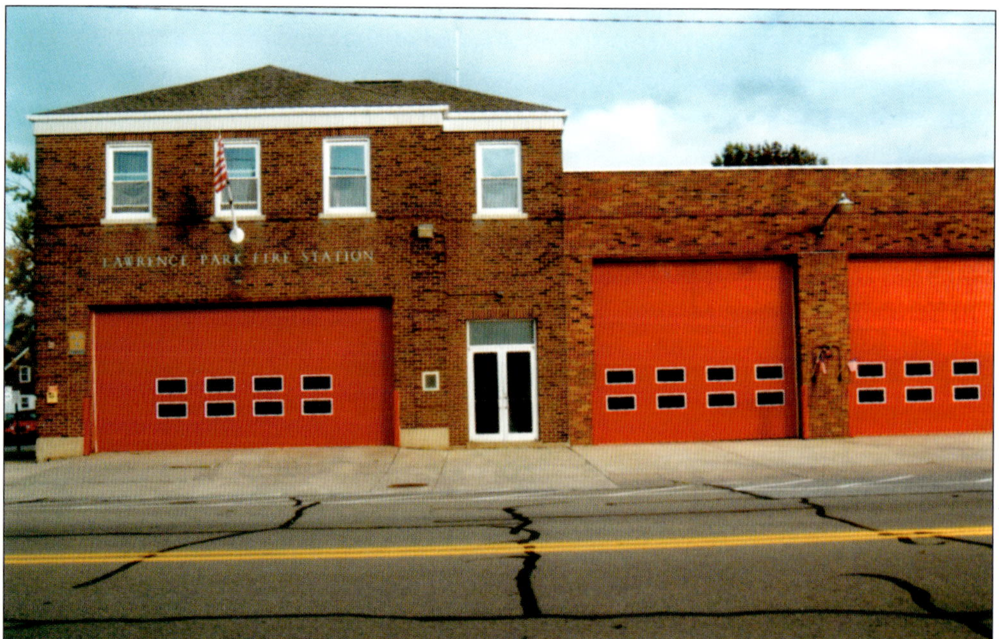

The Lawrence Park Volunteer Fire Department Fire Hall was built on Main Street and Silliman Avenue in 1938. In 1972, an addition provided the high doors for larger fire-and-rescue equipment. The first firehouse was built in the 1920s on Rankine Avenue just off Main Street and is still standing. Volunteer firefighters from both communities not only fight fires and respond to emergencies, but also take part in many community activities.

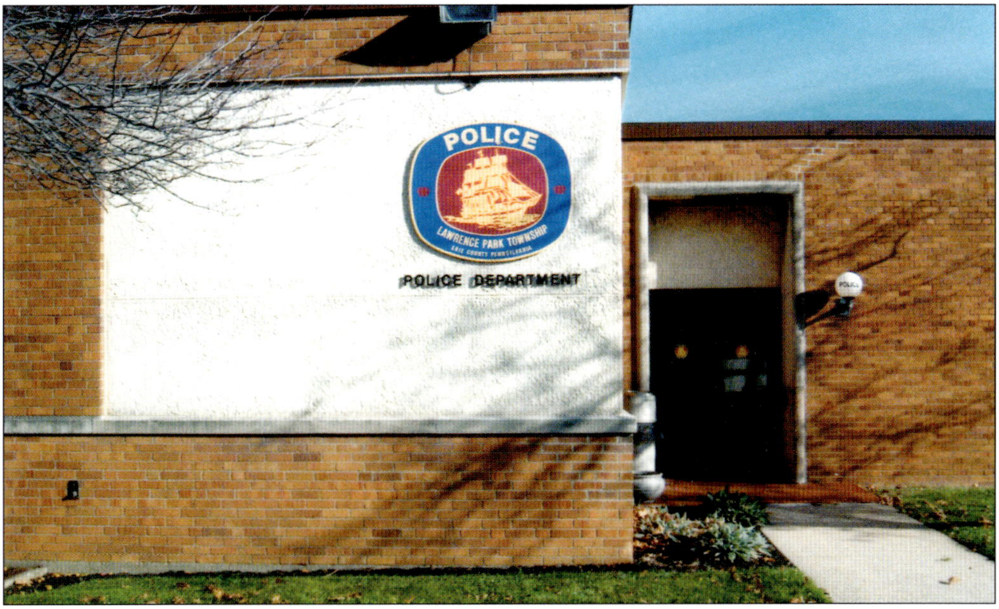

The Lawrence Park Police Department has headquarters in the township building. The police provide many services such as school resource officers, Safety Town, home surveillance, and traffic control. Claude Austin was the second police chief and served from 1925 to 1950, when Ed Strong took over and served until 1981. The ball field behind Iroquois High school is known as the Claude Austin Field.

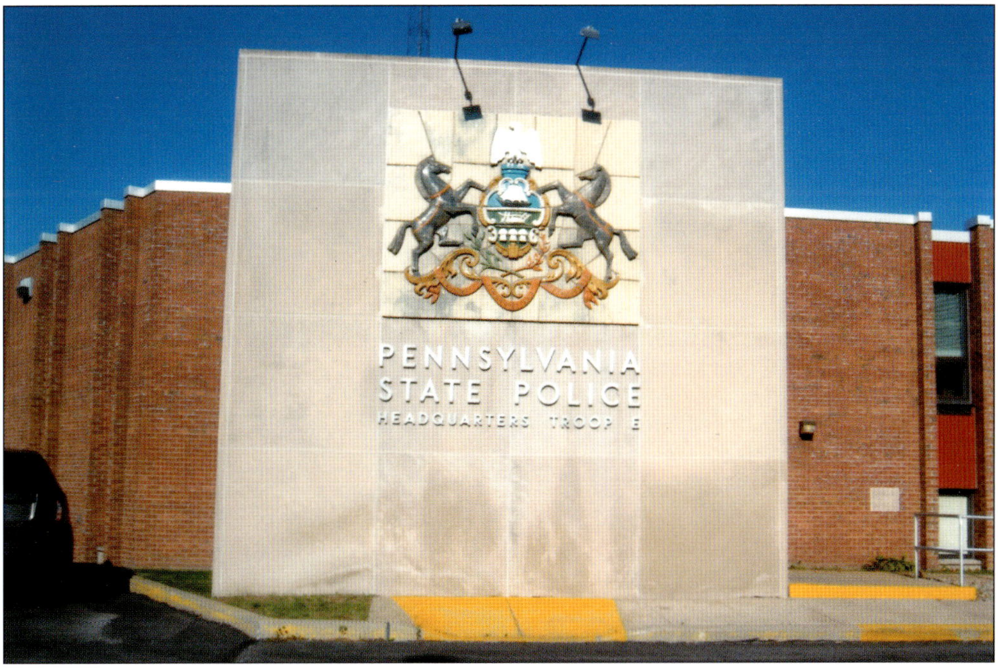

In 1973, the Pennsylvania State Police erected this building on Iroquois Avenue as their headquarters. The state police have had a presence in Lawrence Park since 1926, when they shared facilities with the Lawrence Park Police at 864 Silliman Avenue, the present-day location of Doug Cornelius State Farm Insurance.

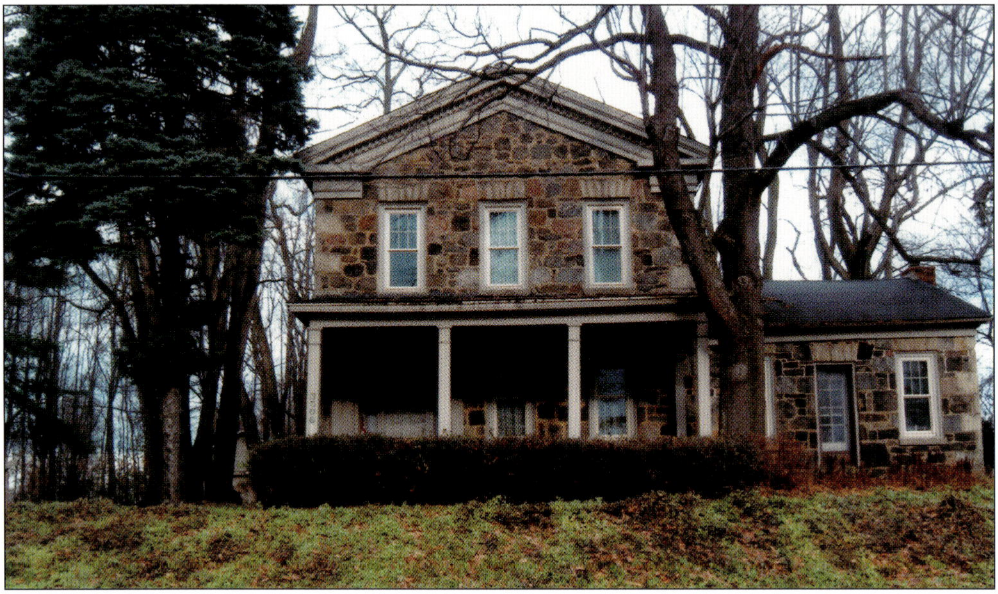

The Stone House, located at the intersection of East Lake Road and Water Street, was built by Michael Crowley in 1832. This beautiful stone home was lovingly restored and lived in by Al and Shirley Diner. It was built on the bank of Four Mile Creek, and local legend hints that it was a station on the Underground Railroad, a movement that aided runaway slaves in reaching freedom. (Courtesy of the Lawrence Park Historical Society.)

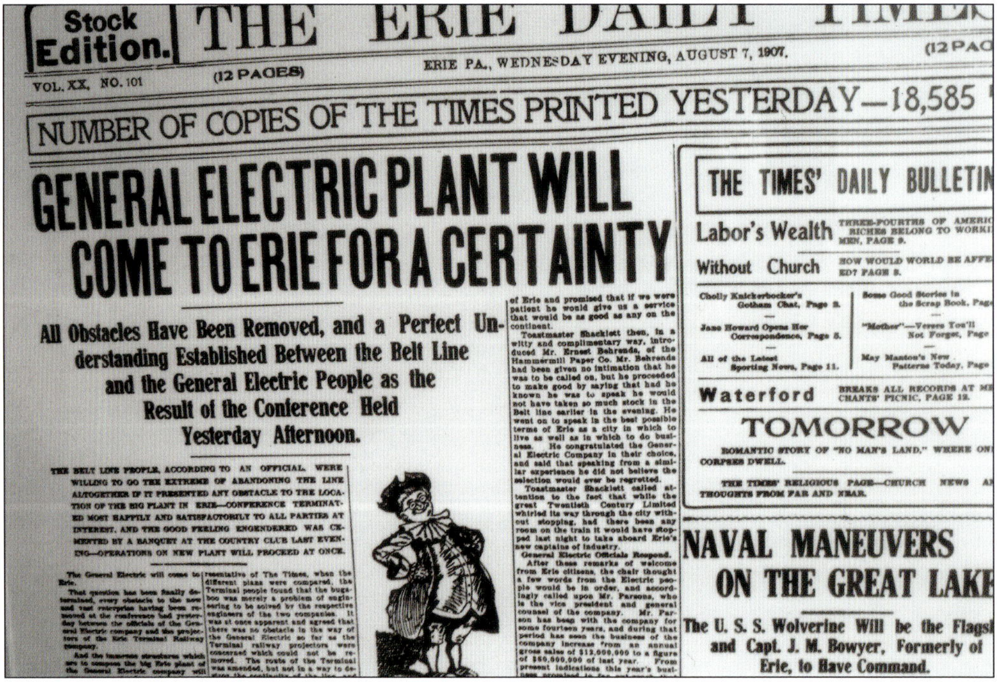

Stock Edition. THE ERIE DAILY TIMES

VOL. XX. NO. 101 (12 PAGES) ERIE PA., WEDNESDAY EVENING, AUGUST 7, 1907. (12 PAG

NUMBER OF COPIES OF THE TIMES PRINTED YESTERDAY—18,585

GENERAL ELECTRIC PLANT WILL COME TO ERIE FOR A CERTAINTY

All Obstacles Have Been Removed, and a Perfect Understanding Established Between the Belt Line and the General Electric People as the Result of the Conference Held Yesterday Afternoon.

THE BELT LINE PEOPLE, ACCORDING TO AN OFFICIAL, WERE WILLING TO GO THE EXTREME OF ABANDONING THE LINE ALTOGETHER IF IT PRESENTED ANY OBSTACLE TO THE LOCATION OF THE BIG PLANT IN ERIE—CONFERENCE TERMINATED MOST HAPPILY AND SATISFACTORILY TO ALL PARTIES AT INTEREST, AND THE GOOD FEELING ENGENDERED WAS CEMENTED BY A BANQUET AT THE COUNTRY CLUB LAST EVENING—OPERATIONS ON NEW PLANT WILL PROCEED AT ONCE.

The General Electric will come to Erie.

That question has been finally determined, every obstacle to the new and vast enterprise having been removed at the conference had yesterday between the officials of the General Electric company and the projectors of the Erie Terminal Railway company.

And the immense structures which are to compose the big Erie plant of the General Electric company will

...resentative of The Times, when the different plans were compared, the Terminal people found that the bugaboo was merely a problem of engineering to be solved by the respective engineers of the two companies. It was at once apparent and agreed that there was no obstacle in the way of the General Electric so far as the Terminal railway projectors were concerned which could not be removed. The route of the Terminal was amended, but not in a way to de-

of Erie and promised that if we were patient he would give us a service that would be as good as any on the continent.

Toastmaster Shacklett then, in a witty and complimentary way, introduced Mr. Ernest Behrends, of the Hammermill Paper Co. Mr. Behrends had been given no intimation that he was to be called on, but he proceeded to make good by saying that had he known he was to speak he would not have taken so much stock in the Belt line earlier in the evening. He went on to speak in the best possible terms of Erie as a city in which to live as well as in which to do business. He congratulated the General Electric Company in their choice, and said that speaking from a similar experience he did not believe the selection would ever be regretted.

Toastmaster Shacklett called attention to the fact that while the great Twentieth Century Limited whirled its way through the city without stopping, had there been any room on the train it would have stopped last night to take aboard Erie's new captains of industry.

General Electric Officials Respond.

After these remarks of welcome from Erie citizens, the chair thought a few words from the Electric people would be in order, and accordingly called upon Mr. Parsons, who is the vice president and general counsel of the company. Mr. Parson has been with the company for some fourteen years, and during that period has seen the business of the company increase from an annual gross sales of $12,000,000 to a figure of $60,000,000 of last year. From present indications this year's busi-

THE TIMES' DAILY BULLETIN

Labor's Wealth — THREE-FOURTHS OF AMERIC... RICHES BELONG TO WORKI... MEN, PAGE 9.

Without Church — HOW WOULD WORLD BE AFFE... ED? PAGE 8.

Cholly Knickerbocker's Gotham Chat, Page 8.

Jane Howard Opens Her Correspondence, Page 5.

All of the Latest Sporting News, Page 11.

Some Good Stories in the Scrap Book, Pag...

"Mother"—Verses You'll Not Forget, Page...

May Manton's New Patterns Today, Page...

Waterford — BREAKS ALL RECORDS AT ME... CHANTS' PICNIC, PAGE 12.

TOMORROW

ROMANTIC STORY OF "NO MAN'S LAND," WHERE ON... CORPSES DWELL.

THE TIMES' RELIGIOUS PAGE—CHURCH NEWS A... THOUGHTS FROM FAR AND NEAR.

NAVAL MANEUVERS ON THE GREAT LAKE...

The U. S. S. Wolverine Will be the Flags... and Capt. J. M. Bowyer, Formerly of Erie, to Have Command.

On August 7, 1907, the people of Erie were delighted to learn from the headlines of the *Erie Daily Times* that the rumors that the General Electric Company would be building a plant in Erie were about to come true. The impact of the General Electric Company Erie Works on the communities of Lawrence Park and Wesleyville has been immense and long-standing.

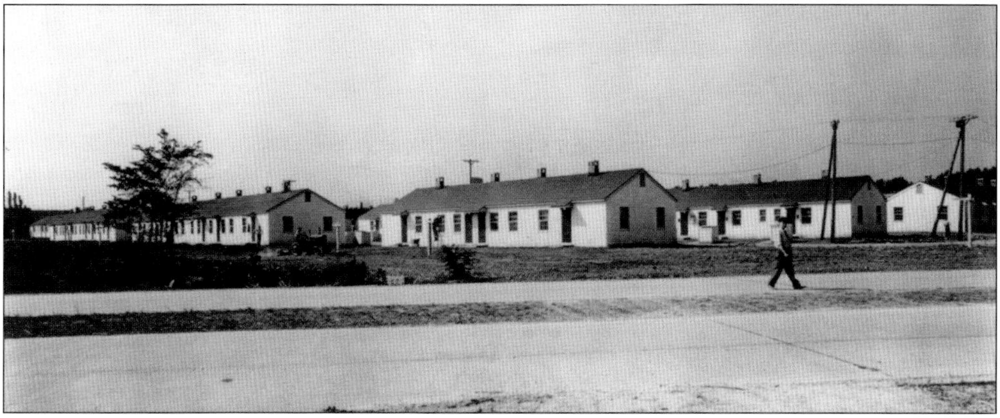

The increased employment at the General Electric plant during World War II necessitated additional housing. In the area south of Iroquois Avenue and Main Street, a development of approximately 300 houses was built of concrete block and painted white and thus called White City. After World War II, when the housing shortage was alleviated, the complex was razed, and between 1964 and 1966 Iroquois High School was built on this site. (Courtesy of the Lawrence Park Historical Society.)

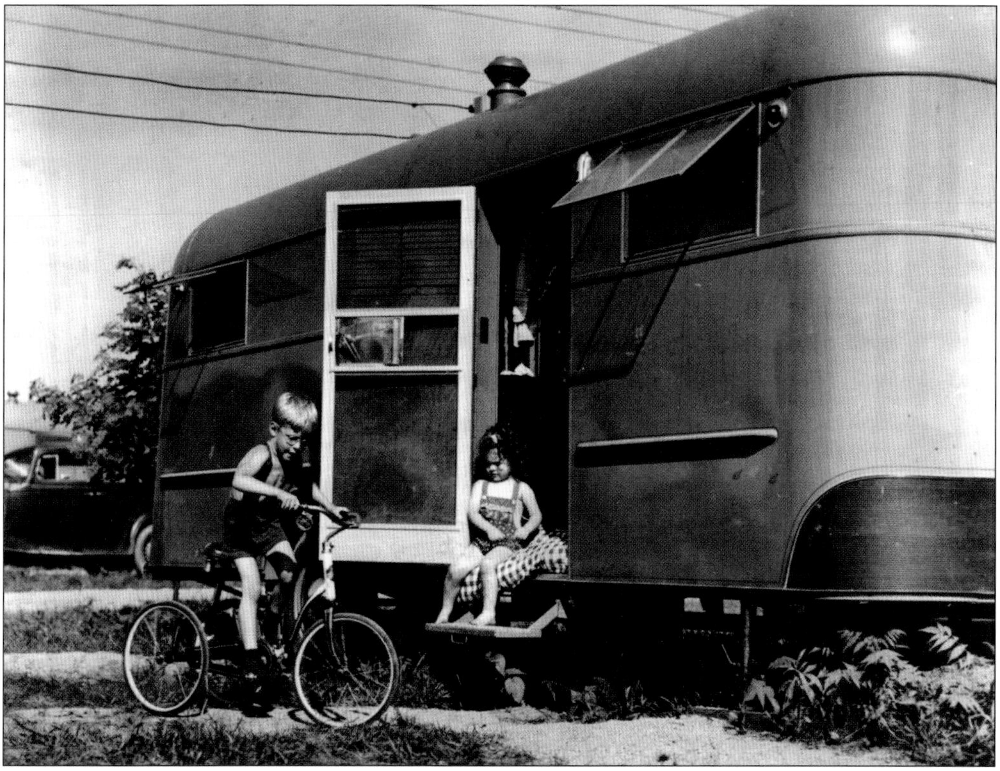

Another effort to provide housing during the World War II years was Hunt's Trailer Park, located across from the main gate of General Electric Company Erie Works on the north side of East Lake Road. These trailers were removed when no longer needed. In 1947, construction of homes in this area marked the beginning of the Lake Cliff Subdivision. The area extends northward to the lake and west to include Halley and Harvey Streets, once known as New Colony. (Courtesy of the Lawrence Park Historical Society.)

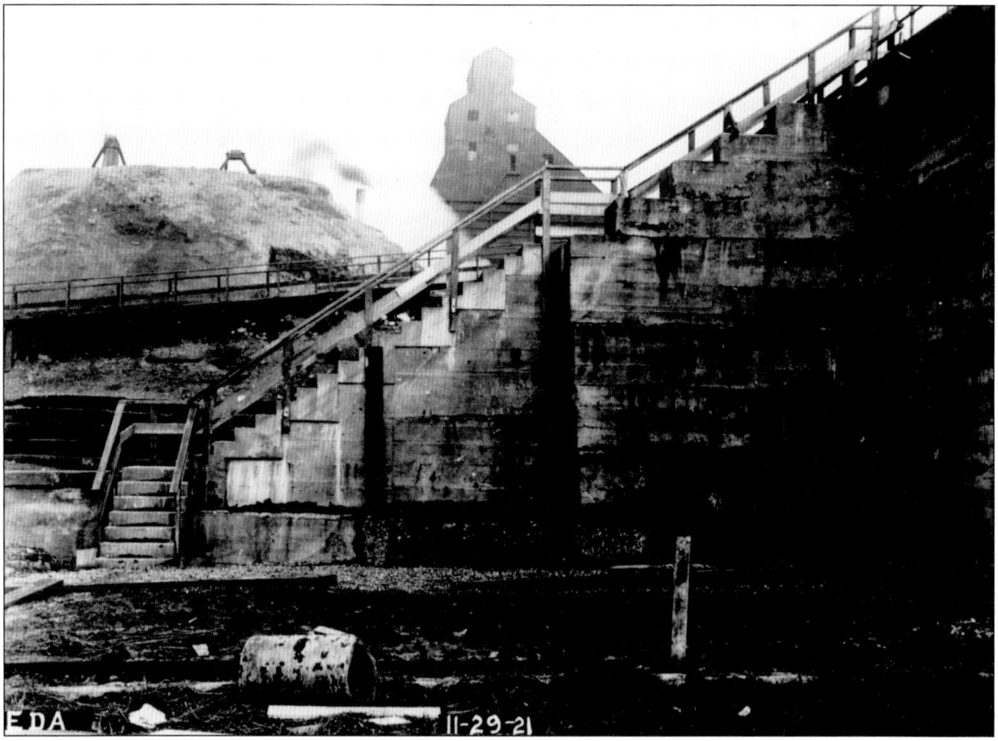

The coal tipple seen in this 1921 photograph disappeared with the demise of coal-fired steam engines, however, the sturdy railroad bridge is still very much in use. A plaque that was once on this bridge identified the road that follows Four Mile Creek and unites Wesleyville and Lawrence Park as "Lawrence Parkway, 1921, signed Erie Co. Commr's, Mill Creek Twp." The road is now known as Water Street. (Courtesy of the Lawrence Park Historical Society.)

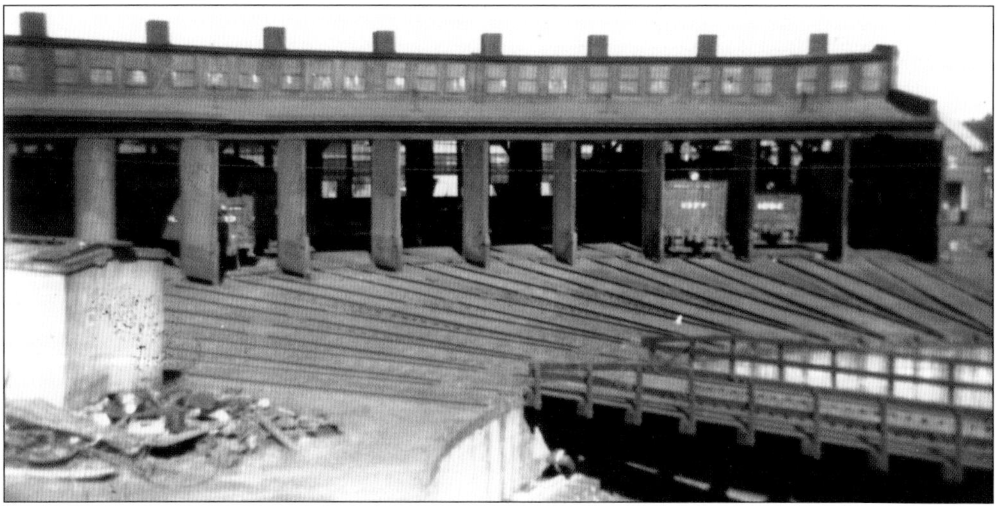
Built in 1913, the roundhouse was part of the Wesleyville Rail Yard and provided a way to reverse directions for steam engines. There was also a bunkhouse, coal tipple, and the Roundhouse Restaurant in this area. For many years after these buildings were razed, the area nicknamed the "Alamo" was a forbidden play area for kids from Lawrence Park and Wesleyville. (Courtesy of the Lawrence Park Historical Society.)

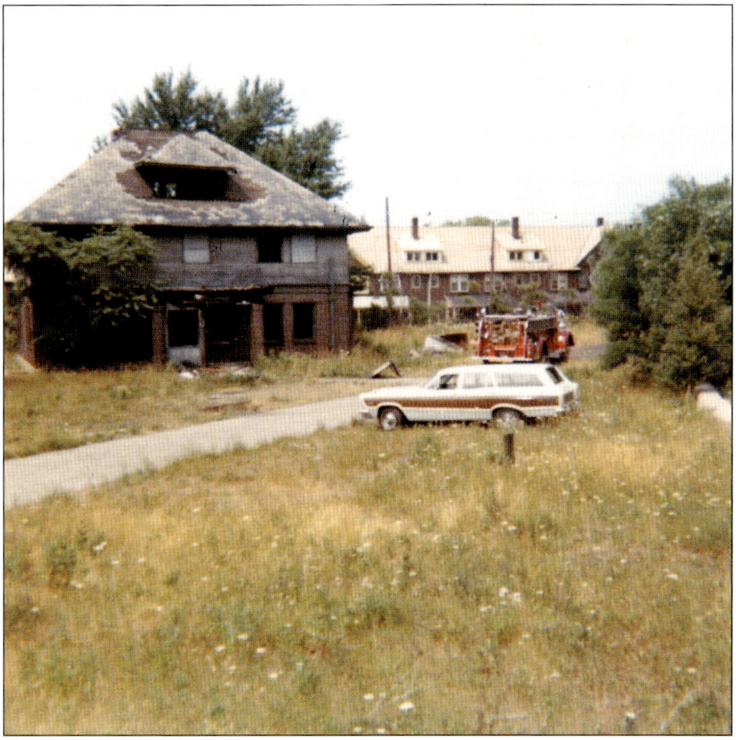

The Roundhouse Restaurant not only fed the railroad crews, but also provided good home-style meals for many residents of Lawrence Park and Wesleyville. There was an underpass at Priestley Avenue in Lawrence Park that gave access to the rail-yard complex. This photograph was taken in 1971 on the day the restaurant was razed by a controlled burn. (Courtesy of the Lawrence Park Historical Society.)

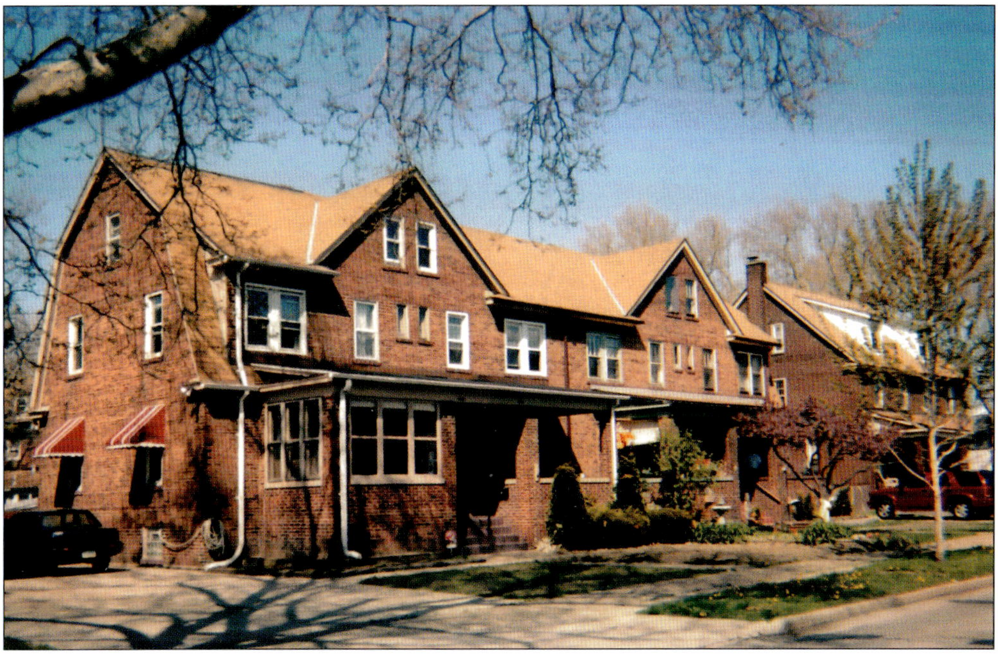

To provide housing for General Electric workers during World War I, a large building program was undertaken in Lawrence Park. In 1917 and 1918, there were 494 row-type homes built as duplexes and in rows of 4, 6, 8, and 10. The sturdy brick row-type homes were built on curving streets with small triangular parks that give Lawrence Park the unique look of an English village. (Courtesy of the Lawrence Park Historical Society.)

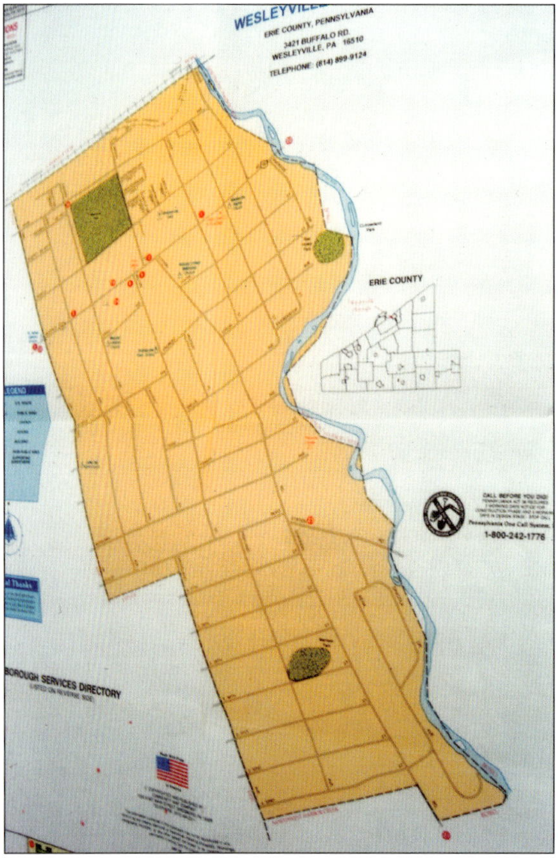

This map of Wesleyville shows its boundaries as the Norfolk & Southern Railroad tracks on the north, Four Mile Creek on the east, Thirty-Seventh Street in College Heights on the south and Bird Drive on the west side. The green spots indicate Memorial Baseball Fields, Hinkler Park, and Morrison Park.

In 1946, to answer the need for additional housing for returning veterans from World War II, Wesleyville began to develop mobile-home parks, and at present there are three parks that provide housing. This one is on Pearl Avenue and stretches from Eastern Avenue to Bird Drive.

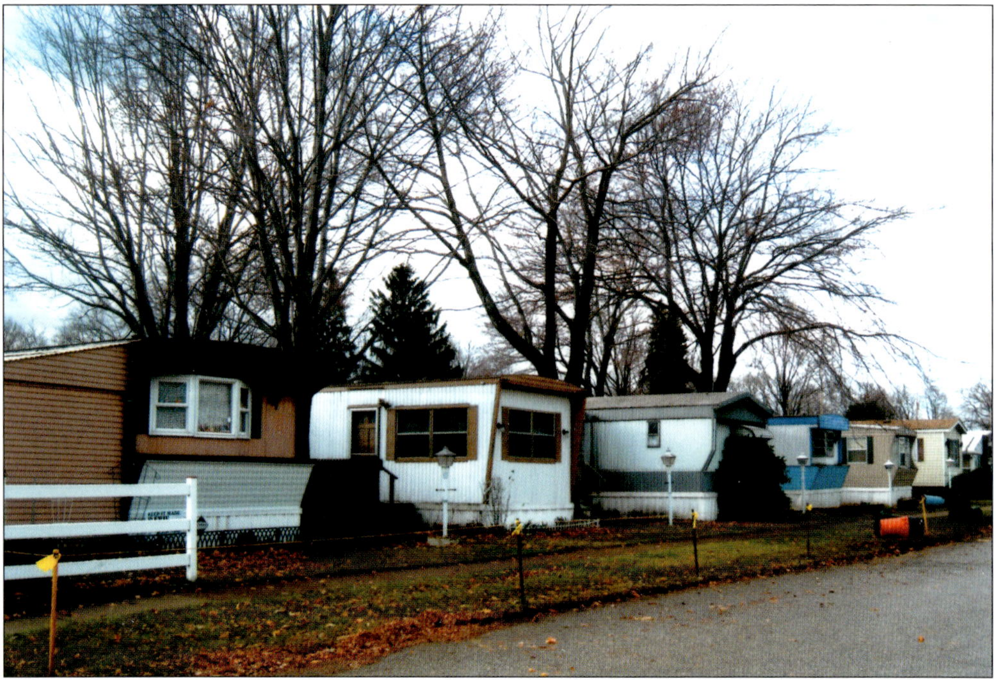

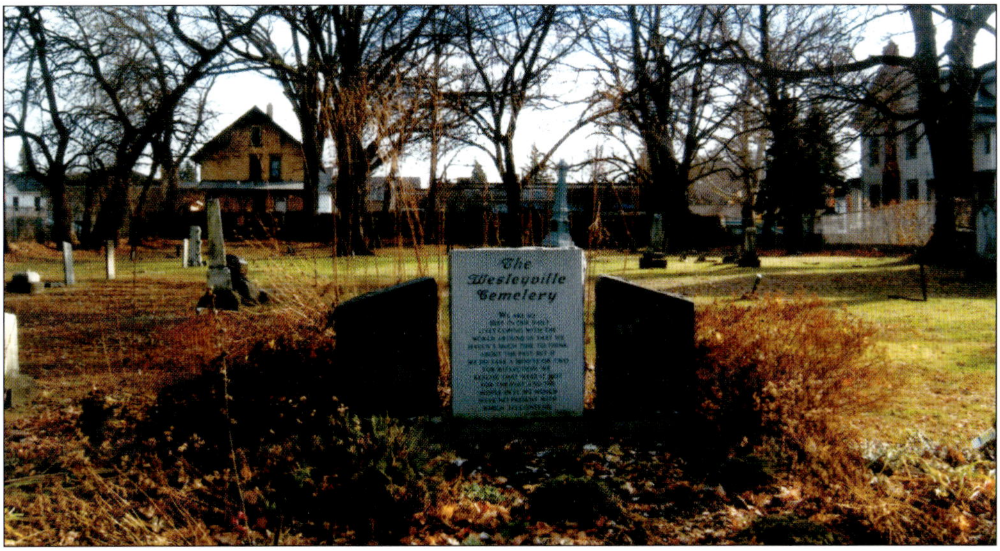

The old cemetery on North Street in Wesleyville was established behind the old Methodist church that stood on Buffalo Road. It has long been rumored that during the 1800s, the old Methodist church was a station on the Underground Railroad, and runaway slaves seeking freedom hid in the attic of the church. Maj. Frederick Fitch and Frank Henry were active in this movement.

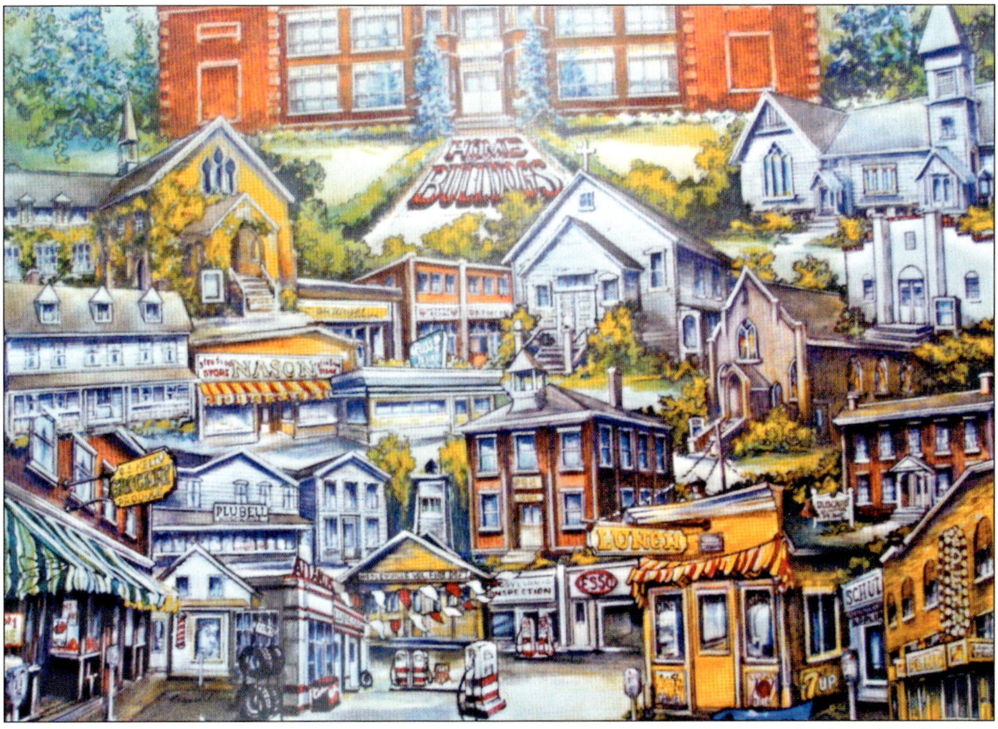

In 1990, as a tribute to his hometown, Ken Nuber painted this mural, *Borough of Wesleyville from 1940 thru 1960*. The town is watched over by the Wesleyville School, home of the Bulldogs. Buildings that can be recognized are Penn Theater; Kelly's; Plubells; Nasons; Market Street School; the Methodist, Baptist, and Lutheran churches; and the old St. James Catholic Church. Ken Nuber graduated from Wesleyville in 1955.

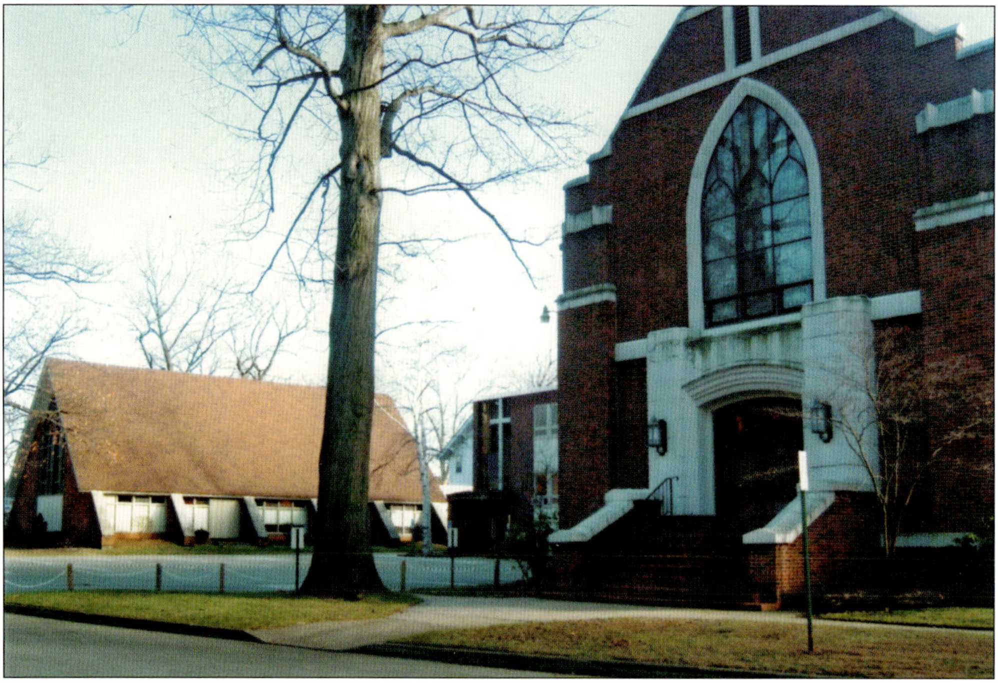

The Lawrence Park United Methodist Church, located across from Elbow Tree Park, was dedicated on May 7, 1922. A growing need for more space for educational and fellowship purposes resulted in building the attached Welker Hall in 1958. In the background is neighboring St. Mary's Episcopal Church, built in 1958. St. Mary's parish hall, which adjoins the church, was built in 1914 and is still used for meetings and social hours.

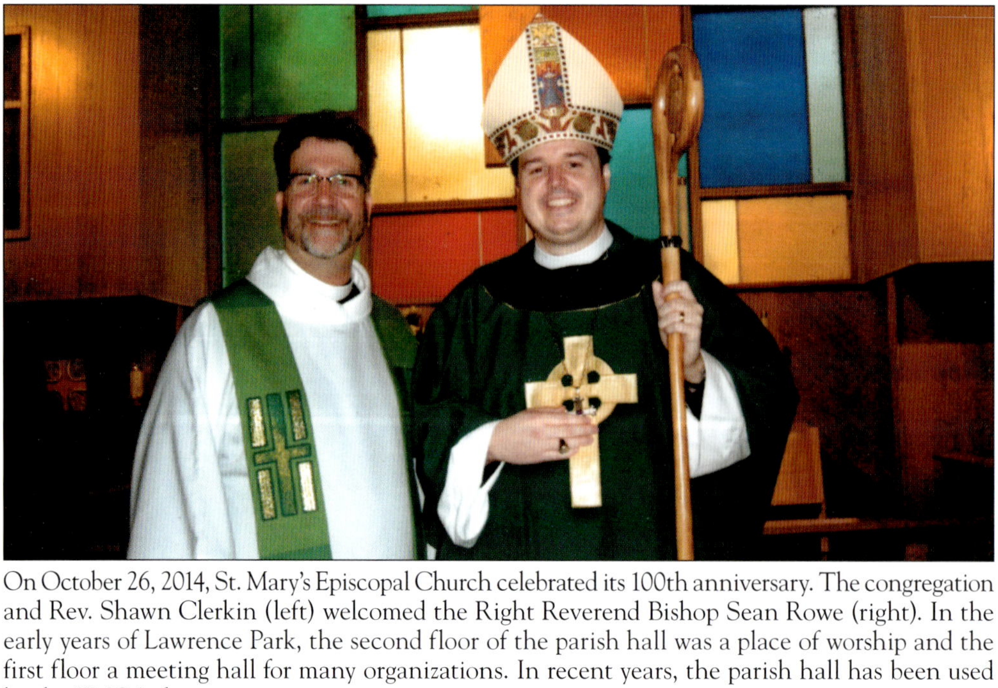

On October 26, 2014, St. Mary's Episcopal Church celebrated its 100th anniversary. The congregation and Rev. Shawn Clerkin (left) welcomed the Right Reverend Bishop Sean Rowe (right). In the early years of Lawrence Park, the second floor of the parish hall was a place of worship and the first floor a meeting hall for many organizations. In recent years, the parish hall has been used by the YMCA day care program.

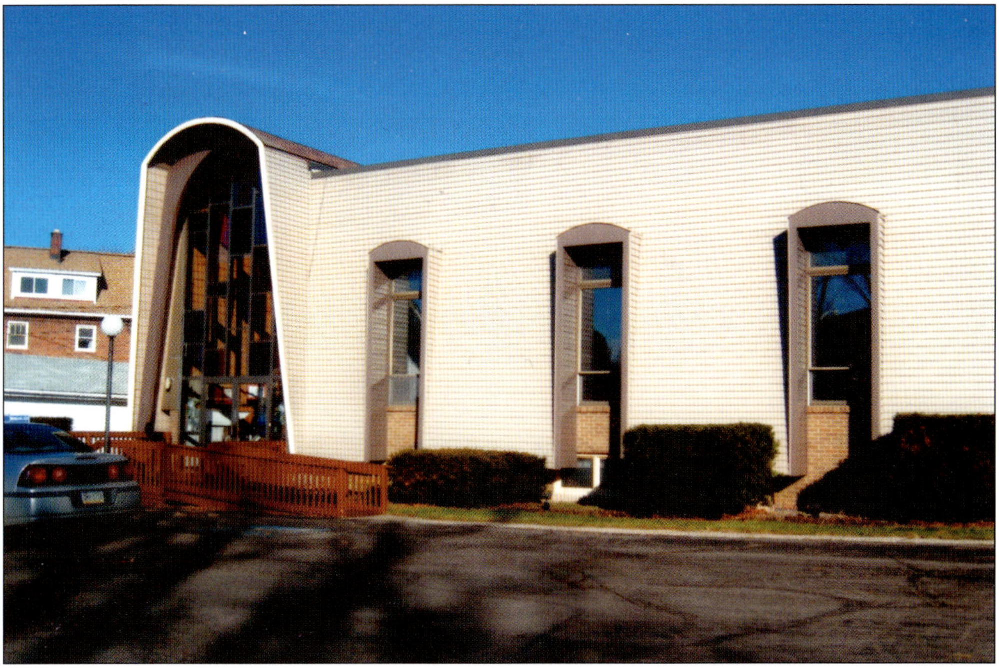

The new Christ the Redeemer Lutheran Church in Lawrence Park was built in 1973 and replaced the old redbrick church that had served the congregation since 1913. In 1983, Christ Lutheran merged with Redeemer Lutheran Church and adopted a new name, Christ the Redeemer Lutheran Church. Many Lawrence Park and Wesleyville youngsters attended a preschool program here from 1974 until recent years.

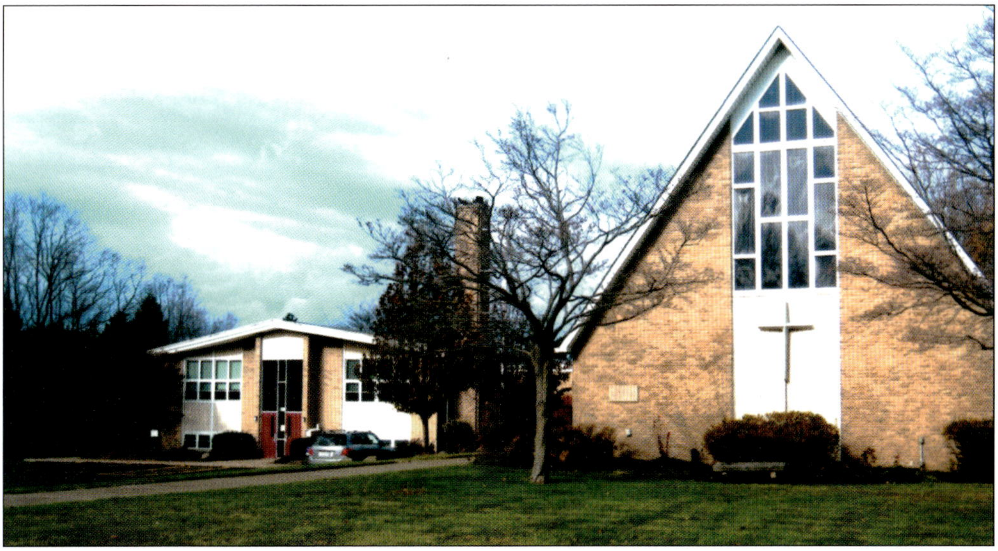

The Eastminster Presbyterian Church was built on East Lake Road near Halley Street in Lawrence Park in 1959. Prior to that, from 1907, the congregation worshipped at their church on Lighthouse Street in Erie. In 1966, a carillon was installed in the new church, and hymns chime out over Lake Cliff and the Lawrence Park Golf Course. Many area youngsters remember the summer camp in the woods behind the church.

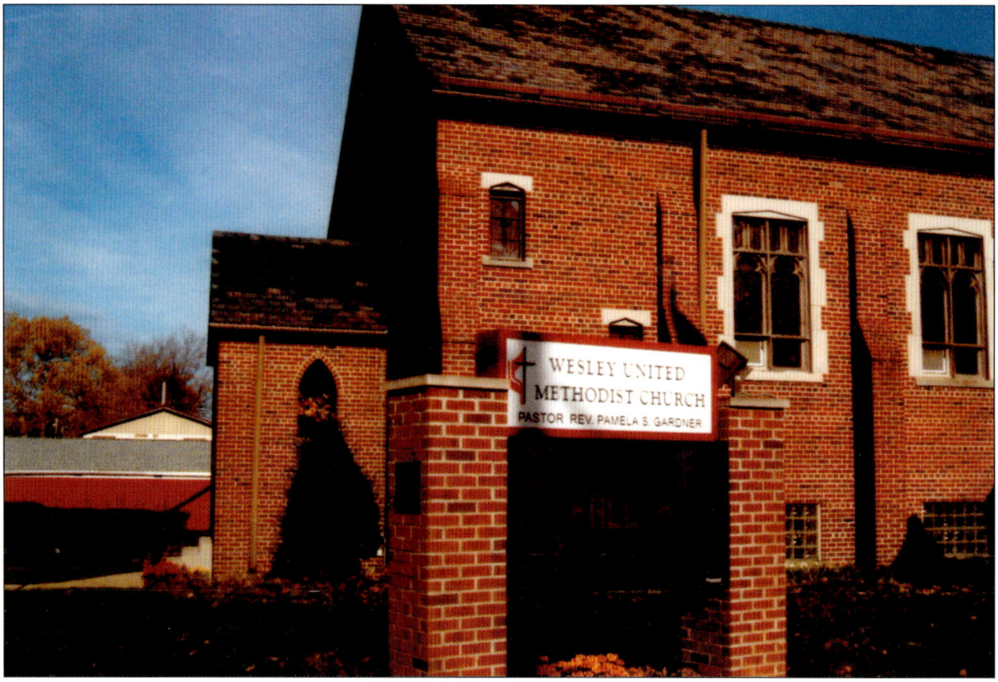

The Wesley United Methodist Church, on Station Road and South Street, was dedicated on September 11, 1927. From 1838 to 1926, the congregation held services in the little redbrick church on Buffalo Road that was a haven for fugitive slaves. At present, the church is not only used for worship, but also is the site of the much-needed Wesleyville Food Pantry, to which many churches contribute.

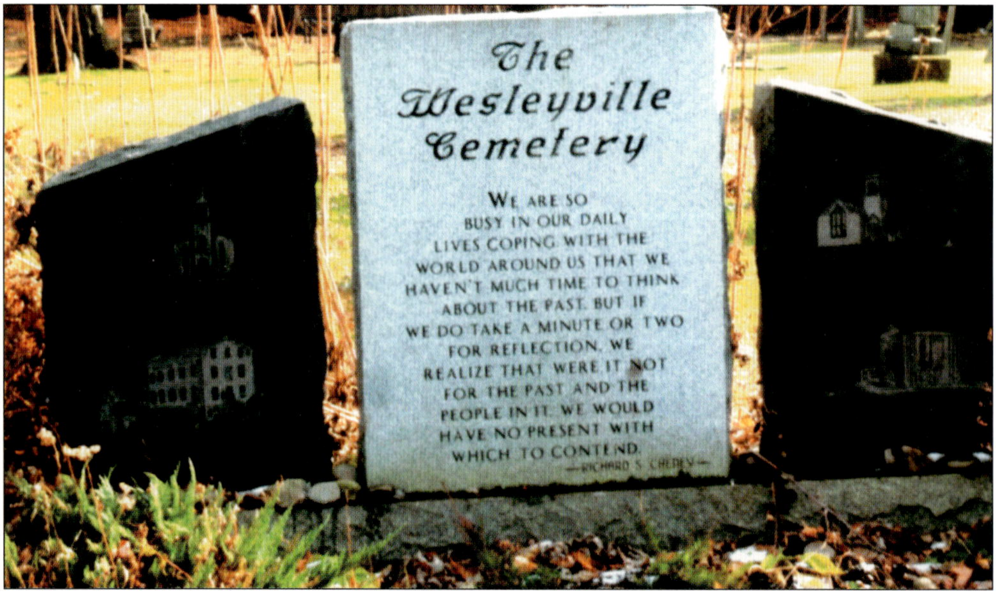

The small cemetery on North Street is still in existence. The cemetery fell into disrepair; however, in 1982, Michael Sensor, an 11 year old, inspired a community effort to repair and restore it. On May 25, 1998, the cemetery, abloom with tulips, was rededicated to Richard Cheney, Wesleyville historian.

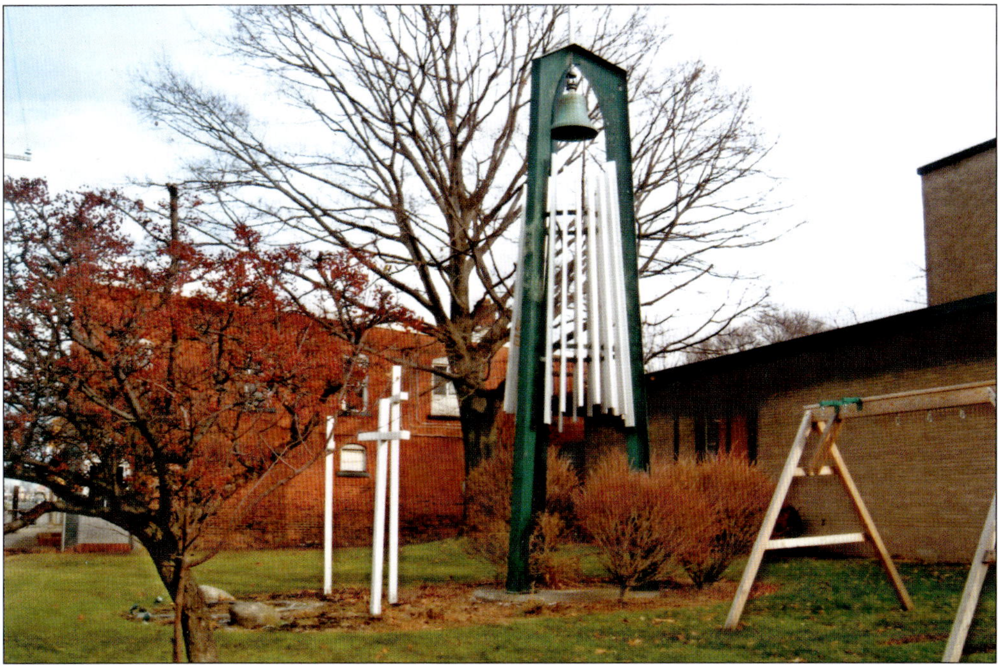

This bell tower graces the yard of the Wesleyville Baptist Church on Buffalo Road and Market Street. The new Baptist church was built in 1965 on the site of the old Market Street School. The bell in the tower is from the old Baptist church, which was constructed at the corner of South and Center Streets in 1891 and rebuilt in 1927 after a fire.

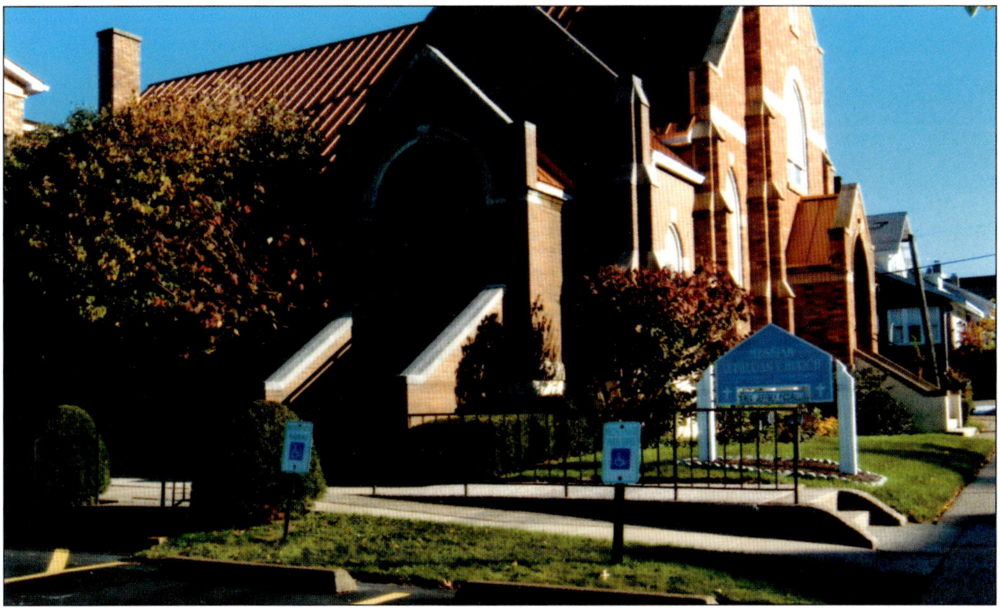

The Messiah Lutheran Church on Eastern Avenue in Wesleyville began in 1916, and the congregation held services in the second-floor meeting room of Chaffee's Hall. The present church was completed in 1921 and renovated in 1973. A number of young people from Messiah Lutheran have entered the Lutheran ministry.

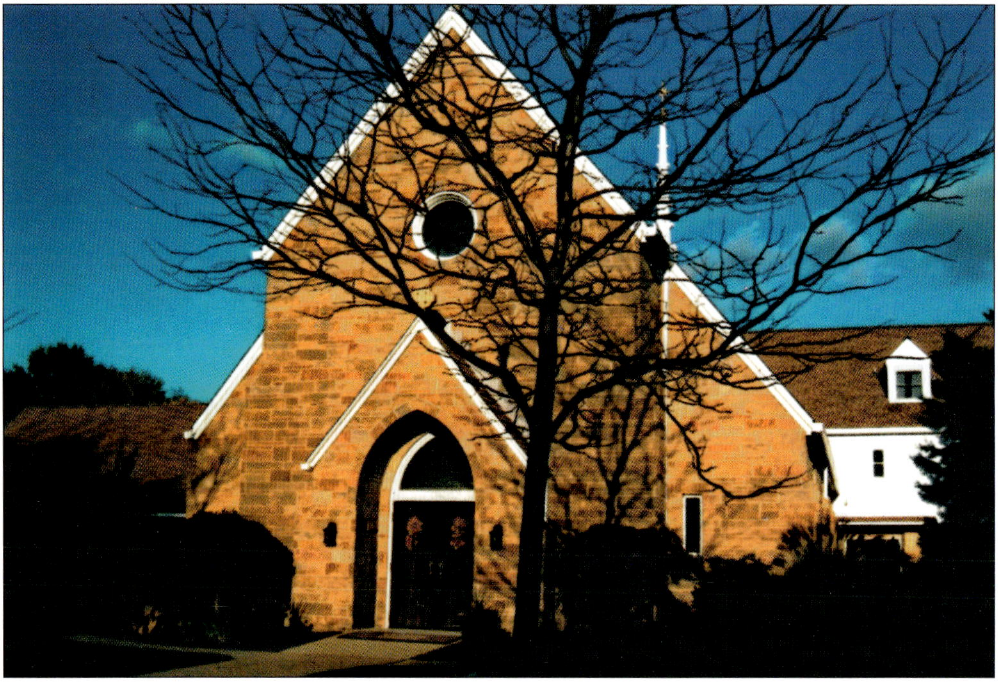

St. Mark the Evangelist Roman Catholic Church was founded in 1938 by Fr. Charles Ward. In the early years, services were held in St. Mary's Episcopal Parish Hall. The church on Smithson Avenue in Lawrence Park was built in 1942, but within a few months, a fire destroyed much of the social hall and main altar. Volunteers from the congregation resolutely rebuilt the damaged area, and the dedication was held on July 16, 1944.

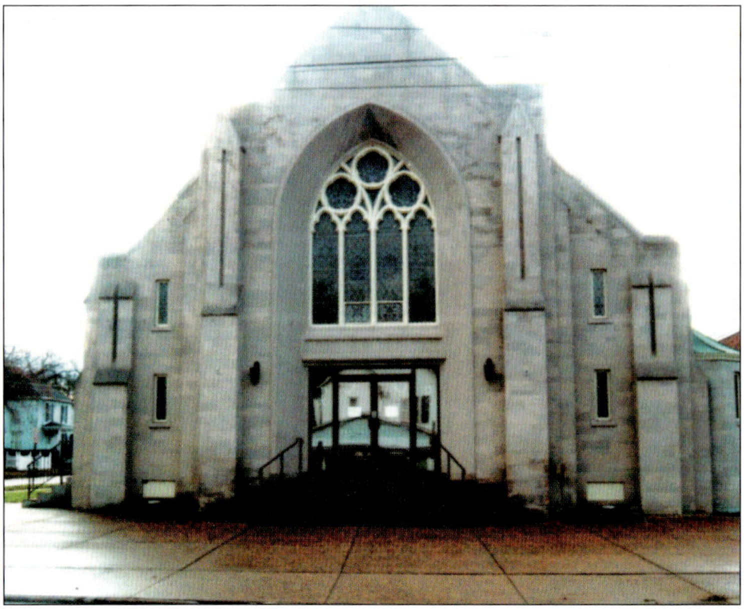

Although St. James Catholic Church is just outside the western boundary of Wesleyville, it plays an important part in the life of the town. St. James Parish began in 1922 in a small frame church set back from Buffalo Road. In 1949, the new stone church seen here, with its beautiful stained-glass windows, was constructed and continues to flourish.

Two

PARKS AND RECREATION

The green spaces and fun places that dot a community are the areas where memories are made. In 1910, a nature park was included in the plans for Lawrence Park. This became known as Elbow Tree Park. As time went on, small triangular parks were named to honor individuals, preserve a school bell, and house a gazebo. Napier Avenue Park, the Barringer Playground, and the Lake Cliff Playground provided many hours of fun and games. Ball games were played in the area behind Iroquois High School. Many sporting events were held on the large field, known as the GE Field or Emerson Field, between Water Street and the Napier Avenue playground. At one time, a large covered grandstand added to the spectators' comfort. Before the erection of the new Iroquois Elementary School, there was a softball field and ice-skating pond on Tyndall Avenue between Morse Street and Iroquois Avenue. Now there is a modern school and community playground.

For many years, Lawrence Park teenagers looked forward to Saturday nights when they could join their friends at Parkers Haven, a recreational activity directed by Ed Poly and held at the union hall. In later years, another teenage youth center emerged on the second floor of the fire hall. Presently, summertime is enlivened by street dances, concerts at the gazebo, and the Fourth of July celebration, complete with a parade and spectacular fireworks.

In 1927, Wesleyville's Penn Theater opened and was the entertainment center for nearly 40 years. After it closed in 1965, the Erie Playhouse moved to the theater and provided another 10 years of live performances. In the late 1950s, Schaffners Teen Age Center was the place where teenagers gathered, and for others there was the Wesley Arcade. In 1946, the Wesleyville Rotary Club erected an honor roll in the park at Center and Market Streets. When this memorial had to be removed, an effort began that resulted in the impressive Veterans Memorial Park at Eastern and North Streets that was dedicated on May 24, 2009. The nearby Memorial Field has hosted Little League ball games for many years. The field includes a playground and tennis courts. Other recreational areas are the Robert Morrison Park in College Heights and the "Red" Hinkler Park next to Four Mile Creek.

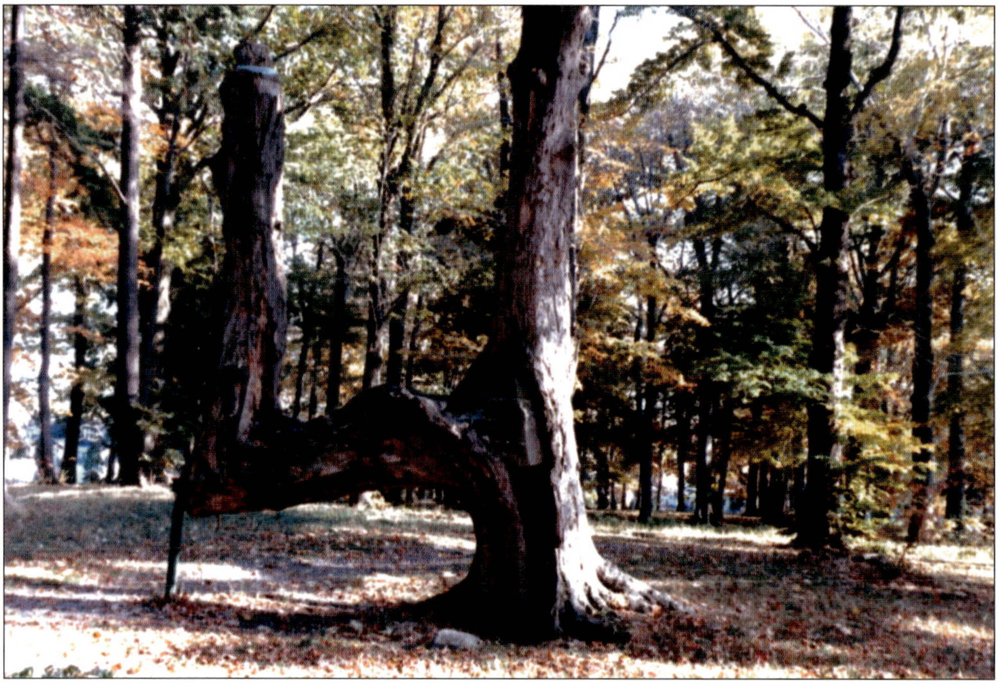

When Lawrence Park was developed by the General Electric Company in 1910, this elbow tree was already growing. It soon became the unofficial emblem of Lawrence Park, and in 2004, the park was officially named Elbow Tree Park. In 2005, the tree became so unstable it had to be cut down, but on May 29, 2006, thanks to the Lawrence Park class of 1955, another elbow tree was planted and is thriving. (Courtesy of the Lawrence Park Historical Society.)

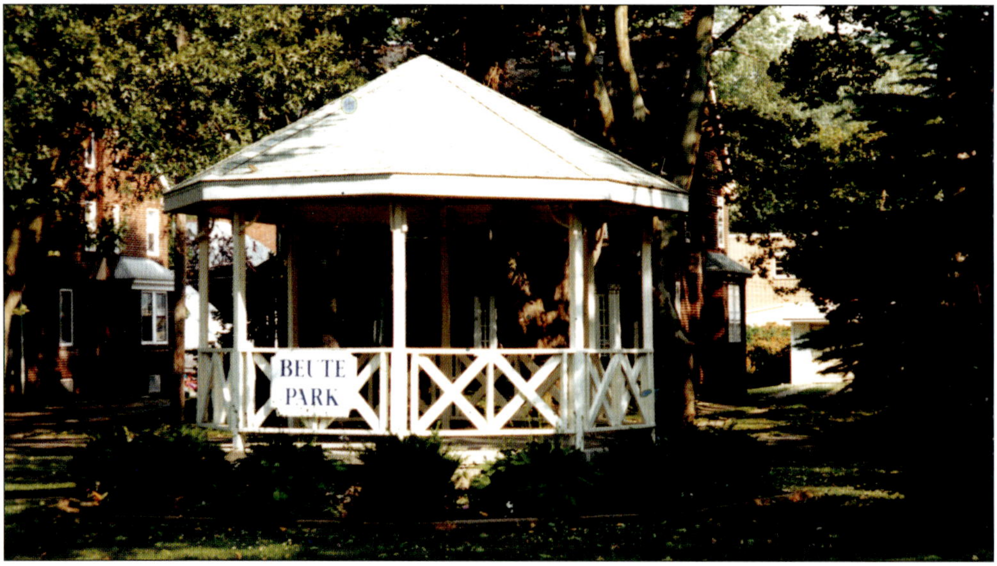

In 1985, the Lawrence Park Commissioners named this small triangular park Beute Park in honor of Erick Beute "for the many years of service and continued effort to make Lawrence Park a better place to live." Erick Beute's trucks were lettered with the name "Beute and Daughters," a reference to his children Patricia, Mercy, Linda, Susan, and Brenda. The gazebo was built by Richard Sanner. (Courtesy of the Lawrence Park Historical Society.)

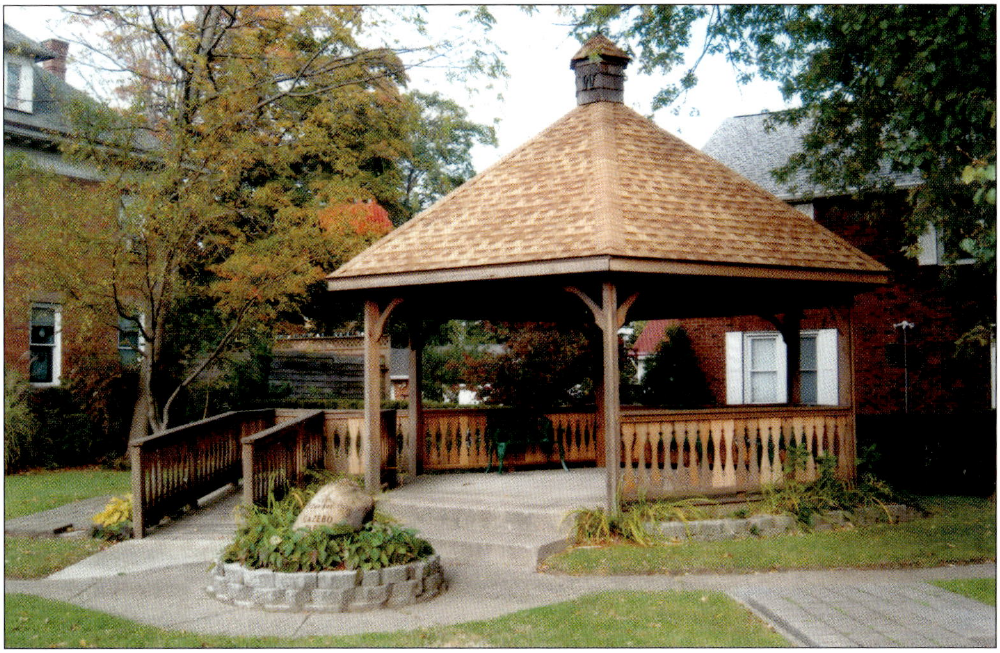

The C.J. "Gus" Dusckas Park got a face-lift and was rededicated on May 25, 2002. In addition to remarks made by state representatives, Richard Brine, a Wesleyville councilmember, gave a tribute to Gus. Also, Gus's daughter Nancy recalled his many contributions to those in need. Gus Dusckas was a friend to all and supported many activities in Wesleyville, Lawrence Park, and Erie.

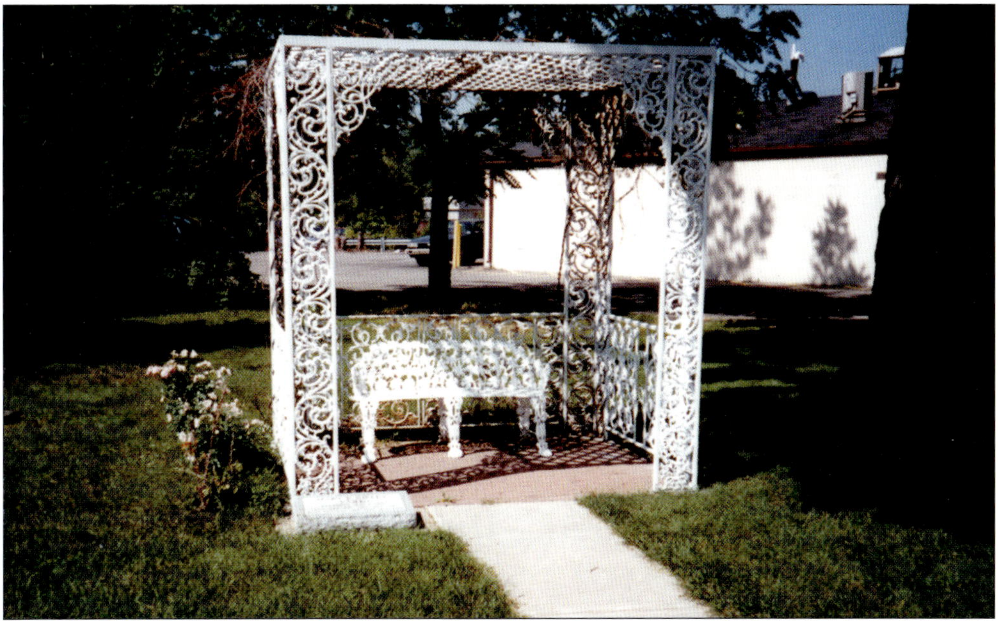

This graceful white arbor was built on the corner of Buffalo Road and Market Street to honor Mary Ripley who, after the death of her husband, Merle, took over his position as Wesleyville Borough secretary and served for 18 years. Also, she was the president of the Pennsylvania Local Government Secretaries Association. A time capsule was buried in this area on July 4, 1976, to be opened on July 4, 2076.

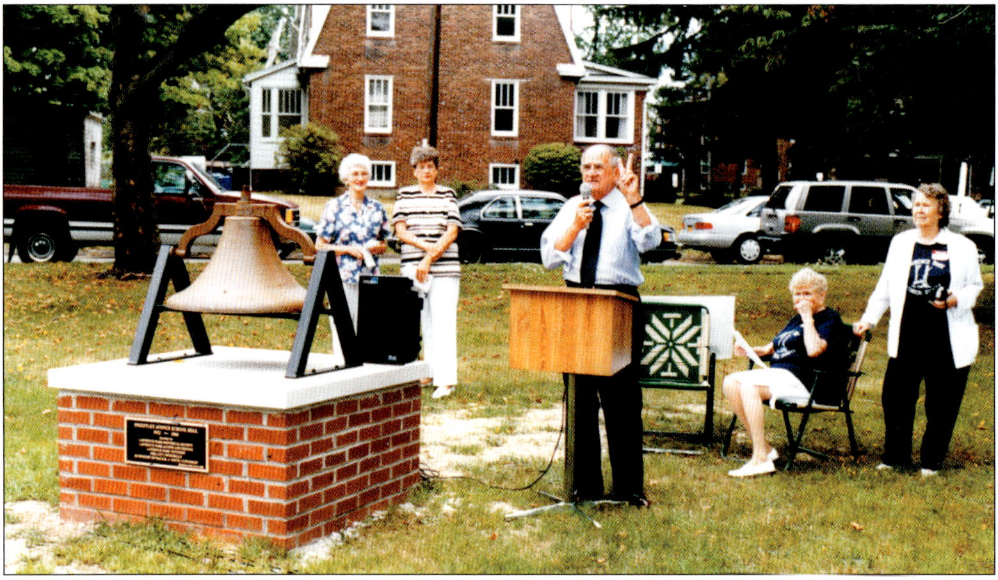

Since 1995, this park at Iroquois Avenue and Priestley Avenue has honored Raymond "Bud" DePlatchett, longtime Lawrence Park commissioner, who is at the microphone in this photograph. Seen in the background are, from left to right, Jean Bailey, Ruth Lewis, Marion Blythe, and Virginia Andersen. The sturdy bell in this park once called students to school at Priestley Avenue School, built in 1913 and razed in 1968. (Courtesy of the Lawrence Park Historical Society.)

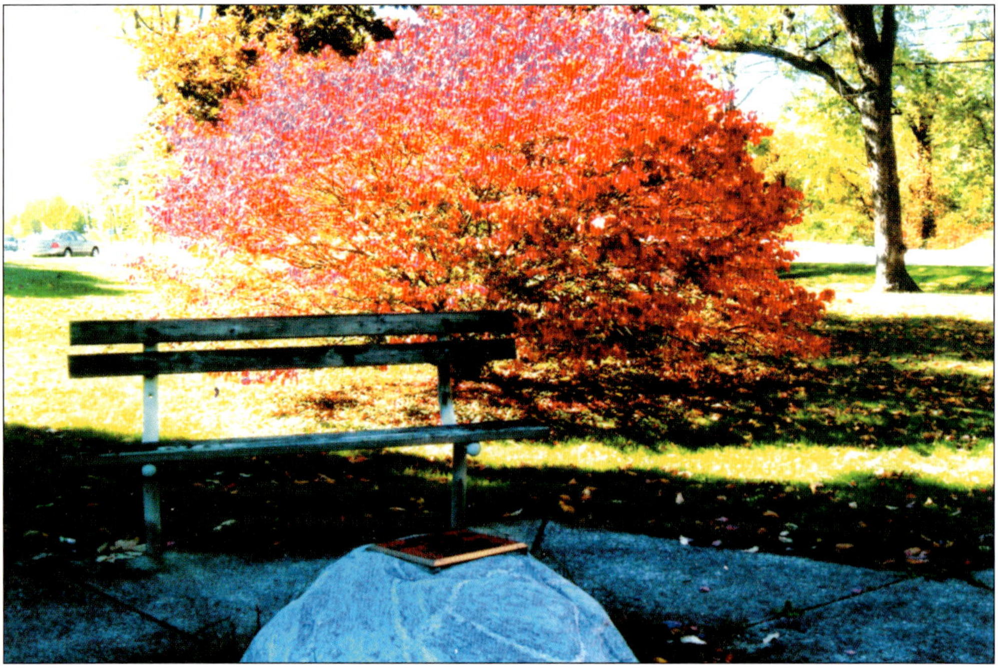

The flaming bush in the park at Iroquois Avenue and East Lake Road symbolizes the life of John Teker, whose name is inscribed on the tablet. John Teker was on the Lawrence Park School Board for 20 years and the Lawrence Park Recreation Board for 38 years. In 1966, the ice-skating pond on Tyndall Avenue was named in his honor. He was an active member of the Lawrence Park Historical Society and the Lawrence Park Fish Club.

In 1952, the stone war memorial was erected in the park at Iroquois and Silliman Avenues. The few words "We Owe So Much To So Few" eloquently express the feelings of the community. This monument replaced the large honor roll board that carried the names of 342 men and women from Lawrence Park who served their country during World War II. The honor roll deteriorated over time and had to be removed. (Courtesy of the Lawrence Park Historical Society.)

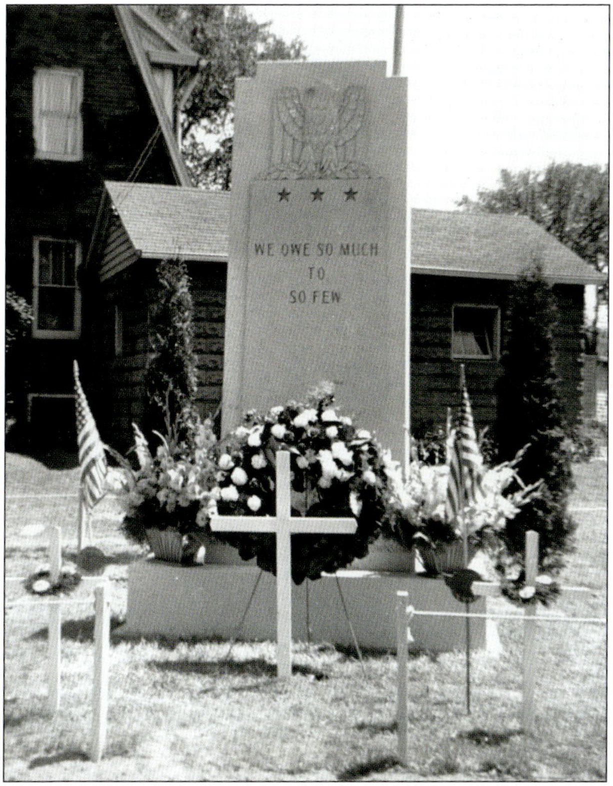

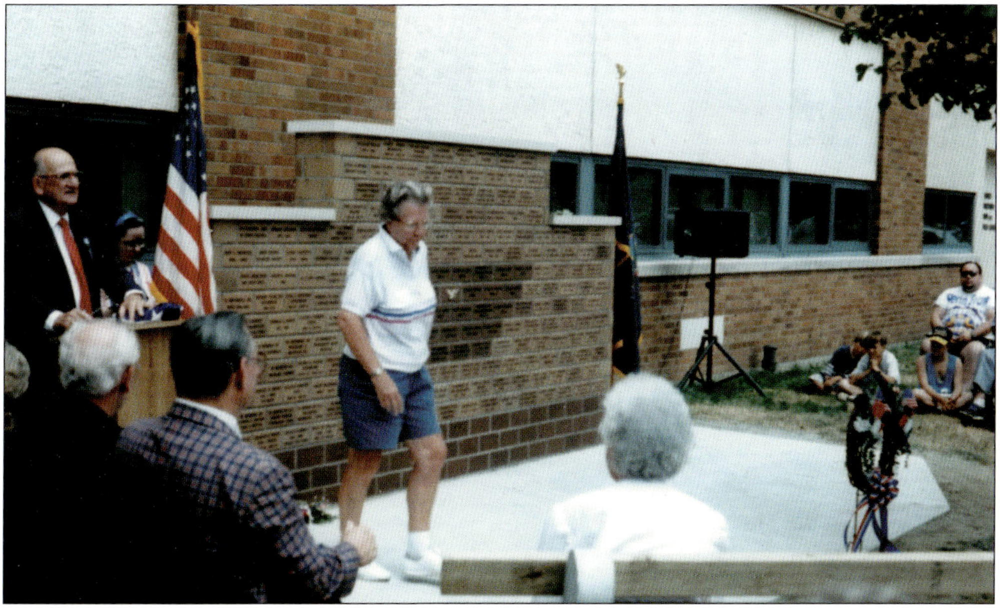

In 1995, the Lawrence Park community dedicated the memorial wall built in front of the township community center. The names of those from the township who gave their lives in the service of their country are inscribed on bricks in the center. In this photograph, Jean Forsythe, well-known Erie and Lawrence Park golfer, laid a wreath to honor her brother William, who was killed at Anzio Beach in Italy on May 27, 1944. (Courtesy of the Lawrence Park Historical Society.)

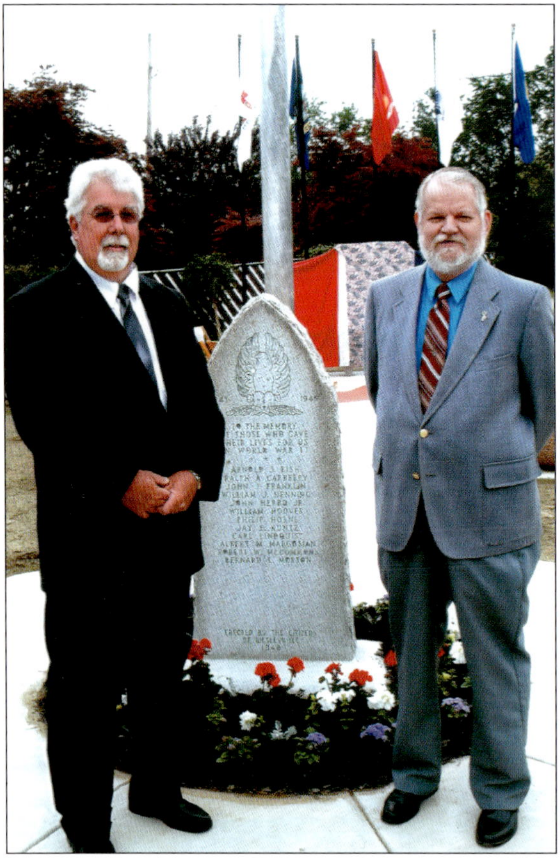

Dedication of the Wesleyville Veterans Memorial Park on Eastern Avenue and North Street took place on May 24, 2009. Two of the members of the committee were Paul Johnson (left), who was mayor from 1991 to 2013, and Bill Wittenberg (right), who had been a councilmember. The committee was spearheaded (via long distance) by Bill Heath. (Courtesy of Wesleyville Borough.)

The handsome memorial plaques at Veterans Memorial Park contain the names of hundreds of veterans who lived in Wesleyville. It replaced the honor roll that the Rotary Club of Wesleyville erected in 1946 in the park at Buffalo Road and Market Street. The Rotary Club also funds the colorful Christmas lights on Buffalo Road.

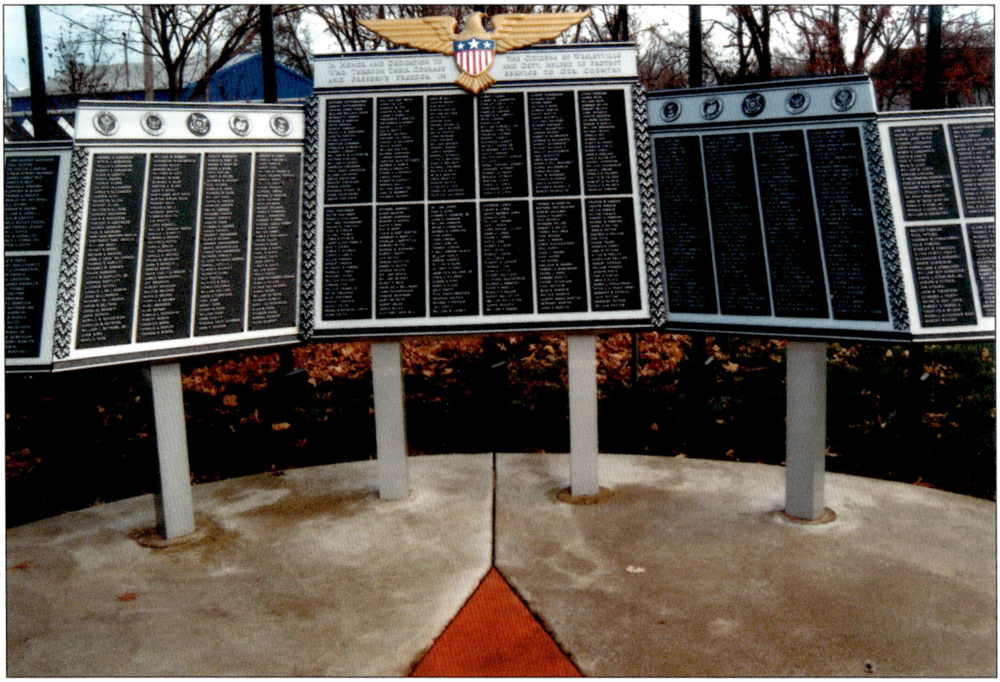

The stone monument at Wesleyville Memorial Park is dedicated to the memory of those who gave their lives in World War II. The monument lists the names of 12 Wesleyville residents and was erected in 1948. Appropriately, it has been incorporated into the new Veterans Memorial Park.

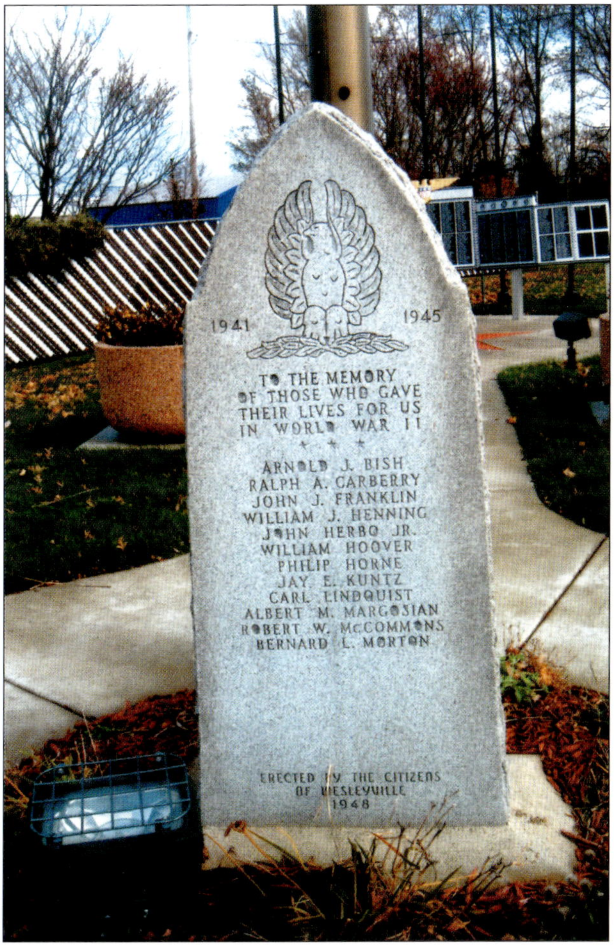

The Wesleyville Memorial Field is adjacent to the memorial park and is a large area that contains three ball fields, a concession stand, and a playground. Many Little League ball games are played here, with participants and fans coming from surrounding communities. Sometimes several games are played at the same time.

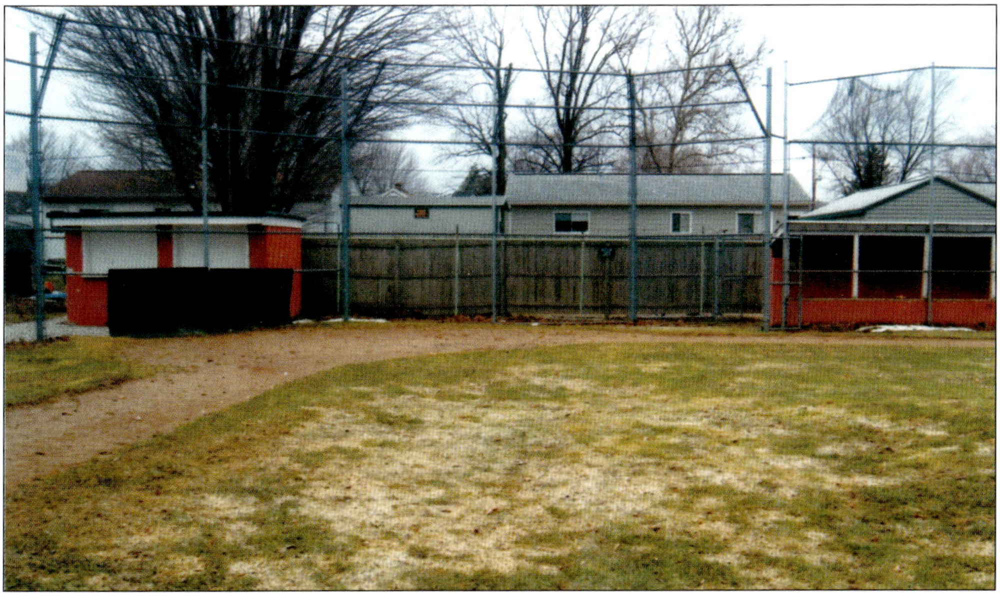

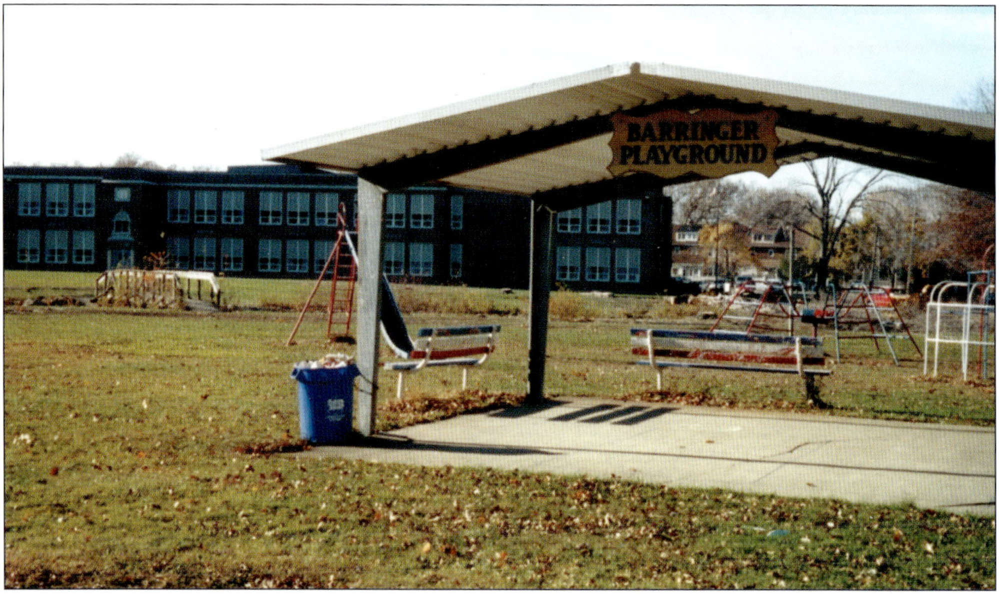

The Barringer Playground at Tyndall and Morse Streets, next to the old Lawrence Park High School, was a playground in the Crotty Subdivision. The residential area was developed by David Crotty in the 1950s, and the playground was named for C. Thomas Barringer, legendary basketball coach at Lawrence Park and Iroquois schools, who lived nearby. (Courtesy of the Lawrence Park Historical Society.)

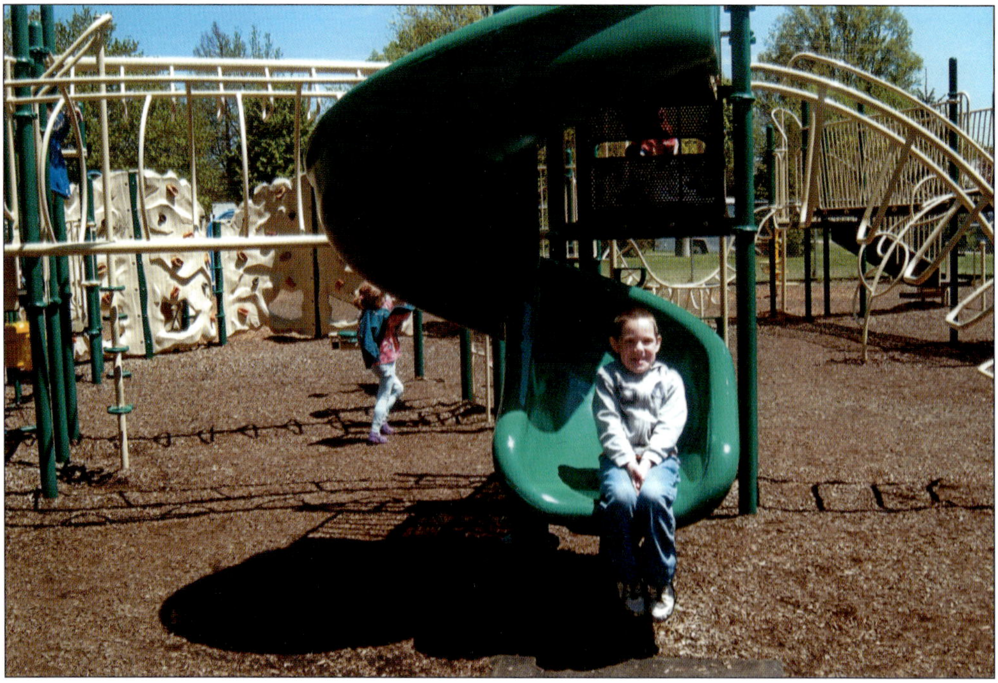

Recess is a time to enjoy the new Iroquois Elementary School playground. Located where the Barringer Playground used to be, this state-of-the-art playground for younger children is used by the school and community. On the other side of the school building is a play area for older students that is equipped with basketball hoops and outdoor Ping-Pong tables.

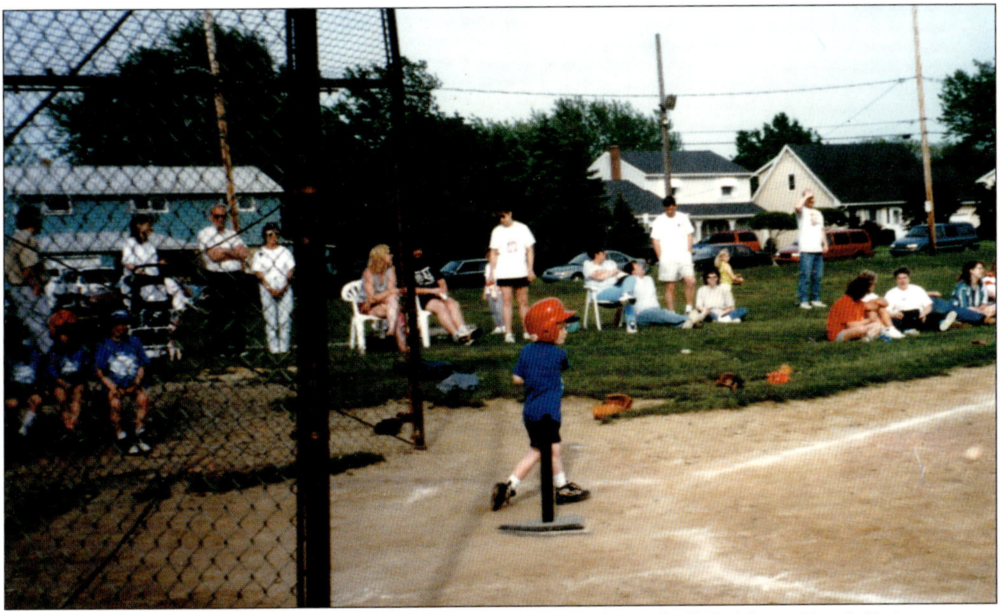

Before the new Iroquois Elementary School was built, this T-ball field on Tyndall Avenue in Lawrence Park was where aspiring ball players got their start. Fans either brought their own chairs or found a comfortable spot on the ground. Many young players went on to play on the Claude Austin Field behind Iroquois High School, which was dedicated in 1958 to Claude Austin, police chief from 1925 to 1950. (Courtesy of the Lawrence Park Historical Society.)

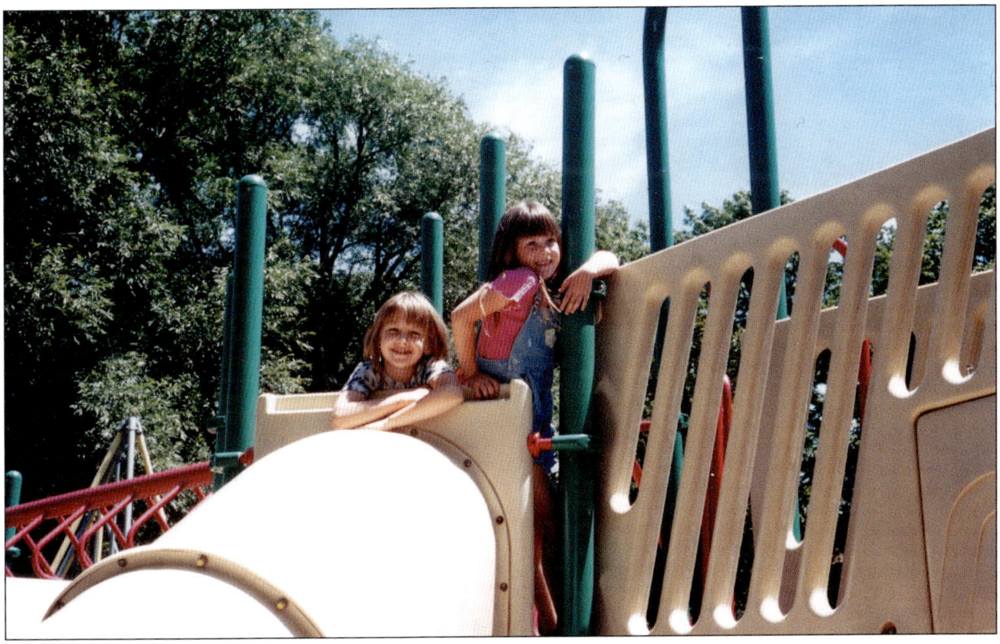

In 1999, the Lacey girls enjoyed the Napier Avenue playground that has served the community since the very early days of Lawrence Park. Located in the basin that is created by Four Mile Creek on the west side and the high bank where Napier Avenue is located, the park has been upgraded to contain modern playground equipment, basketball courts, and a picnic shelter. A supervised program is conducted in the summer. (Courtesy of the Lawrence Park Historical Society.)

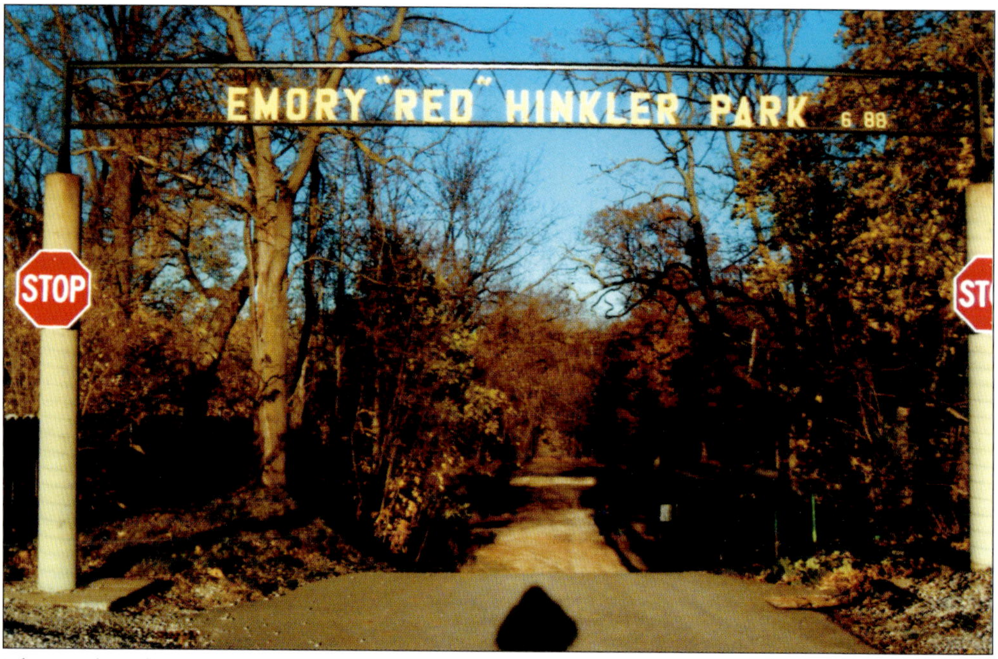

The Wesleyville park that is located between Riverside Drive and Four Mile Creek was renamed Hinkler Park in honor of Emory "Red" Hinkler, who was supervisor of streets in Wesleyville for 36 years. The park was formerly known as Edison Park.

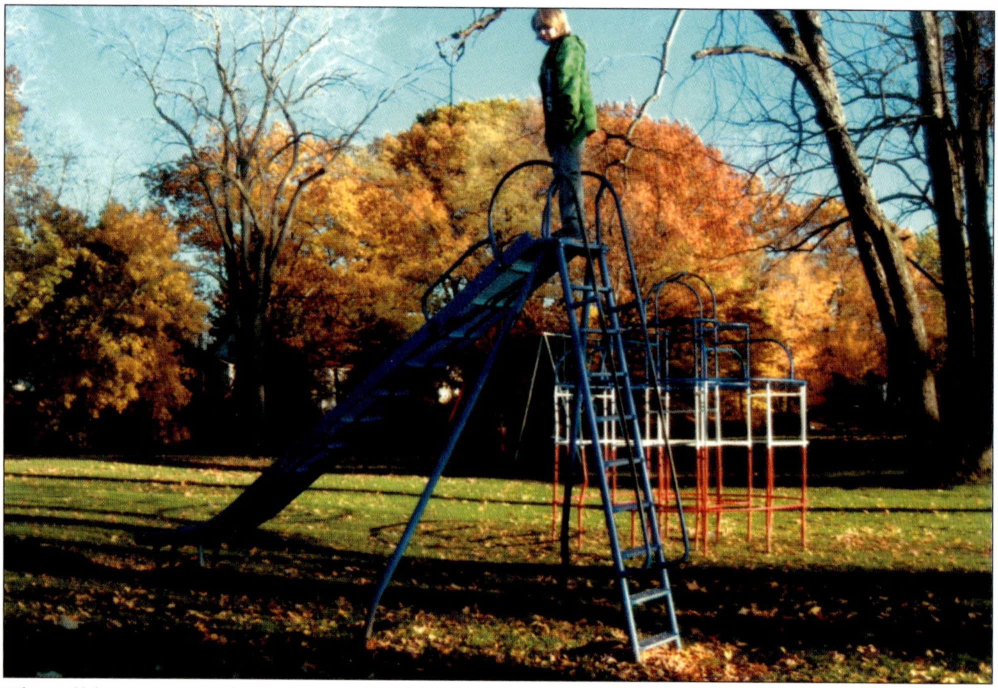

The tall boy seems to be surveying Hinkler Park as he gets ready to slide. Playground equipment and a large picnic shelter make a delightful place for groups to gather. Four Mile Creek flows just beyond these colorful trees as it makes its way toward Lawrence Park and eventually Lake Erie.

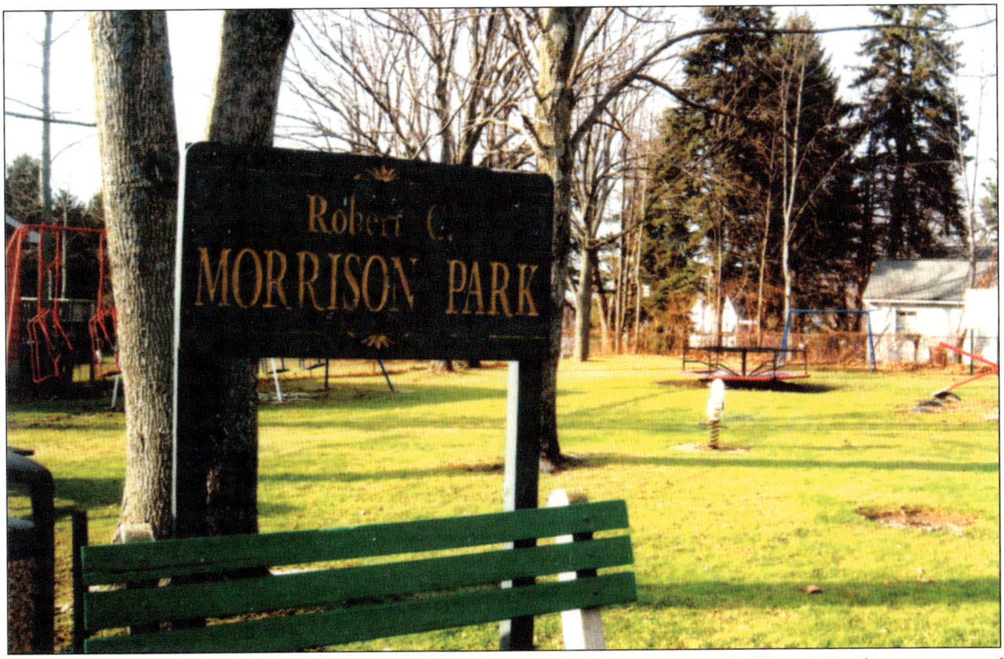

Robert G. Morrison Park provides green space and a play area in College Heights, a part of Wesleyville. Robert Morrison was a member of the borough council in the 1950s and again in 1991. He served on the Pennsylvania Board of Probation and Parole for 24 years.

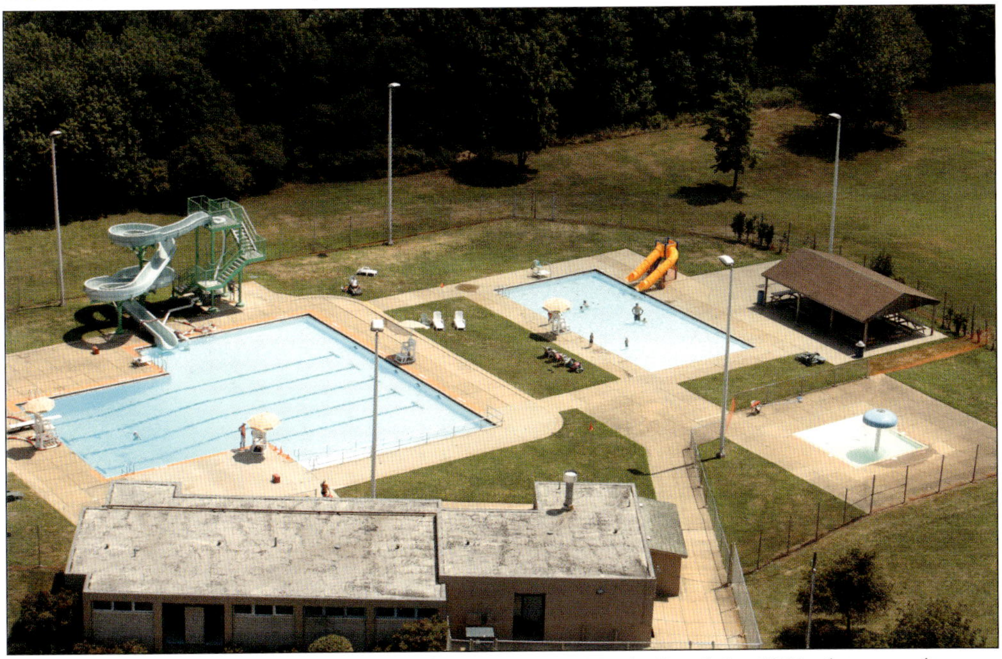

The Tri Community Pools are next to the YMCA on Nagle Road. In 1976, this complex was begun by the joint efforts of community-minded men from Wesleyville, Lawrence Park, and Harborcreek. The pools are managed by an authority composed of nine members, three people from each community. In 1996, the addition of slides added to the fun, and a picnic pavilion built by General Electric volunteers gives shelter for all. (Courtesy of Mark Bell.)

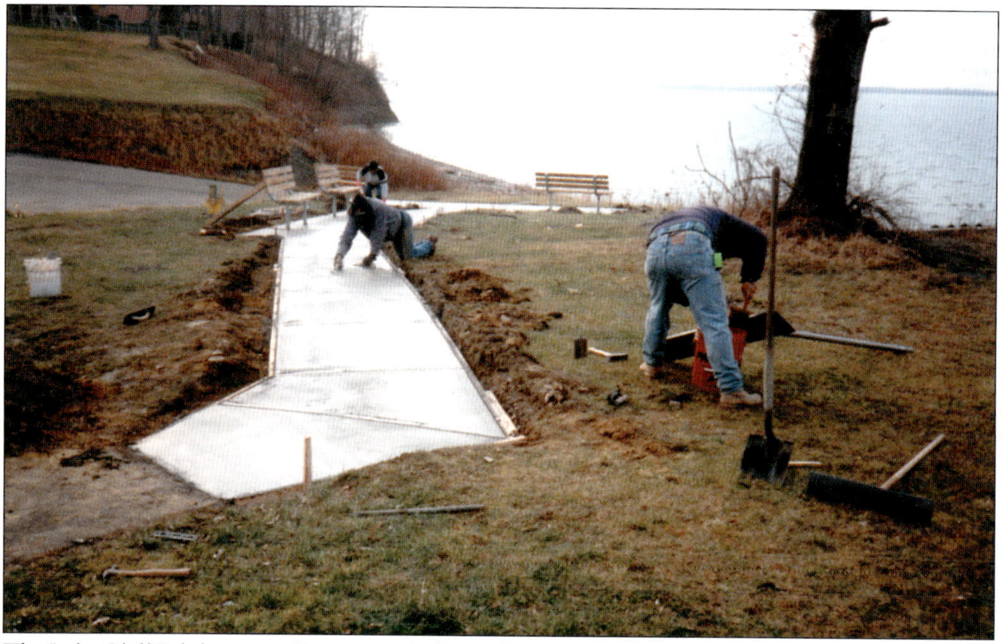

The Lake Cliff Subdivision of Lawrence Park was designed to have a swath of green space stretching from the playground to the lakefront. Here, work is being done on the walkway of the small park that is adjacent to the boat ramp. This park provides an ideal spot to watch beautiful Lake Erie sunsets. (Courtesy of the Lawrence Park Historical Society.)

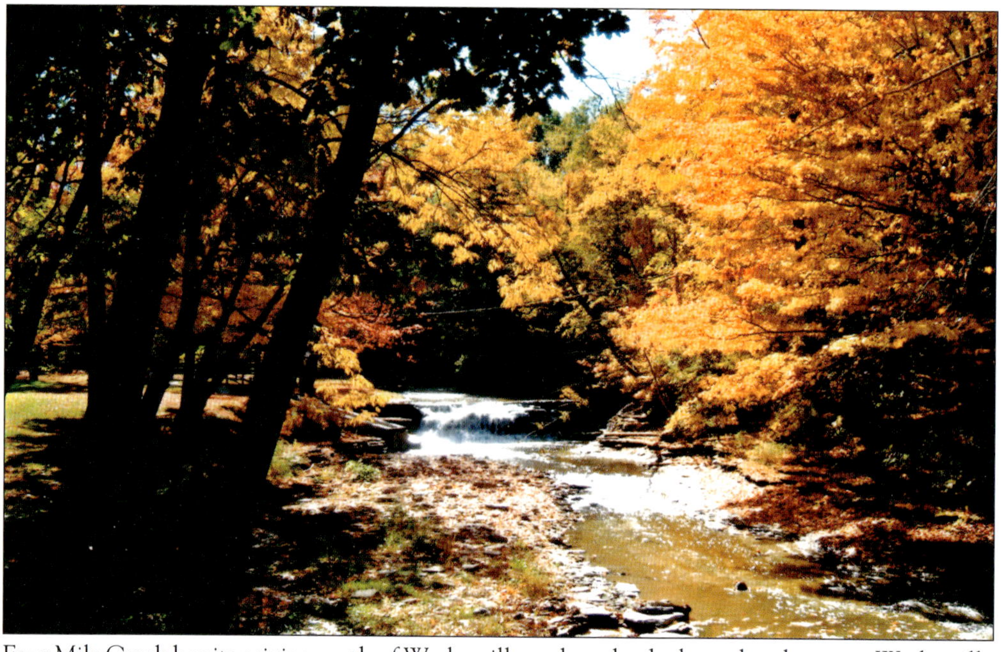

Four Mile Creek has its origins south of Wesleyville and marks the boundary between Wesleyville and Harborcreek. It flows through Lawrence Park, its banks creating green space between the General Electric factory and the residential area. It then continues on through the Lawrence Park Golf Course. This lovely waterfall is the background for many photographs, and the area creates a beautiful setting for weddings.

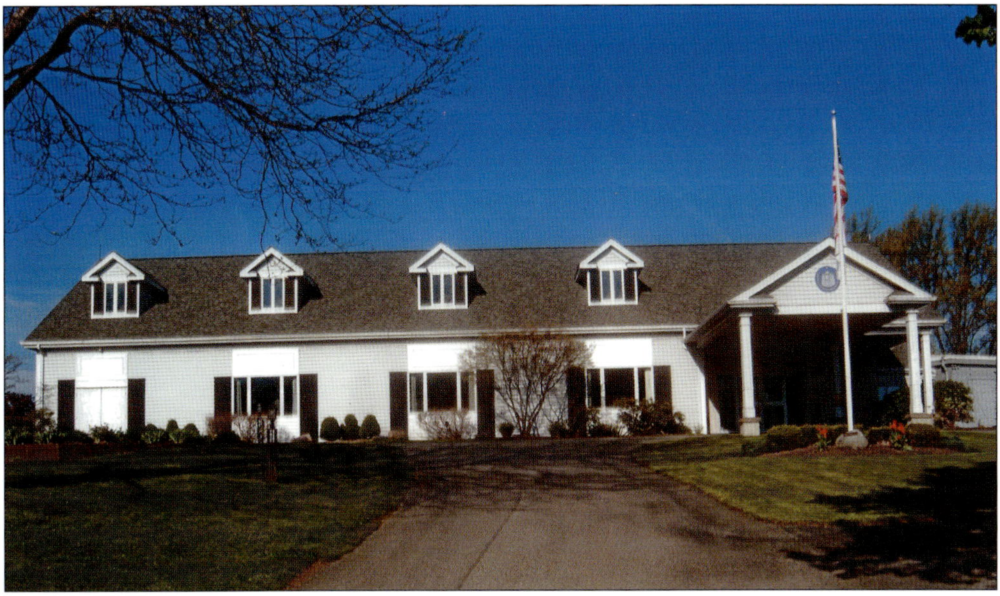

In 1989, a new Lawrence Park Golf Clubhouse was built to replace the farmhouse that had been used as a clubhouse. In addition to being used by members and for celebrations, the banquets for WILP (Wesleyville, Iroquois, Lawrence Park) are held here. Yearly since 2008, the WILP Hall of Fame has honored the best of local athletes and sports supporters.

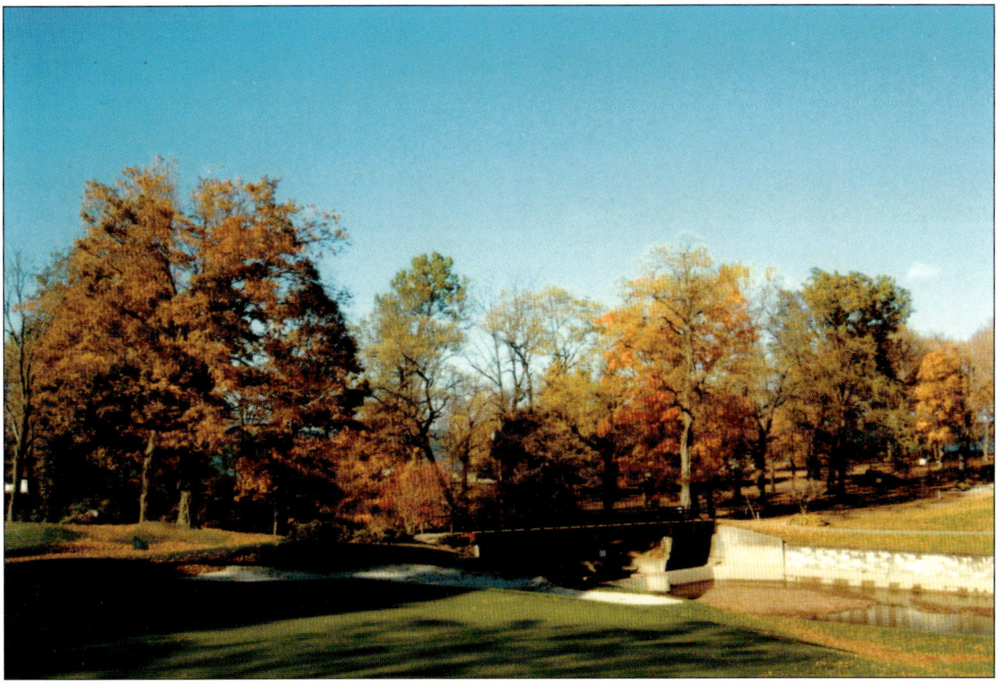

In 1921, a group of volunteers from General Electric Company began to develop the Lawrence Park Golf Course. By 1942, a second nine was constructed. In 1967, the members of the club purchased its 125 acres from General Electric Company. The nines have been reversed since the original construction, so this photograph shows the No. 9 green and gives a glimpse of the "golf ball–eating" pond created by damming Four Mile Creek.

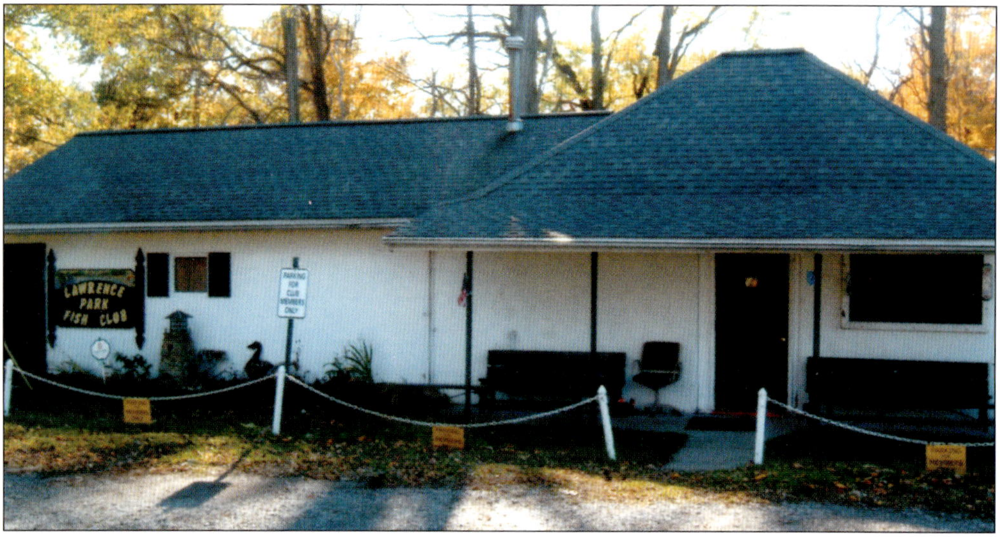

The Lawrence Park Fish Club began in 1946 through the efforts of local fishermen. It has provided a boathouse, clubhouse, and more recently a delightful picnic and playground area located on the bank of Lake Erie. The north end of the clubhouse is the only remaining building of Four Mile Creek Amusement Park, which provided entertainment for thousands from 1902 to 1919.

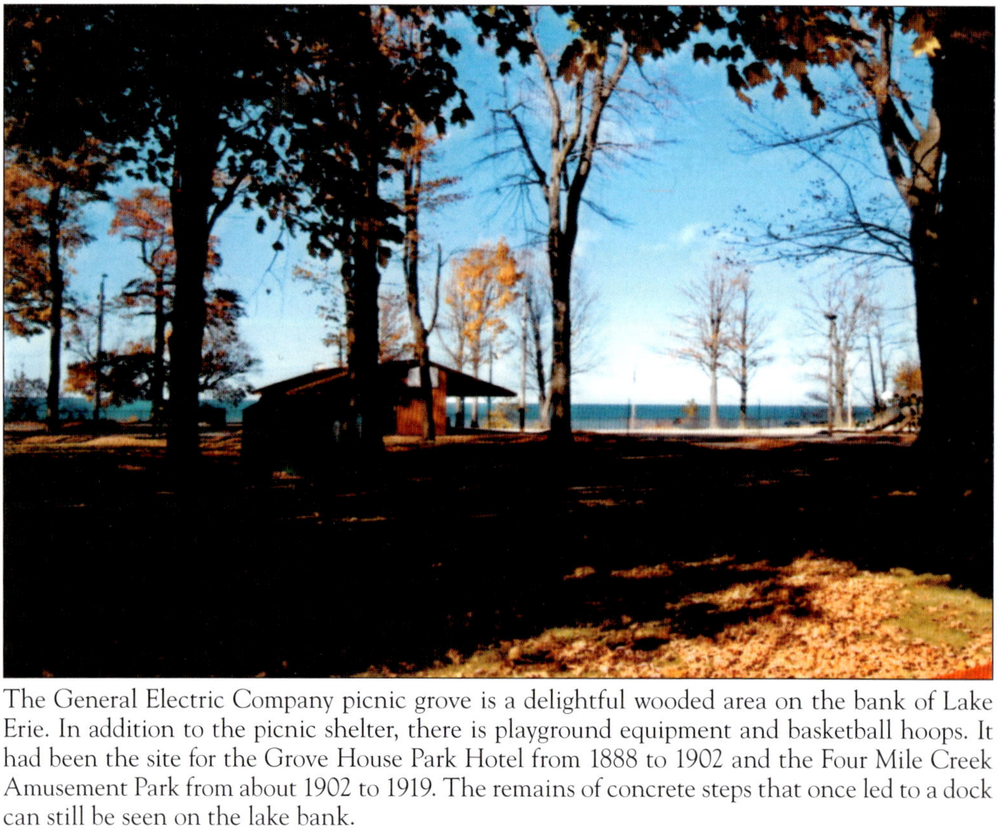

The General Electric Company picnic grove is a delightful wooded area on the bank of Lake Erie. In addition to the picnic shelter, there is playground equipment and basketball hoops. It had been the site for the Grove House Park Hotel from 1888 to 1902 and the Four Mile Creek Amusement Park from about 1902 to 1919. The remains of concrete steps that once led to a dock can still be seen on the lake bank.

Three

Schools

As early as 1810, there was a small school on Buffalo Road in Wesleyville. In 1894, the brick school was built on Market Street, and in 1919, the large brick school was constructed on Willow Street. This building and a portable housed all Wesleyville students until 1966.

In Lawrence Park, the Priestley Avenue school was built in 1913 and housed all grades until 1924, when the junior-senior high school was constructed on Morse Street and grades 9 through 12 transferred there. The primary school, built in 1953, was home to kindergarten through third grade. This building was eventually sold and is now the Lawrence Park Township Community Center.

After much discussion, the school districts of Lawrence Park and Wesleyville merged to become the Iroquois School District. The Bulldogs of Wesleyville and the Tigers of Lawrence Park became the Iroquois Braves. The new Iroquois High School was built on Iroquois Avenue on the site that had been the location of White City. The $3.1 million building was not quite finished in time for the first class of 1965–1966 so the new high school operated as one school in two buildings. There were class officers in each building and homecoming and prom kings and queens from each structure. However, the athletic teams merged to become a powerhouse. Iroquois football teams won the Erie County League championship in both 1965 and 1966. Similar success was had by basketball and baseball teams in those early years. The Priestley Avenue school and the Wesleyville portable trailer were torn down in 1967. The former high schools were renovated for use by elementary students.

In 2007, the new Iroquois Elementary School was completed, and the old Lawrence Park school, with its many memories, was demolished. The old Wesleyville school that also held many memories was sold.

To capture the essence of 50 years of the Iroquois School District is difficult; however, it is hoped that by focusing on highlights of various sports and activities readers will recall many memories. Schools are much more than buildings. Teachers, administrators, fellow students, athletics, extracurricular clubs, and activities also contribute to the school experience. Although each individual has different memories of school, it is hoped that these pages will engender pleasant reminiscing.

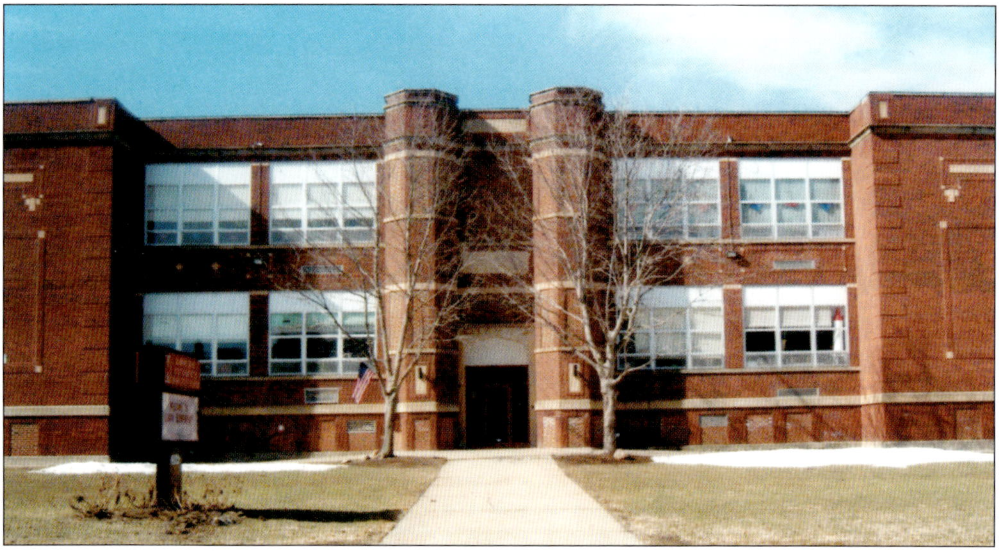

The venerable Wesleyville School holds many memories for generations of students from its beginnings in 1912 until 2007, when the last local students left the building and entered the new Iroquois Elementary School. William McKee was principal until his retirement in 1975, when Bob Wall took over. The building was sold to Harborcreek Youth Services in 2010.

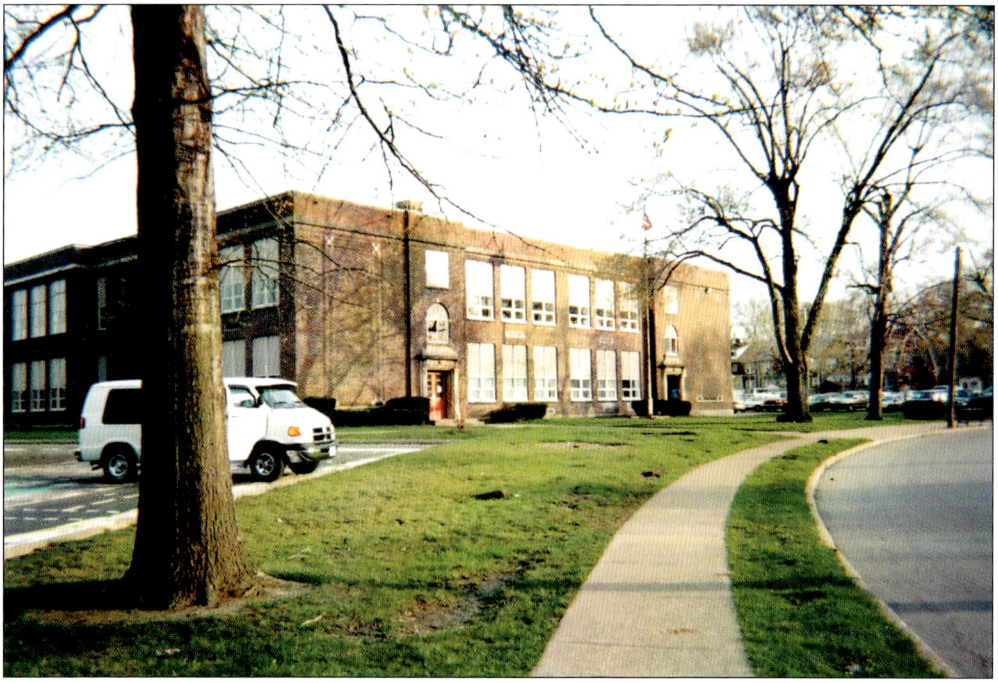

The Lawrence Park School was built in 1924 and served as a junior-senior high school until 1966, when the new Iroquois High School was ready for occupancy. Supervising principal was Harry K. Rhodes, and principal was Dan Skala, who served from 1931 to 1974. It was a sad day when the school, with its many memories, was demolished to make way for the new Iroquois Elementary School. (Courtesy of the Lawrence Park Historical Society.)

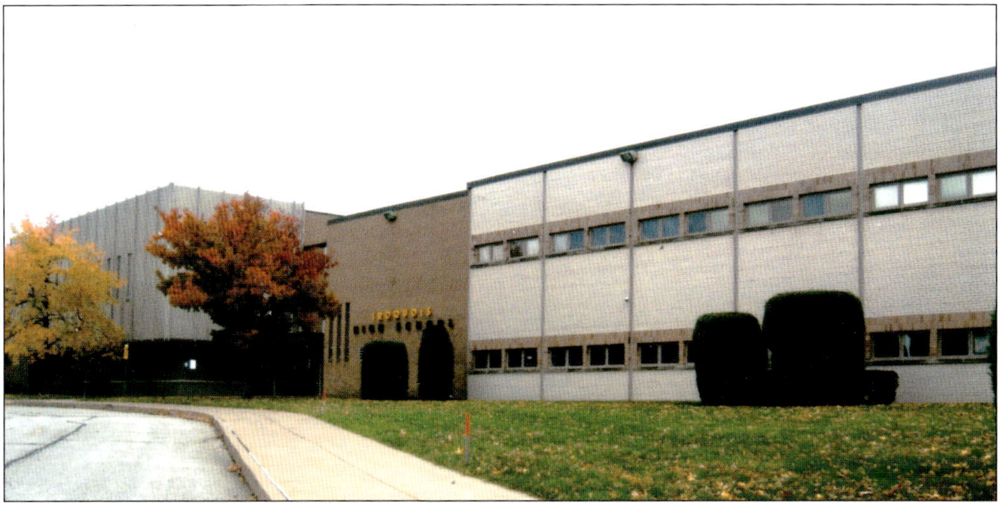

Construction of Iroquois High School started in 1963 but was delayed, so in 1965–1966, the first year for the high school, it operated as one school in two buildings. There were class officers and homecoming and prom kings and queens from each building. Jim Manafo suggested the name Iroquois, and Ron Brooks, the music director, wrote the school song. (Courtesy of the Lawrence Park Historical Society.)

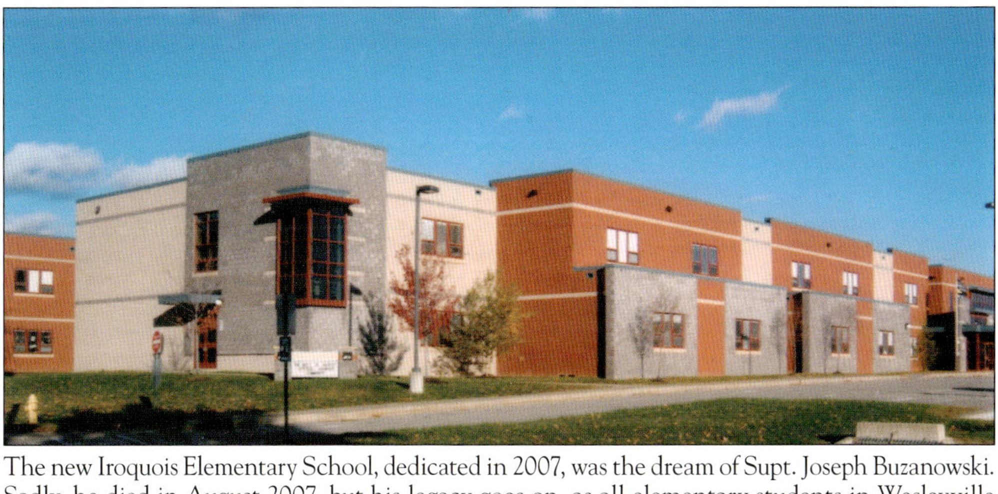

The new Iroquois Elementary School, dedicated in 2007, was the dream of Supt. Joseph Buzanowski. Sadly, he died in August 2007, but his legacy goes on, as all elementary students in Wesleyville and Lawrence Park now attend this state-of-the-art school. In August 2007, many volunteers helped move the elementary school supplies from Wesleyville and Lawrence Park schools to the new Iroquois Elementary School.

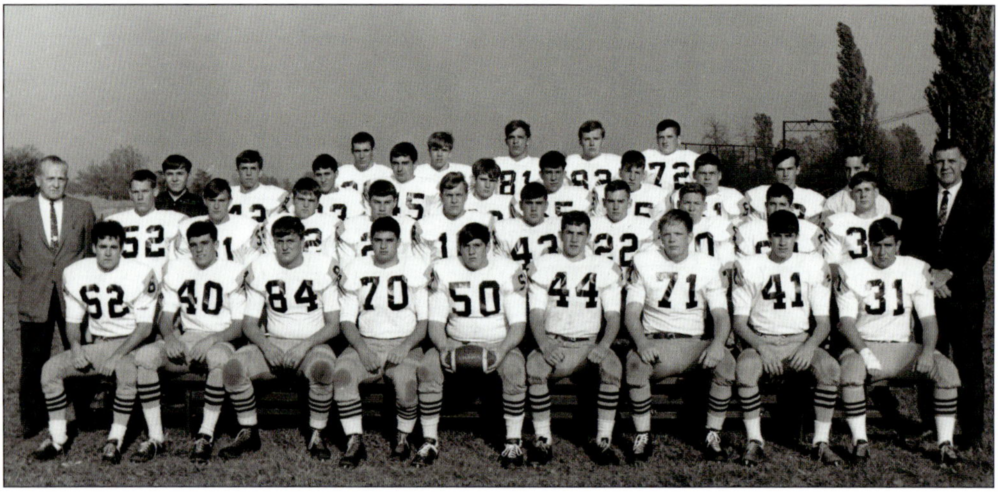

The 1966 football team captured the Erie County League championship, as did the 1965 team. Both teams were coached by Jim Manafo (left) and Ed Poly (right). In 2012, the 1966 football team was inducted into the Wesleyville, Iroquois, and Lawrence Park Hall of Fame. The 1965 team used a two-platoon system with the exception of Denny York, Gil Seus, Chuck Dengel, and Tony Major, who played both offense and defense. (Courtesy of Charlie Curtis.)

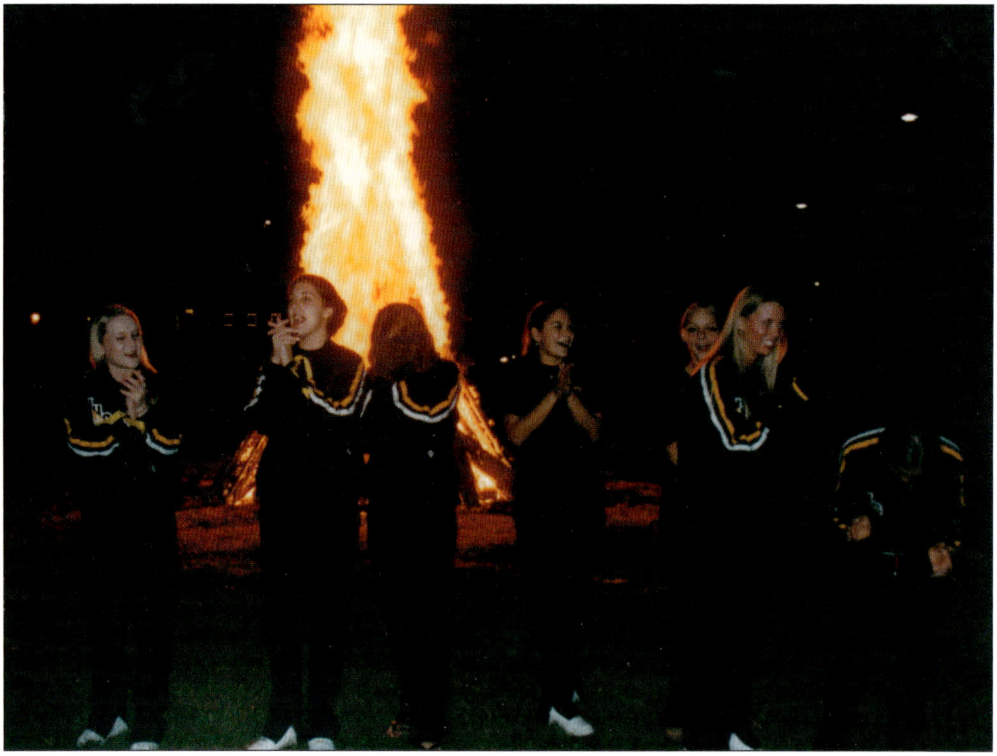

One of the time-honored traditions is the bonfire and rally the night before the homecoming football game. The football cheerleaders surround the blaze as they cheer on the team. In 1976, volunteers built bleachers; however, in 1998 they became unsafe and had to be removed. Spectators stood or brought their own chairs until 2001, when new bleachers were built. In 2009, the sod field was replaced by turf. (Courtesy of Gerard Drozdowski.)

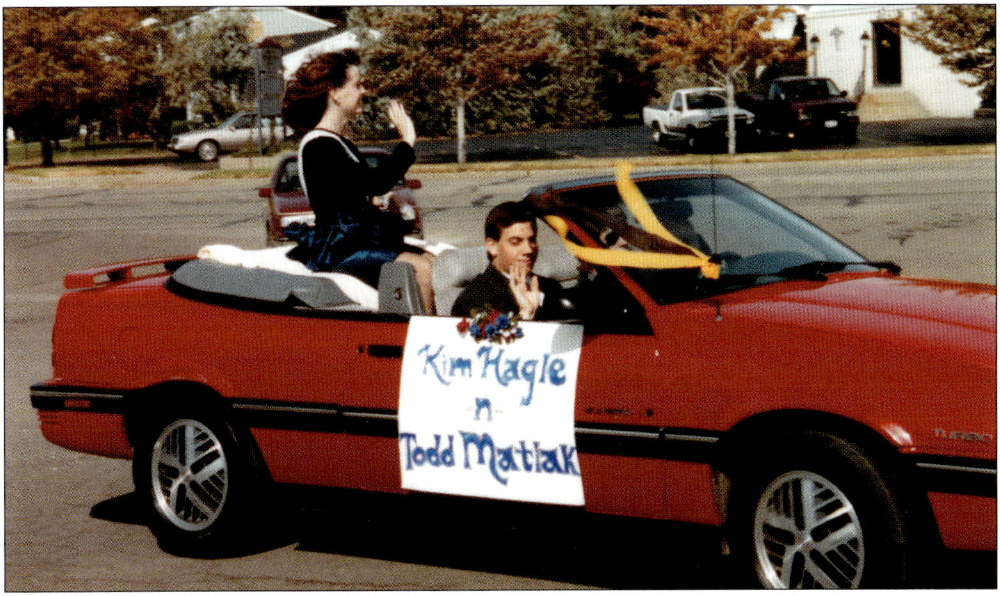

Another tradition is the homecoming court parade prior to the big game. Kim Hagle and Todd Matlak were part of the court in 1992. King Sean Day and Queen Cheryl Hagle presided over the festivities. At the first homecoming game in 1965, King Dick Bonniger and Queen Nancy Adams from Wesleyville and King Bob Ball and Queen Linda Burrows from Lawrence Park presided. (Courtesy of the Lawrence Park Historical Society.)

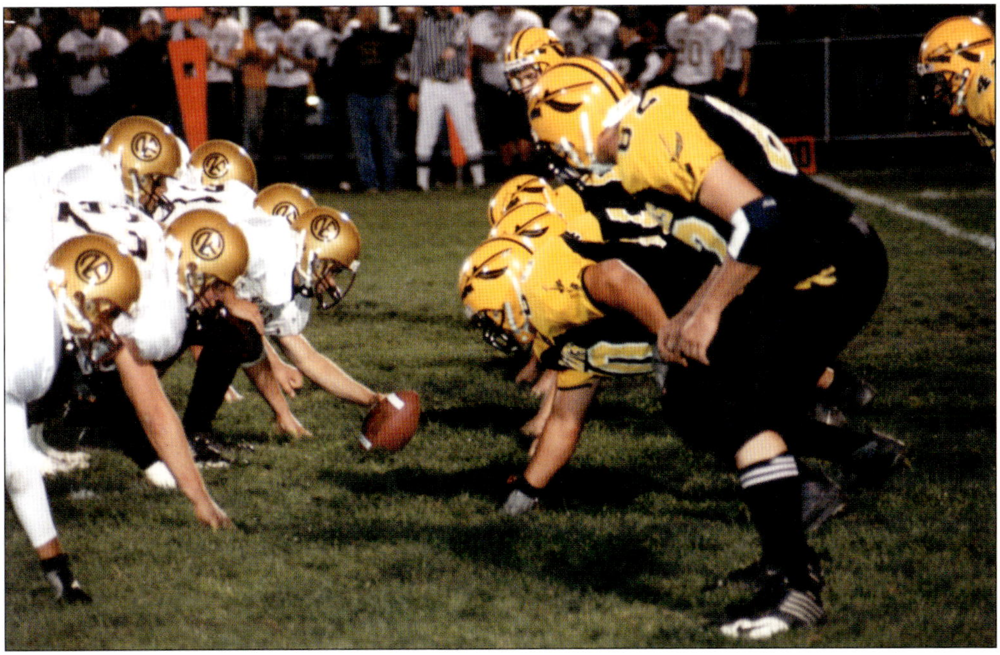

Two football teams get ready for action. The 1991 team, coached by Phil Glass, won the District 10 title. Scott Schnars recalls that there was illness caused by fumes from a gasoline leak on the bus while going to the playoff game against Smethport. The Iroquois team, favored to win, lost a heartbreaker. However, in 1990 and 1995, the team won District 10. (Courtesy of Gerard Drozdowski.)

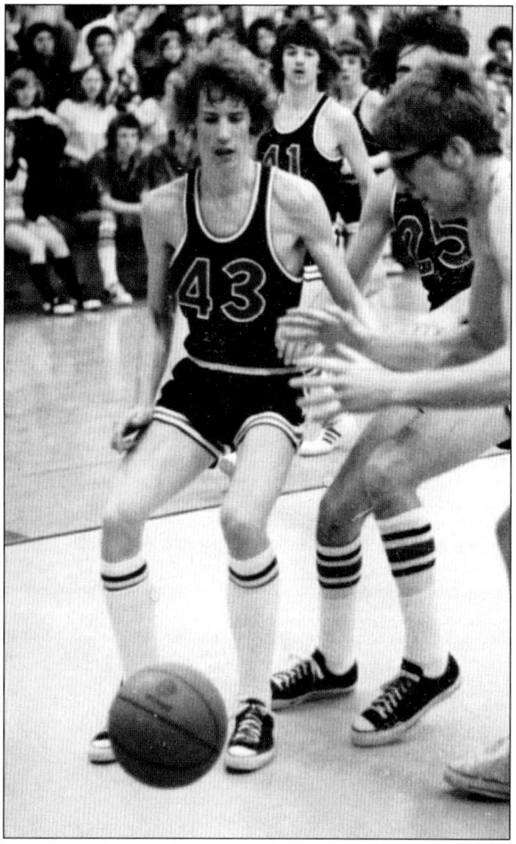

Dick Brickell (right) is about to pounce on a loose ball. Brickell and his teammates Gary Dietrich, Owen Bernatowicz, Scott Barringer, Greg Kurt, and Dick Chilcott won the Erie County League title in 1974–1975 with a perfect season and gave coach Tom Barringer his 200th win. (Courtesy of the Lawrence Park Historical Society.)

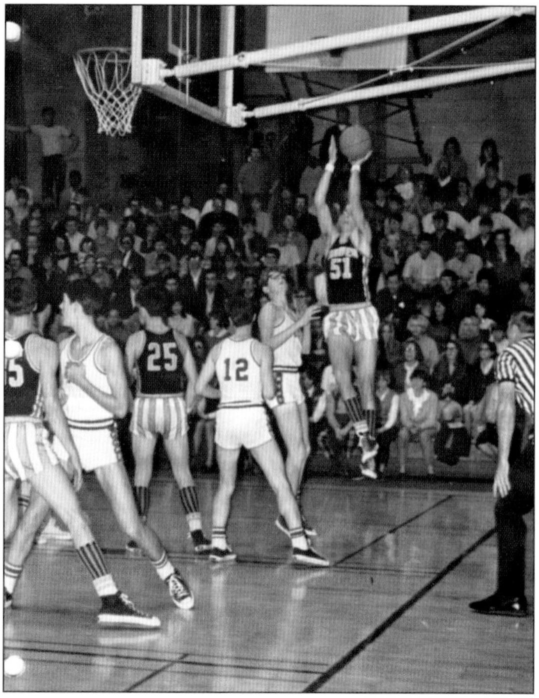

Jim Brickell goes to the hoop as the 1969 basketball team enjoys another winning season. They won the Erie County League title in 1967, 1968, and 1969 and District 10 in 1968 and 1969. In 1969, Don Wilson was high scorer in Erie County. The team was coached by C. Thomas Barringer and Harry Farnbaugh. The basketball teams went on to win many more championships. (Courtesy of the Lawrence Park Historical Society.)

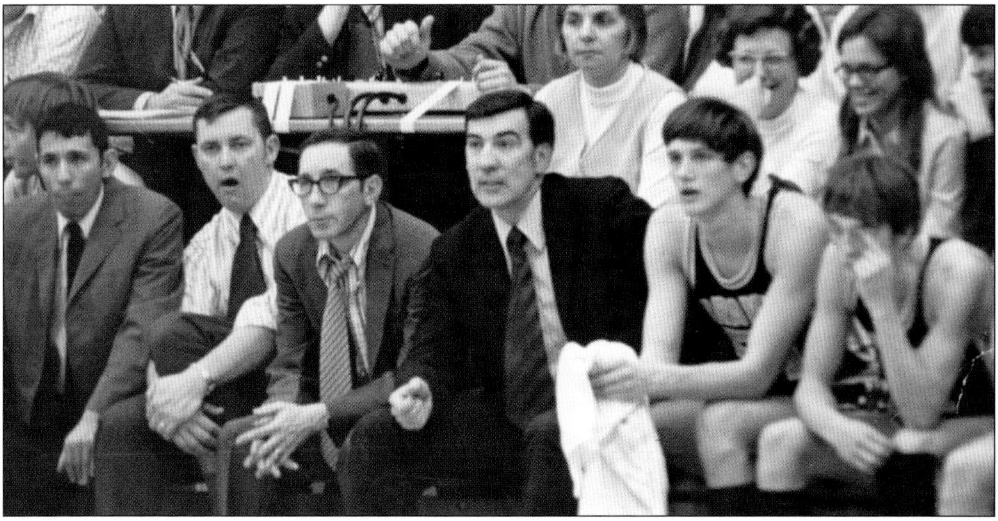

Coaches and fans are tense while watching a basketball game in the 1970s. Seated from left to right are Lenny Lombardo (assistant coach), John Post (athletic director), Dick Parry (assistant coach), C. Thomas Barringer (head coach), and two unidentified players. In 2014, the athletic field was dedicated to John Post, longtime athletic director. (Courtesy of the Lawrence Park Historical Society.)

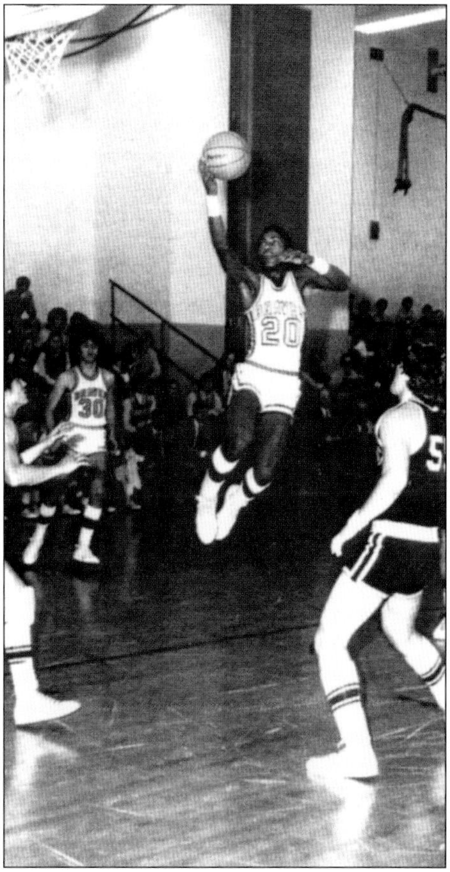

Vic Butler, a member of the 1973–1974 basketball team, shows his skills at jumping as he seeks to put the ball through the hoop. The basketball teams in 1970, 1972, 1973, and 1974 were District 10 champions. They also prevailed as Erie County League champions in 1975, 1983, and 1984. In 1972, young Tom Barringer celebrated scoring 1,000 points. (Courtesy of the Lawrence Park Historical Society.)

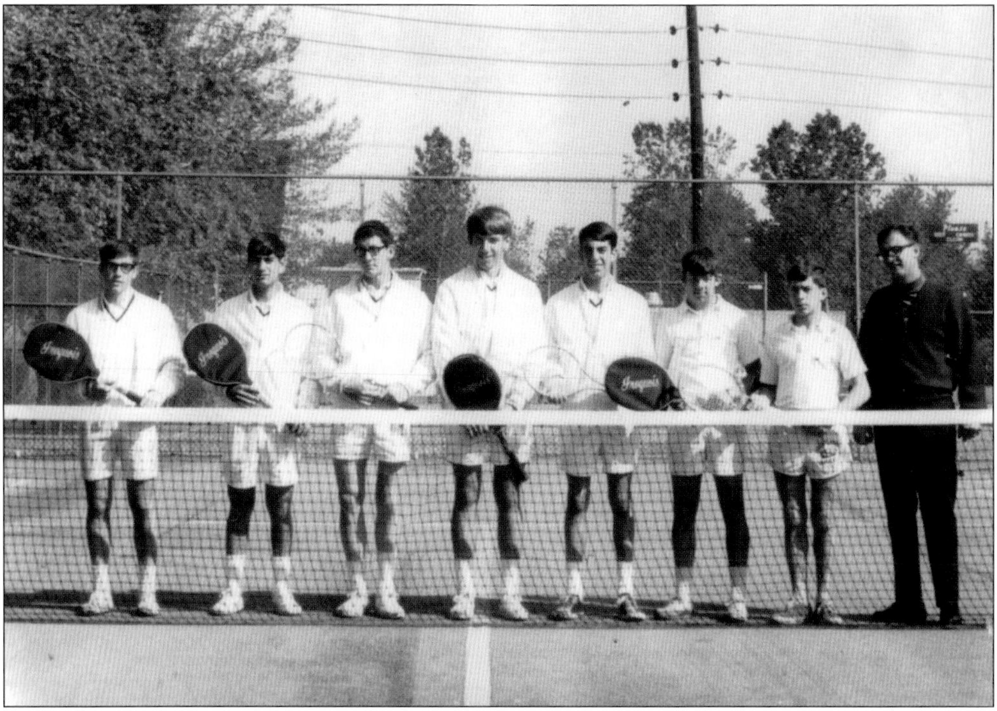

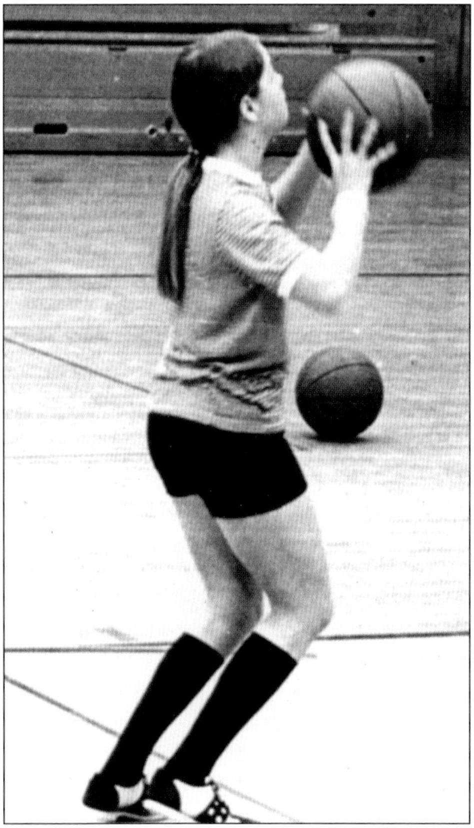

The 1968 tennis team, coached by Jim Perrotto (far right), is pictured here. Members are, from left to right, Tim O'Neil, Bob Thomas, Kent Peightal, Albert Perry, Brad Rankin, Daniel Roberts, and Craig Turnbull. The girls' tennis team won the Erie County League in 1978 and 1980 and Metro in 1975, 1976, and 1977. Outstanding players were Terry Catherine, Debbie Chilcott, Sharon Ferretti, Laurie Ferretti, Shelly Brown, and Debbie Seybold. Tennis and golf were cut from the athletic program in 1985. (Courtesy of Jim Perrotto.)

The first year for a girls' basketball team was 1972. Iroquois girls were Erie County League champions in 1983, 1984, and 1985 and also won District 10 in 1984. There were no girls sports prior to this; however, the girls enjoyed Girls Athletic Association, sponsored by Phyllis McLane. The 1979–1980 team featured Mez Chilcott, Mary Armbruster, Tricia Guise, and Lisa Jacobitz. (Courtesy of Gerard Drozdowski.)

D. Thompson is carefully considering his next shot. Golf had been a popular sport for many years, but in 1985, golf and tennis were cut from the school budget. However, in 2009, coed golf teams with coach Mike Kujawinski once again took to the links and entered into District 10 competitions. (Courtesy of Gerard Drozdowski.)

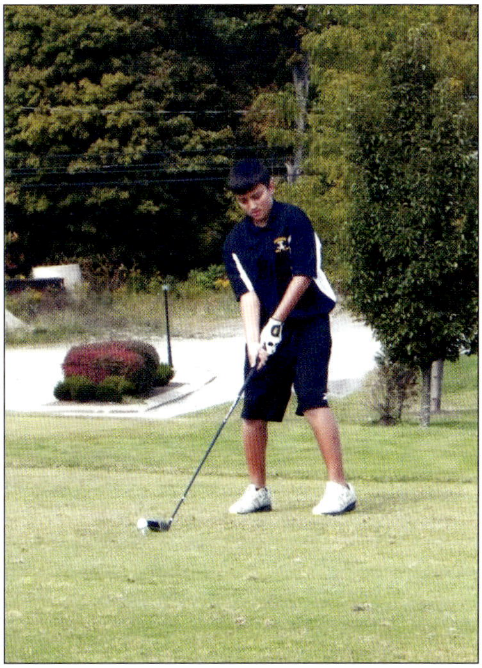

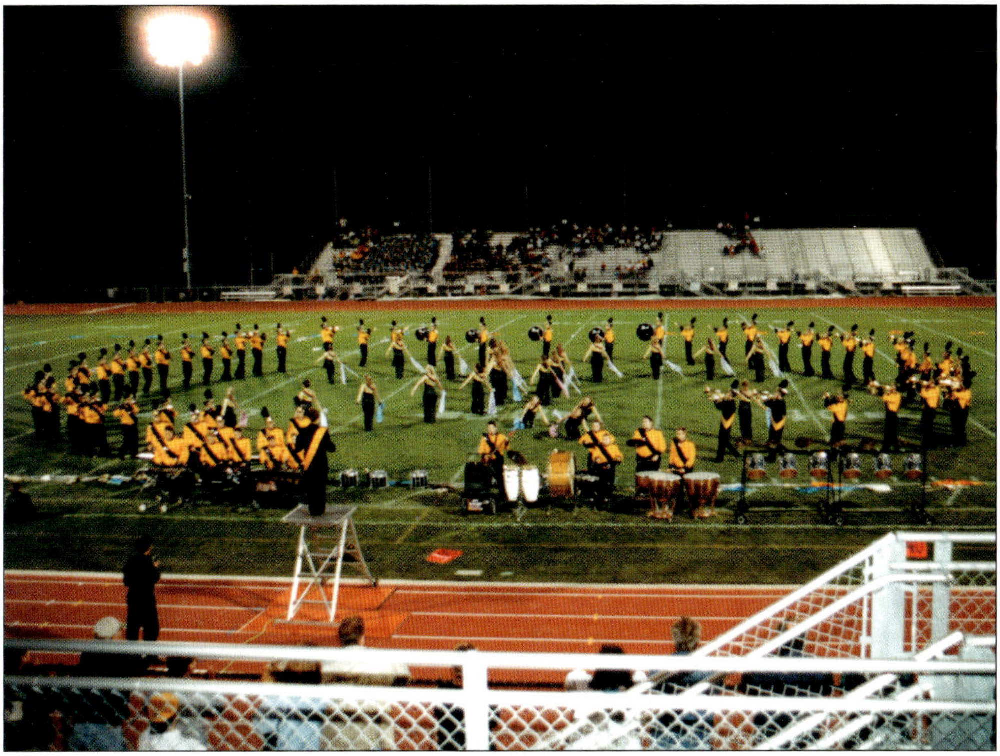

The Iroquois Marching Band has been under the direction of Robert Chase since 1992 and has won a roomful of trophies in Lakeshore Marching Band Association competitions. The band has increased its membership from about 40 members to over 100 members. Hardworking band boosters assist the band in many ways. (Courtesy of the Lawrence Park Historical Society.)

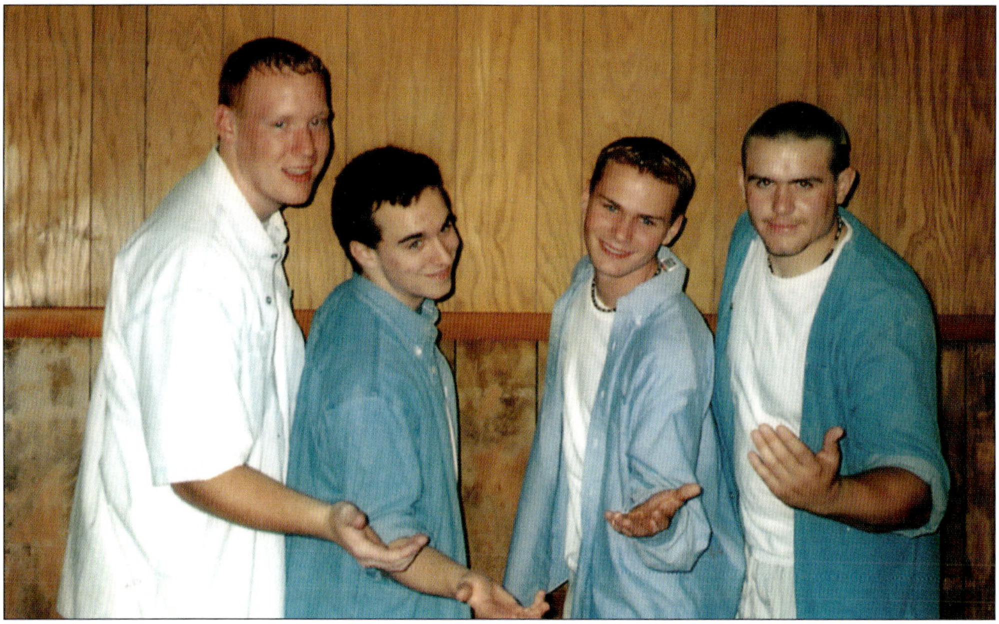

A Spring Concert in the Courtyard in 2000 called on the vocal talents of, from left to right, Bob Applebee, Jonathan Beveridge, Mark Weindorf, and Kevin Loftus. The Iroquois choirs and drama clubs have presented many beautiful concerts and entertaining musicals. (Courtesy of Roberta Stoughton.)

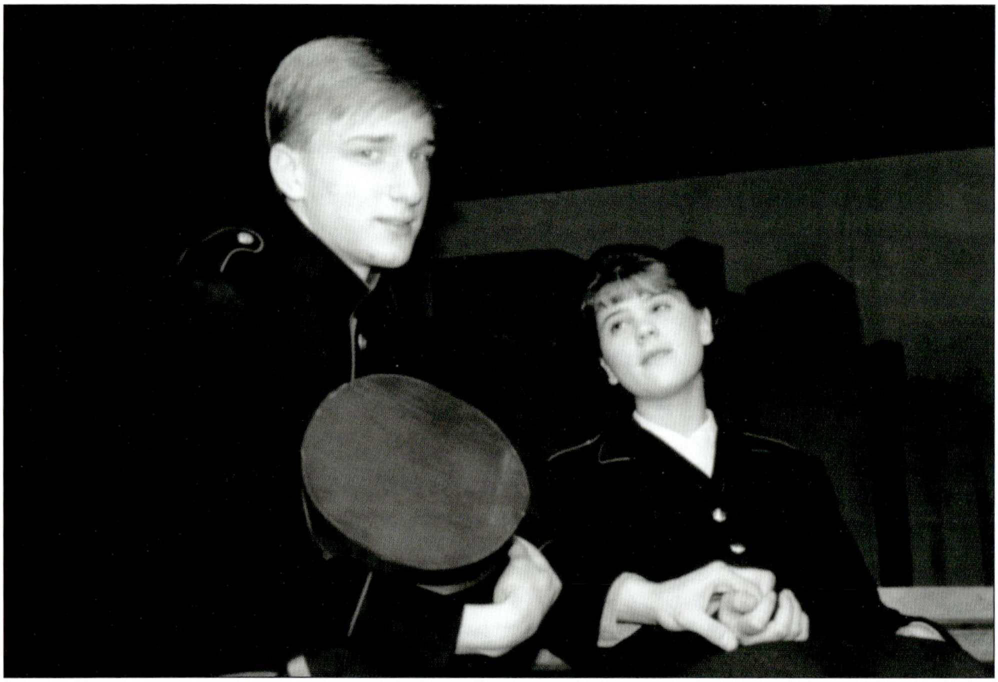

In 1993, the drama club produced the popular *Guys and Dolls* under the direction of Roberta Stoughton. Shown here are Steve Pelkowski and Denise Mankoski who starred in the show. This entertaining show was also produced in 2003 by another group of talented Iroquois students. (Courtesy of Roberta Stoughton.)

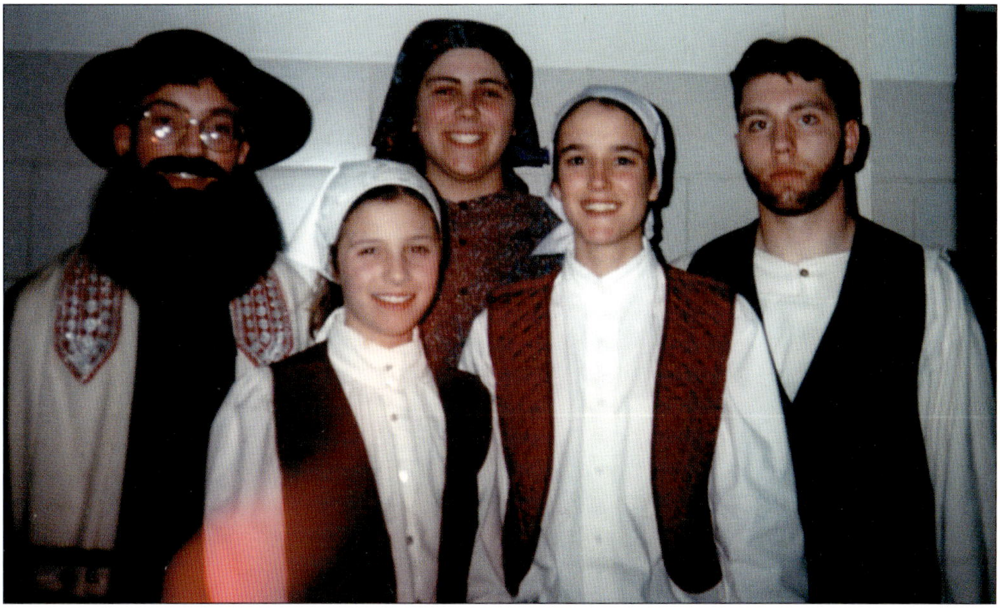

Yet another drama club production was the ever-popular *Fiddler on the Roof.* The part of Tevye was played by Troy Brydon and Golda by Laura Tryon. Lisa Salter, Rachel Stewart, and Kyle Millet also had major roles in this time-honored musical that entertained students and the community. (Courtesy of Roberta Stoughton.)

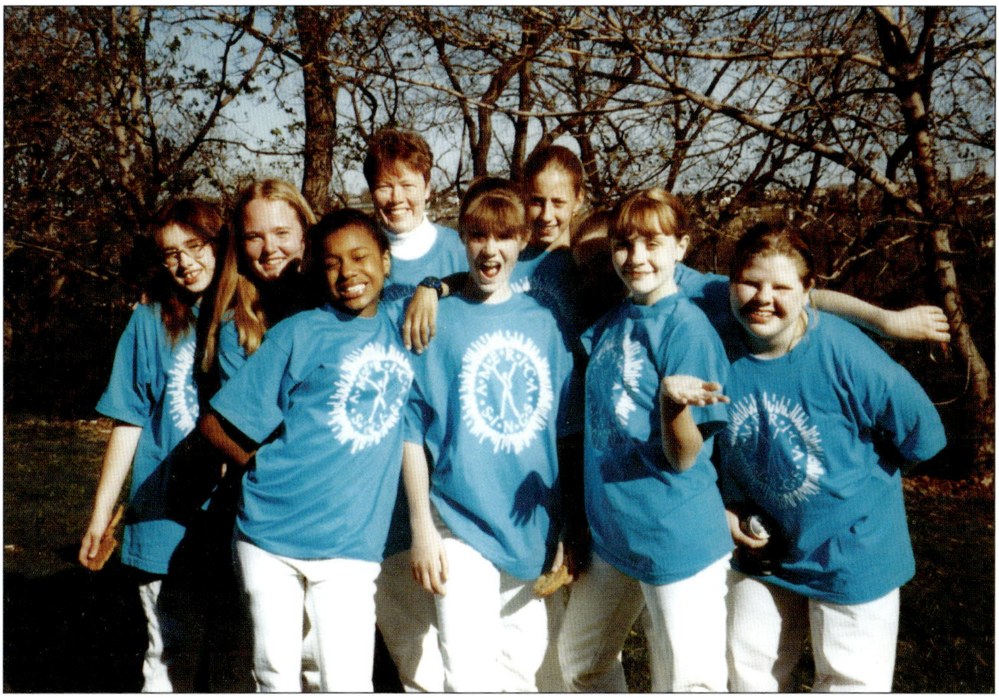

In 1997, under the direction of Roberta Stoughton, 100 students participated in the America Sings program in Pittsburgh. Iroquois vocalists joined the combined voices of 2,500 singers who were urged to utilize their time and talents to help others. In 2002, Iroquois students participated in Music in the Parks in Toronto, Canada. (Courtesy of Roberta Stoughton)

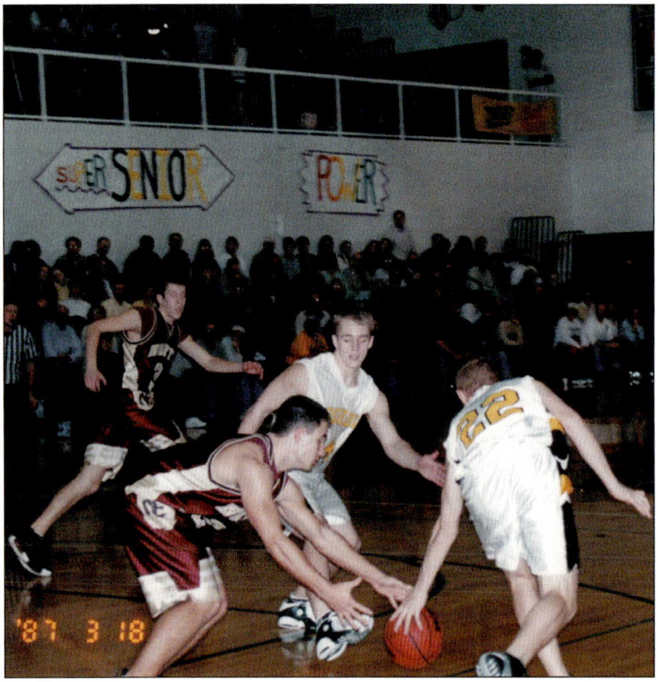

Jordan Eller steals the ball in a 2005 basketball game. The team played in District 10 playoffs and fell only slightly short in the state playoffs. Jordan Eller and Matt Merry led the team in scoring. Others on the team were Justin Smith, Will Crotty, Dan Howell, Stephen Barringer, Ryan Lutton, Dan Barringer, and Tony Cassaady. (Courtesy of Gerard Drozdowski.)

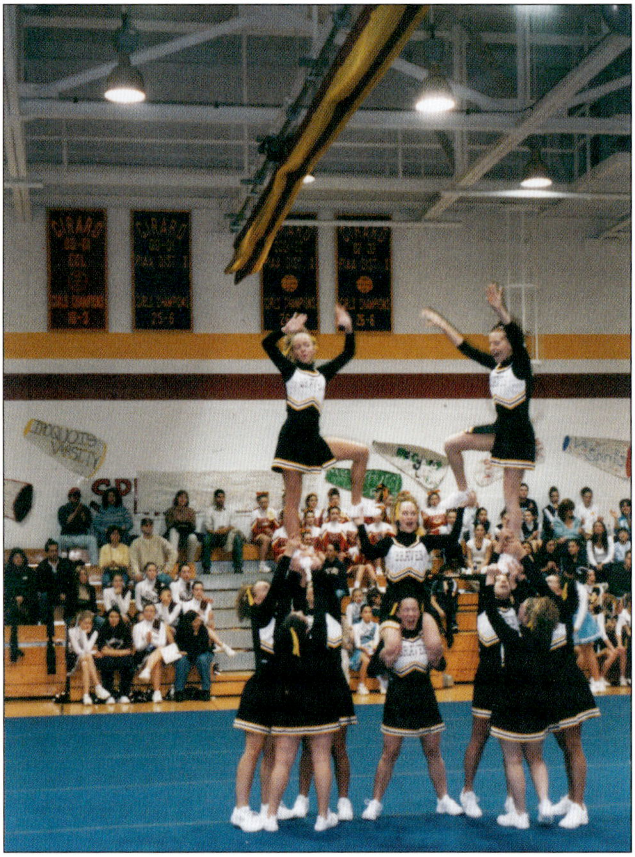

Cheerleaders are athletic and fearless as they create enthusiasm in the crowd. Iroquois has several squads of cheerleaders for football, basketball, and wrestling. The girls practice their routines for long hours and also put a lot of effort into decorating the halls during spirit week. (Courtesy of Gerard Drozdowski.)

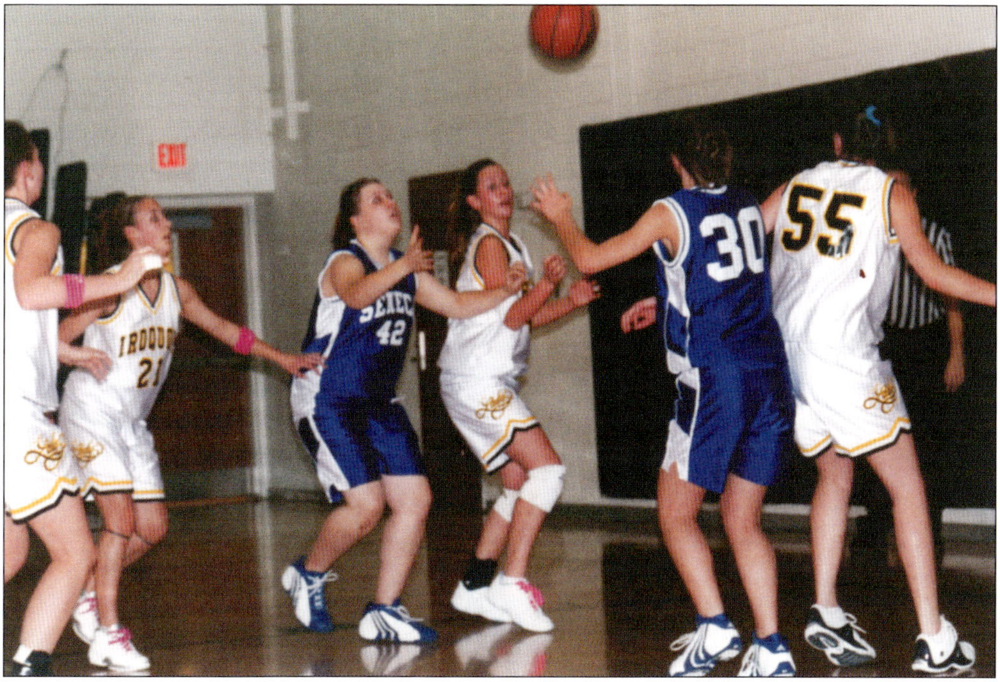

The girls' basketball team won the Erie County League championship in 1983 and 1985. They won the District 10 championship in 2004 and had a spot in the District 10 playoffs in 2005. Players who have scored over 1,000 points are Wendy Turco (1983), Shelly Brown (1985), Tammy Bokol (1986), Amy Krajnik (1999), and Jackie Artise (2005). (Courtesy of Gerard Drozdowski.)

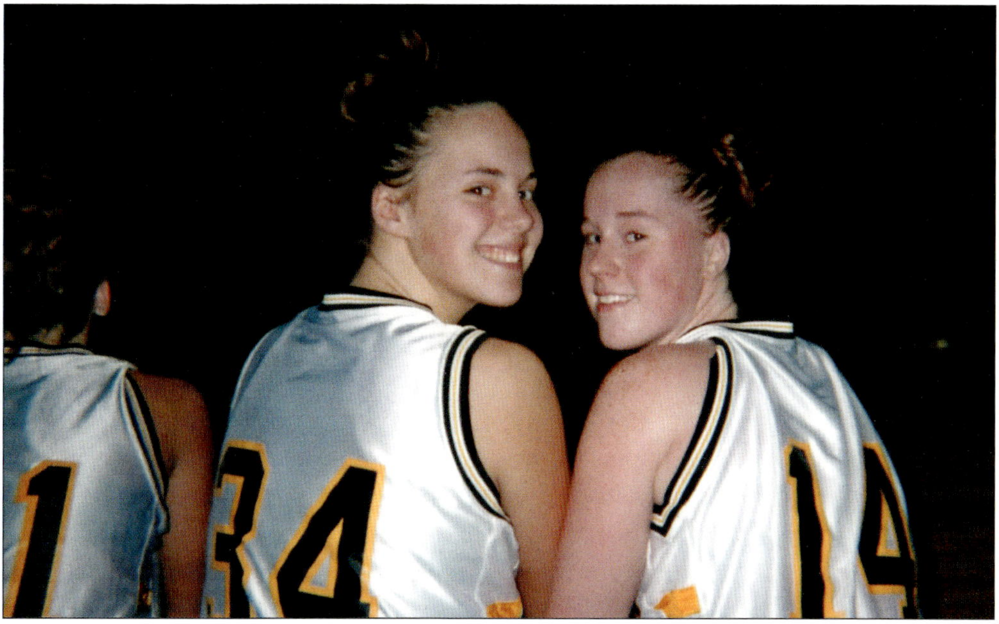

The winning smiles of Nicole Wilson (left) and Katie Barringer (right) indicate they are enjoying the game. Wilson also was a track-and-field star, and in 2005, she placed second at state competition in discus. In 2005, Wilson scored her 1,000th point in basketball, and in 2015, Rosemary Campbell, another basketball standout, also scored 1,000 points. (Courtesy of Gerard Drozdowski.)

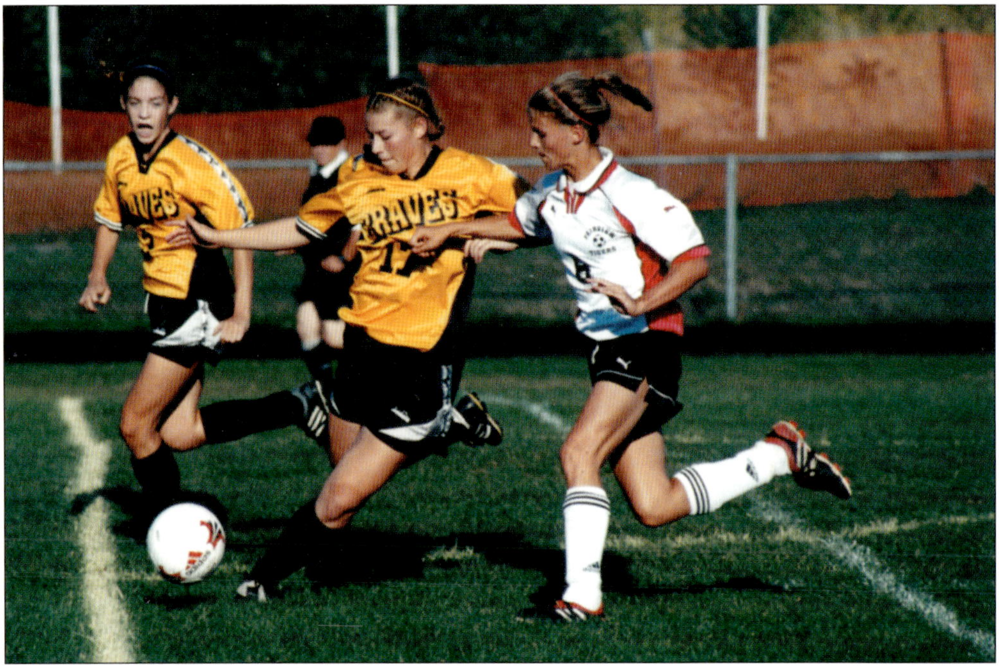

Sarah Krajnik looks like she is about to score as Devin Eller (far left) runs beside her. Goalie Liz Hall was named team MVP, and all-county honors went to Hallie Robertson. The 2003 team narrowly missed a playoff spot, and in 2010, the team was the regional champion. The girls' soccer team began in 1991 and in 1995 advanced to District 10 playoffs. (Courtesy of Gerard Drozdowski.)

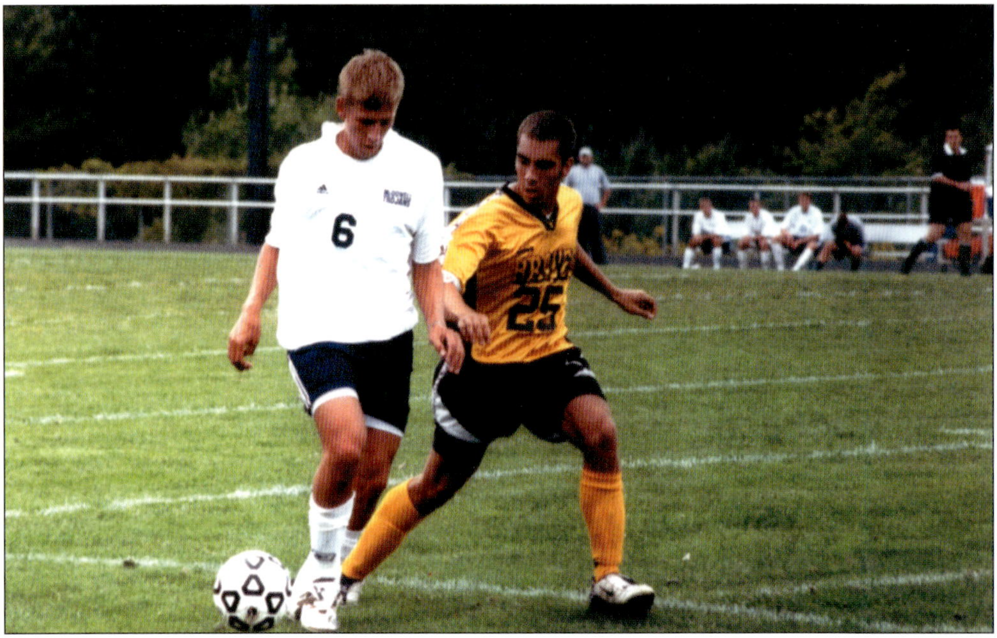

The Iroquois boys' soccer team was Erie County League champion in 1997 and 2002. They also won District 10 in 1996, 1997, 1999, 2001, and 2002. In 2001, the team was second in the state under captains Mike Marche, Cory Baird, Kevin Falk, and Matt LaPaglia. (Courtesy of Gerard Drozdowski.)

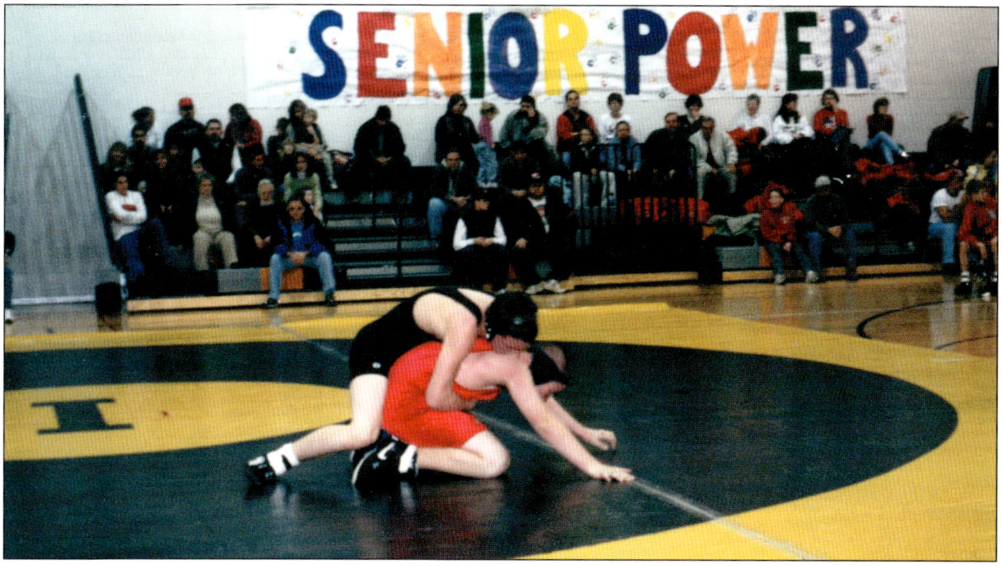

The wrestling teams were coached by Jack Sinnott from 1965 to 1978. They were Erie County League champions in 1969, 1970, 1971, 1972, and 1974. Well known in the world of wrestling were Craig and Tom Turnbull, Ed Trimmer, and Larry Trimmer, who was a state finalist in 1971. In 1992, Sean Day placed third at state. In 1994–1995, when wrestling was to be cut from the budget, concerned community members kept the program going. (Courtesy of Gerard Drozdowski.)

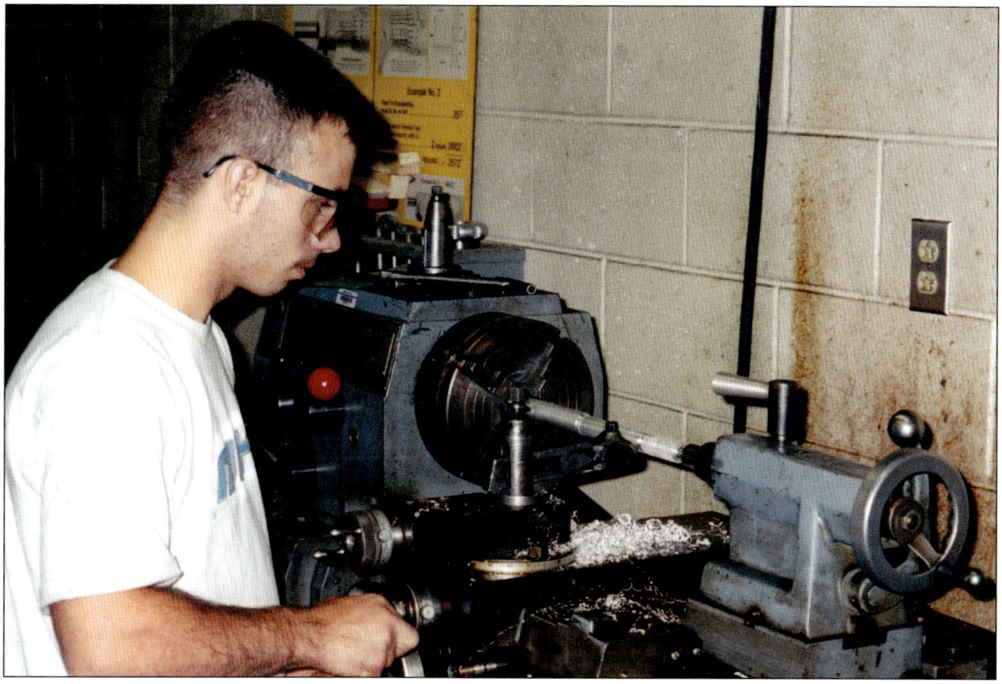

The Erie County Technical School offers students the option of learning occupations in any one of 18 areas by choosing to enroll in this excellent program. Over the years, various attendance patterns have existed; some years it was two weeks at Erie County Technical School (ECTS) and two weeks at Iroquois. At present, students attend a half day at Iroquois and a half day at ECTS. (Courtesy of Gerard Drozdowski.)

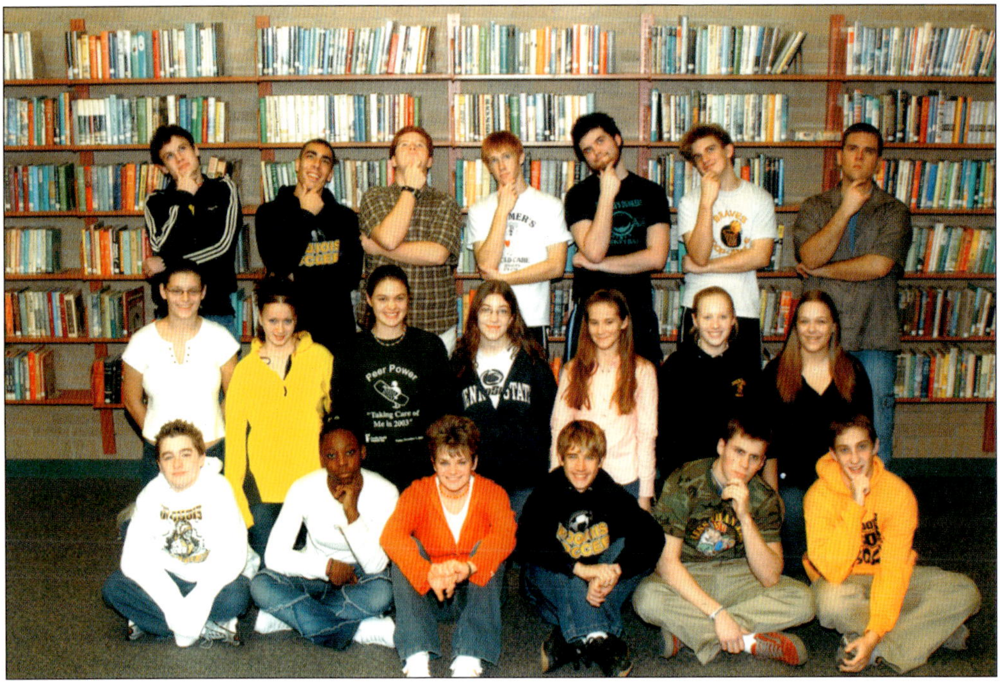

The library has always been a haven for information and a quiet place to study, especially when Lynda Knauff ("Sarge") was in charge. This group looks like serious book lovers. In the 1970s, there was a career resource room adjacent to the library. The speech and debate teams spend time doing research in the library, and in 2015, the Iroquois Book Club team won the Battle of the Books. (Courtesy of Gerard Drozdowski.)

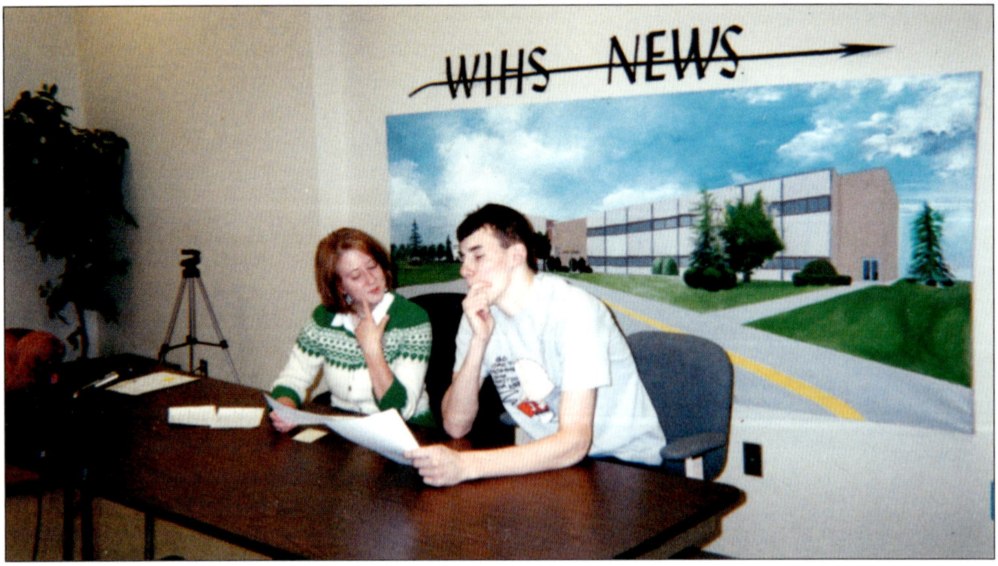

Will Crotty and Stacey Weismiller look as though they are pondering the breaking news of the day. Other groups that spend long hours gathering and disseminating news are the staffs of the newspaper, the *Smoke Signal*, and the yearbook, the *Bravero*. Some years, the *Manito*, a literary magazine, was also published. Until 1980, printing was done in the graphics class with Charles Leehan, instructor. (Courtesy of Gerard Drozdowski.)

Art and music are available to all students in both the elementary and high schools, and it is a favorite subject for many students. In this photograph, a student is working on a large, impressive painting. Some of the art teachers who have encouraged budding artists were Les Fobes, Mark Bowen, Karen Corle, and Bryan Toy. (Courtesy of Gerard Drozdowski.)

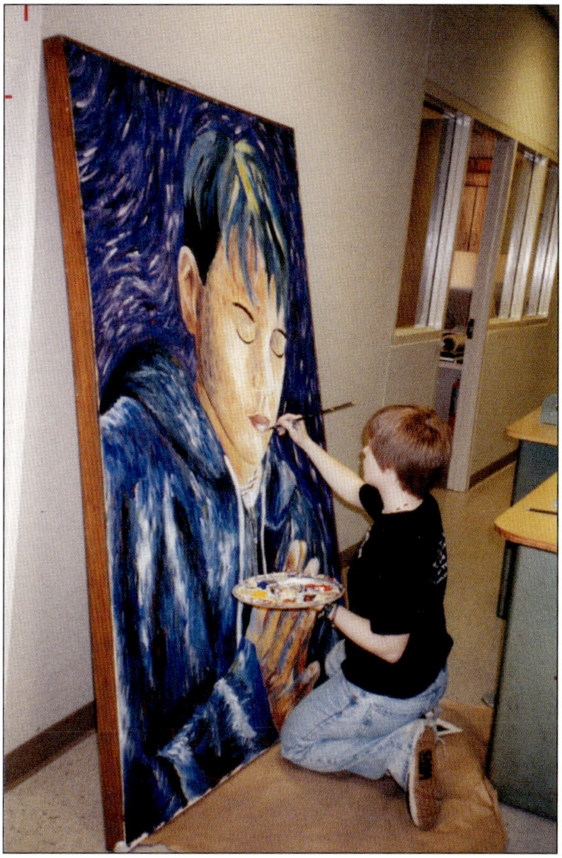

The Christmas Tree Assembly is one of the many activities sponsored by the student council. In 1972, the student council helped to revise the dress code, especially after girls who had worn slacks to school were sent home as rules stated it had to be 15 degrees before girls were allowed to wear slacks. William Parrish, principal, thought it was 18 degrees, but it was 15 degrees. He heard from some irate parents. (Courtesy of Gerard Drozdowski.)

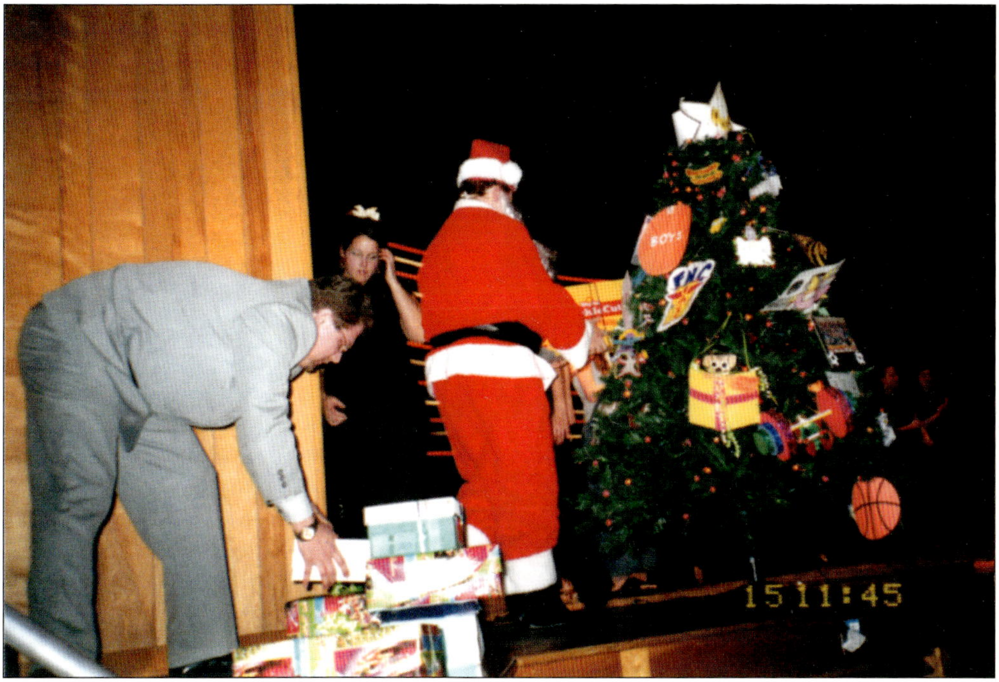

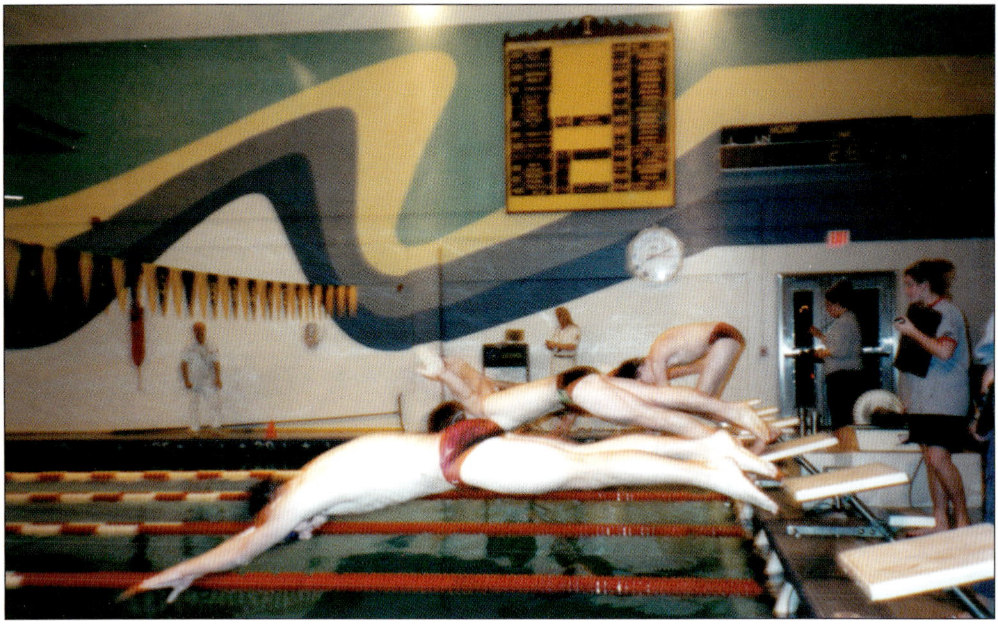

In the early years at Iroquois, when there were sliding glass doors that opened to the outside, Dave Tompkins coached the swim team. In 1993, the auditorium was dedicated to "Dr. David Tompkins, teacher, coach, and principal 1961 to 1993." Swim teams have set many records under the direction of Bob North and, recently, Mike Kujawinski. In 2010, Rachael Regan advanced to state competitions.

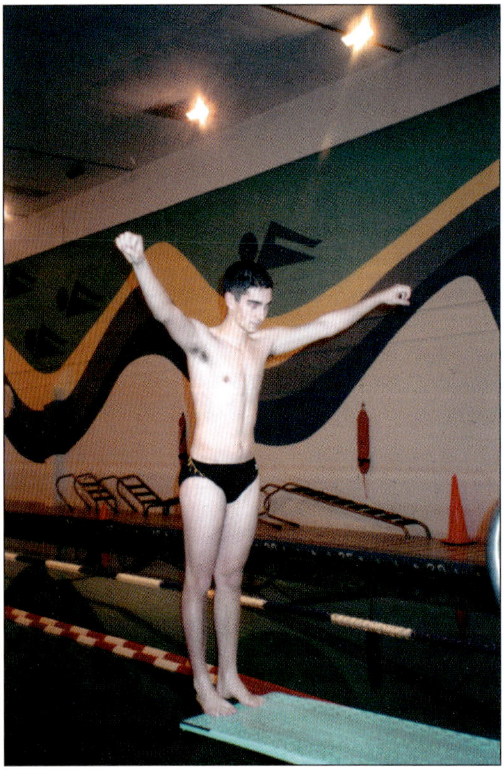

Kyle LaPaglia is poised to do a back dive. LaPaglia, Vinny Massella, and Kyle Mulligan qualified for state competitions. Some of the other outstanding divers were Jessica Norman, Brenna Pease, May Smith, Brianna Downs, and Nicki Hodges. Dave Mulligan was the diving coach for many years. Recently, the pool bottom was resurfaced and raised, so the pool can no longer be used for diving.

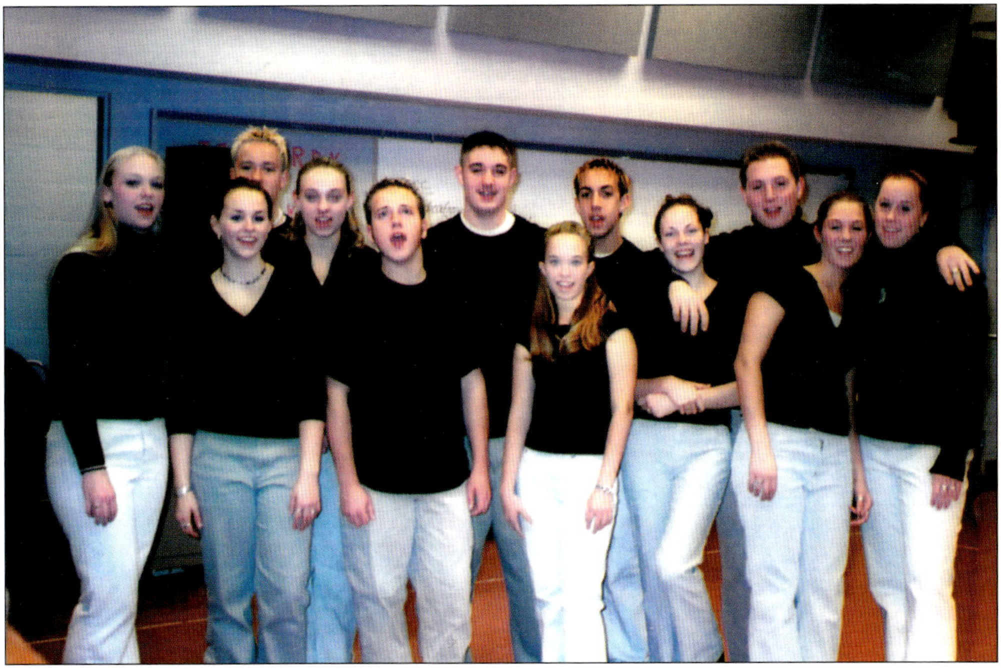

The 2002 Iroquois Show Choir participated in the dedication of the gymnasium to C. Thomas Barringer, legendary basketball coach who led the Iroquois teams to 14 Erie County League championships in his 23 years as a coach. The Iroquois Show Choir, under the direction of Roberta Stoughton, performed at many school and community affairs. (Courtesy of Roberta Stoughton.)

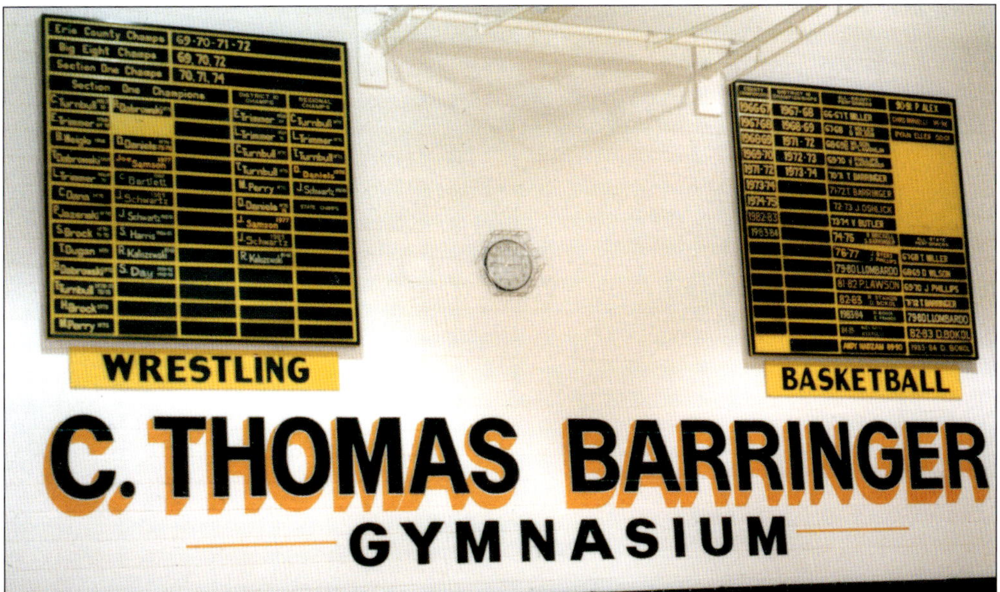

The dedication of the gymnasium to coach C. Thomas Barringer was a fitting tribute, as he coached many winning teams. His famous words to the team, "What's your job!" are still echoing in the gymnasium. This dedication was a part of the remodeling project that, among other things, moved the office from the Iroquois Avenue side of the building to the gymnasium-auditorium side. Students remember confusion in the halls and dust in the air. (Courtesy of Gerard Drozdowski.)

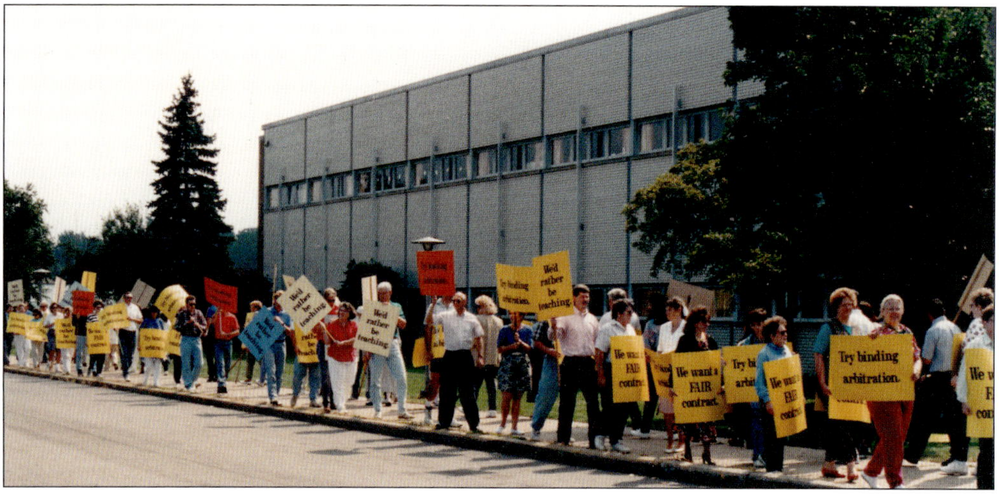

The opening of the 1994–1995 school year was eagerly anticipated by football players, as volunteers had installed the long-awaited lights on the athletic field. However, when teacher negotiations broke down, a teacher strike closed the school until October 6. A disappointed football team played only three games. (Courtesy of Gerard Drozdowski.)

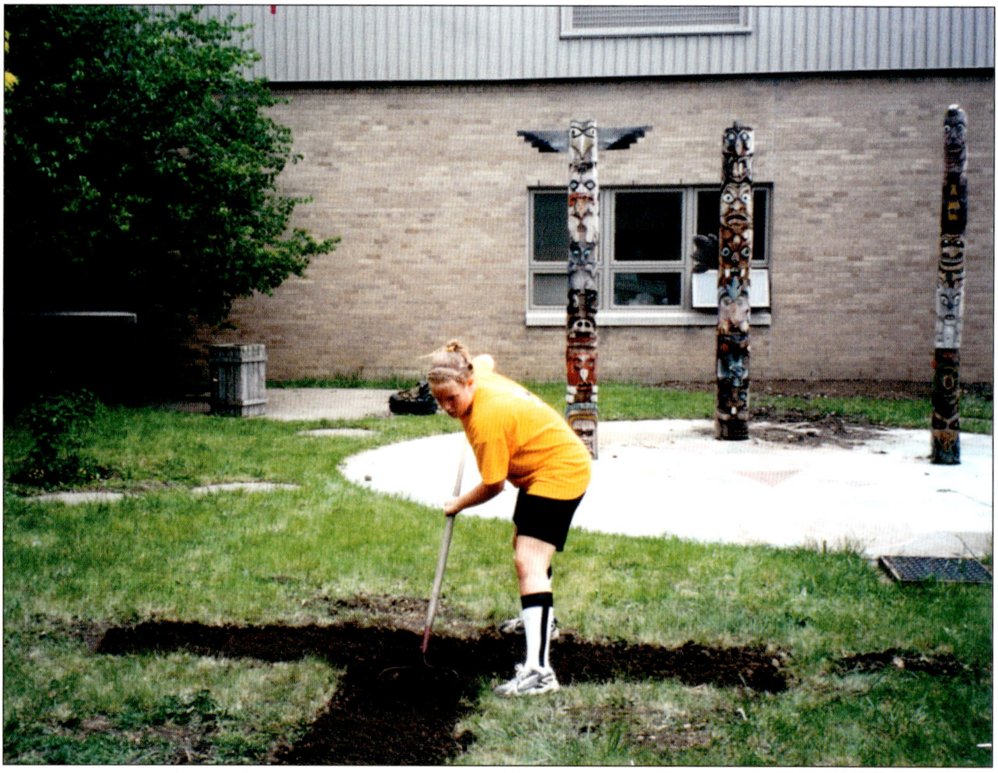

An energetic student is doing extra duty as groundskeeper in the Totem Pole Courtyard at Iroquois High School. In 1980–1981, Kathy Kaliszewski and Kim Kalista helped carve totems representing mascots from all the county schools. The totem poles disappeared for a time, but fortunately they reappeared to once more decorate the courtyard. (Courtesy of Gerard Drozdowski.)

Smiles and medals grace Toni (left) and Jackie Artise (right) as they completed a fall cross-country run in 2003. Dick Bonniger has been cross-country coach for many years. Some of the outstanding runners were Ron Reuss, Bill Manny, Mike Barlett, and Lindsey Phillips. (Courtesy of Gerard Drozdowski.)

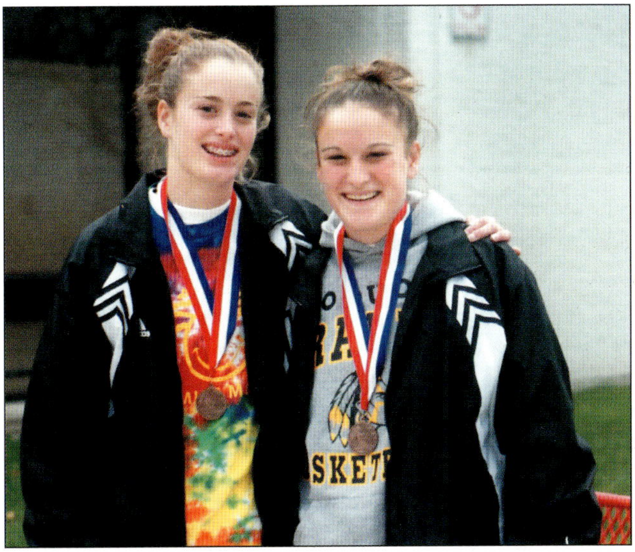

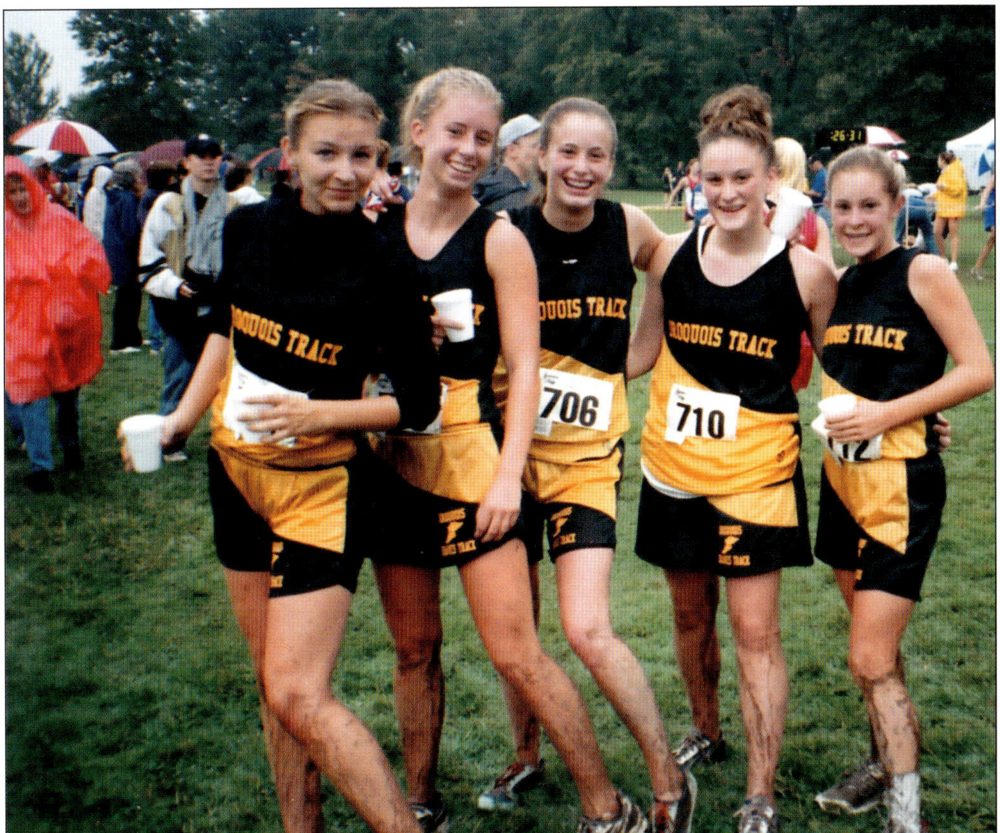

No, it is not a chorus line, but a group of cross-country runners showing their muddy legs after a meet in 2003. From left to right are Linsey Danielson, unidentified, Toni Artise, Jackie Artise, and Bridget Mullaney. Cross-country is a grueling sport with no bands or cheerleaders. (Courtesy of Gerard Drozdowski.)

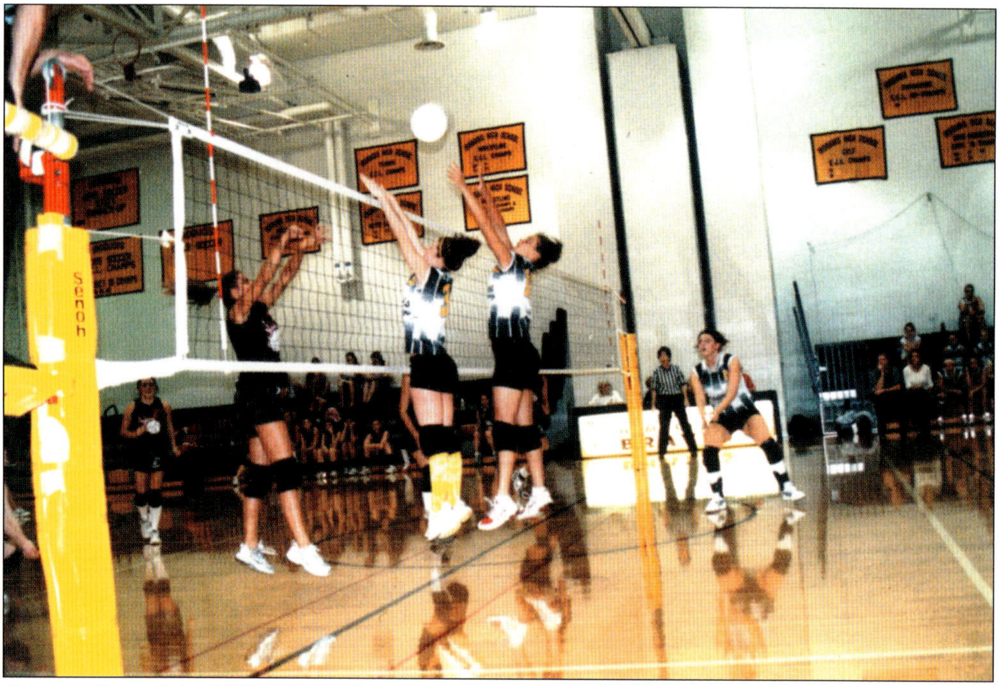

Two members of the 2003 volleyball team are about to spike the ball as it soars over the net. Senior members of the team that competed in District 10 playoffs were Trish McLaughlin, Jenna Crotty, Nicole Guise, and Sarah Barringer. Iroquois volleyball teams were state runner-ups in 1984 and won the Erie County League in 1985, 1988, and 1990. (Courtesy of Gerard Drozdowski.)

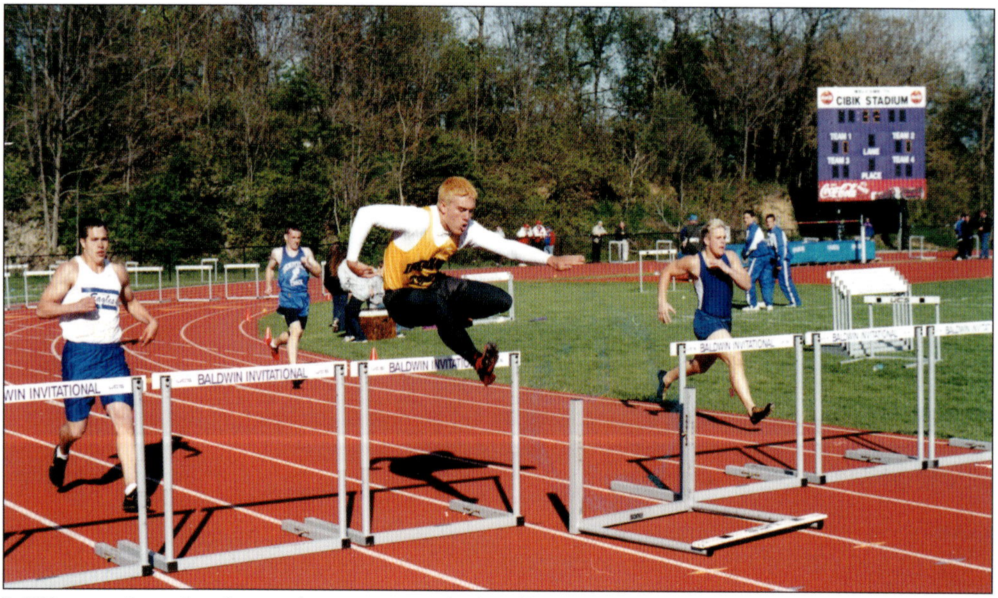

Jeff Strayer shows his form as he soars over the hurdles. He and his teammates Doug Trojanowski, Matt LaPaglia, and Scott Burick placed at the Erie County meet. In 1991, Bob Corey was Iroquois's first-ever state track champion. Rich Harper placed fourth in the 400-meter, and the 1,600-meter relay team placed fifth. In the 1980s, Fenn Allen was an outstanding track star. (Courtesy of Gerard Drozdowski.)

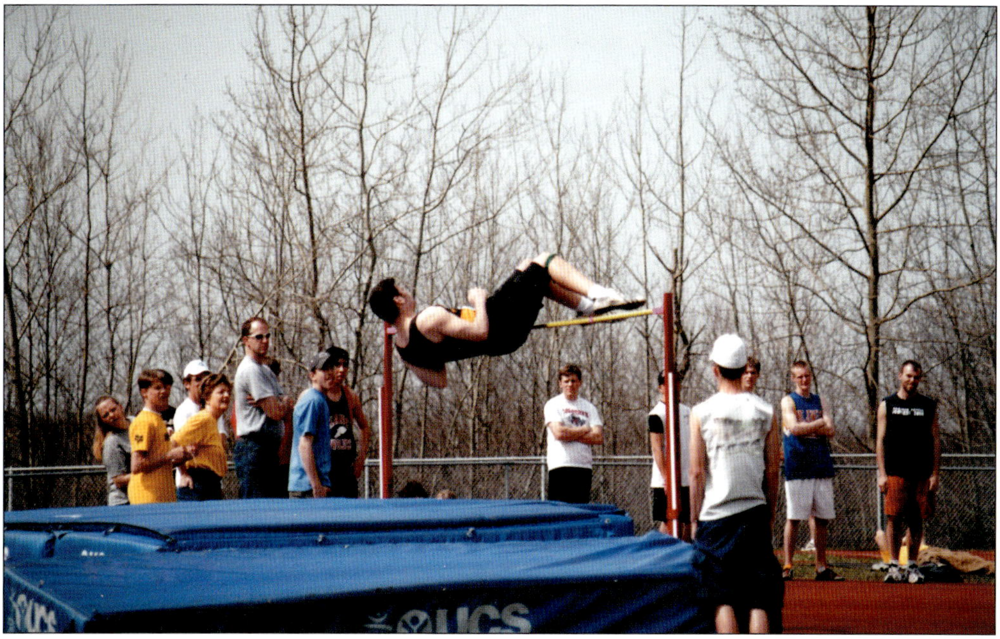

Kenneth Cox, class of 2004, clears the bar in a track meet. There are several field events at which Iroquois athletes have excelled: Hubert Brock in discus in 1973, Ron Head in high jump in 1984, and Brian Sharp in long jump in 1985. The track coach in the early days of Iroquois was Russ May, followed by Chuck McKay and Craig Sluga. (Courtesy of Gerard Drozdowski.)

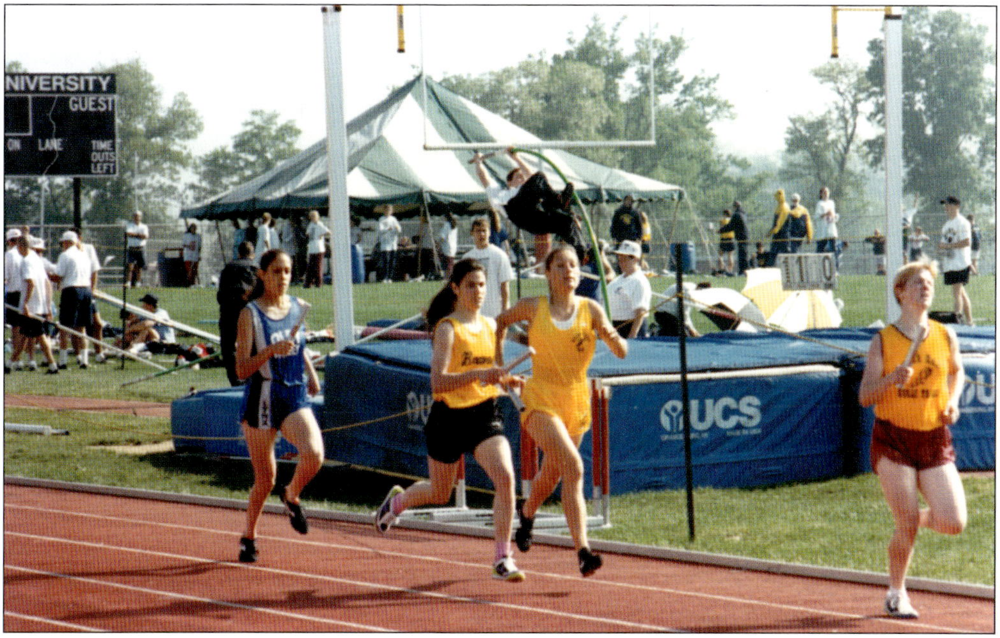

Girls' track was added to the sports roster in 1993. In 1996, the 3,200-meter girls relay team was third at state competitions. Its members were Alison Falk, Amy Hazen, Kelli Hazen, Melissa Popoff, Melissa Grant, and Rebecca Downing. In 2001, Leah Kerstetter won the 800- and 1,600-meter runs at state. State qualifiers in 2004 were Brianna Downs, Jackie Artise, Nicole Wilson, Megan Fellows, Toni Artise, Colleen Burick, and Caryn Krahe. (Courtesy of Gerard Drozdowski.)

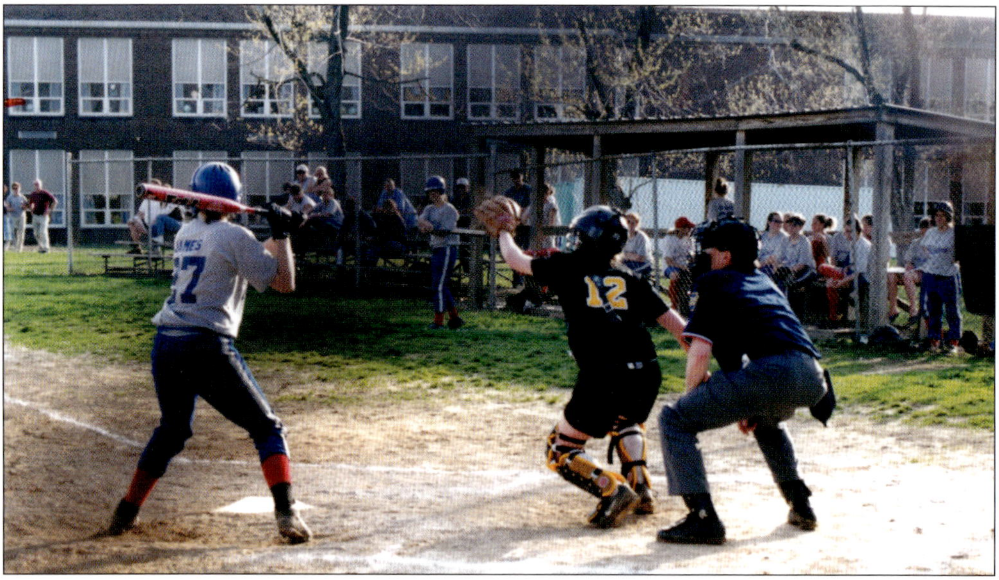

The 1982 softball team, with the outstanding pitching of Mary Butler, achieved a dream come true, a state AA title. (The entire 1982 team was inducted into the WILP Hall of Fame in 2014.) The 1983 and 1991 teams repeated winning the state title. In 1990 and 2006, the team lost at state by just one run. (Courtesy of Gerard Drozdowski.)

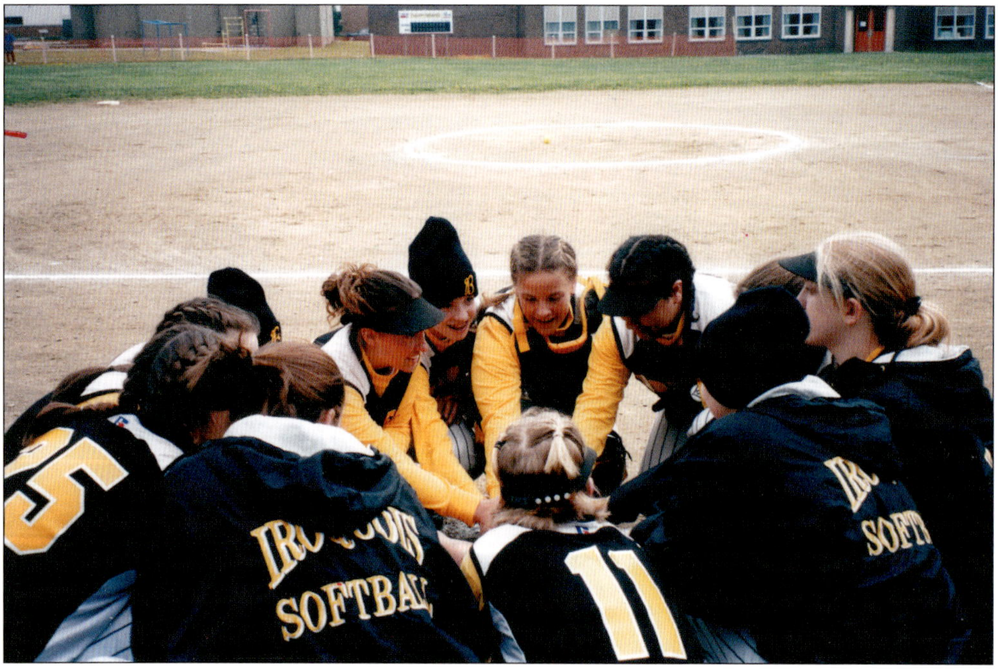

Softball teams are a close-knit group, as seen in this 2002 photograph. Soup suppers and trips to Charleston, South Carolina, help. The softball teams won District 10 titles 12 times between 1978 and 2007. Some of the members of the 2007 team were Becky Zill, Kelce Cook, Kayla Troop, Lindsey Phillips, Sarah Johnson, Samantha Cunningham, and Karey Bartlett. Bernie Fitch and Mickey Allen coached the softball teams for many years until 2001, when Fitch retired. Currently, the team is coached by Julie Parker. (Courtesy of Gerard Drozdowski.)

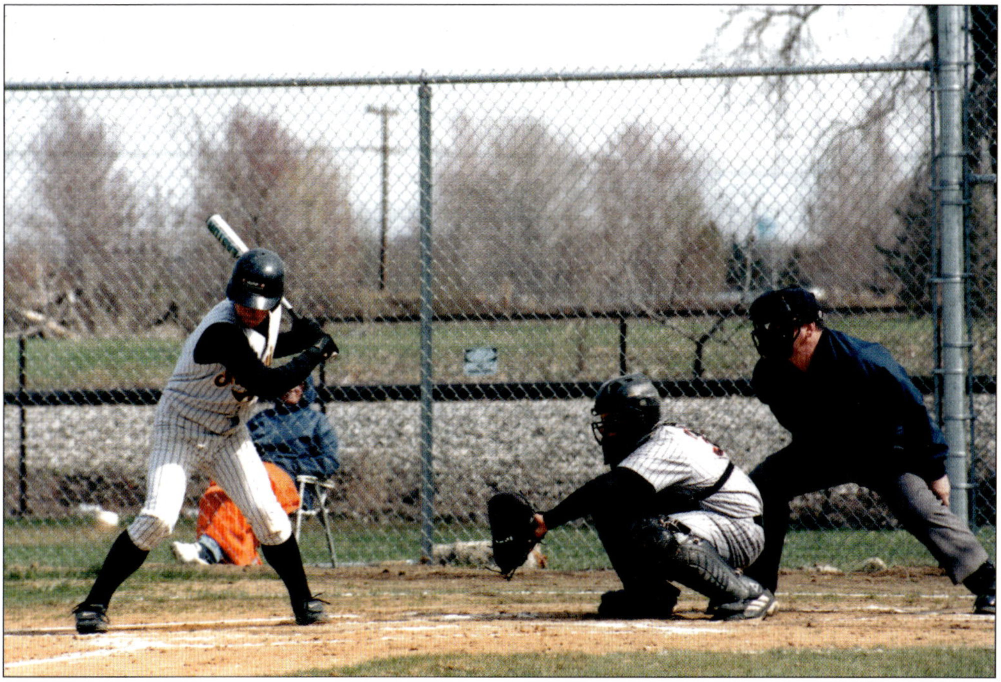

Baseball teams, coached by Harry Farnbaugh from 1966 to 1980, won Erie County League championships five times from 1969 to 1977. The teams coached by Phil Glass continued with six more ECL championships in 1983, 1986, 1987, 1990, 1992, and 1996. Coach Glass's final coaching year was 2003. He was also the student council sponsor for many years. (Courtesy of Gerard Drozdowski.)

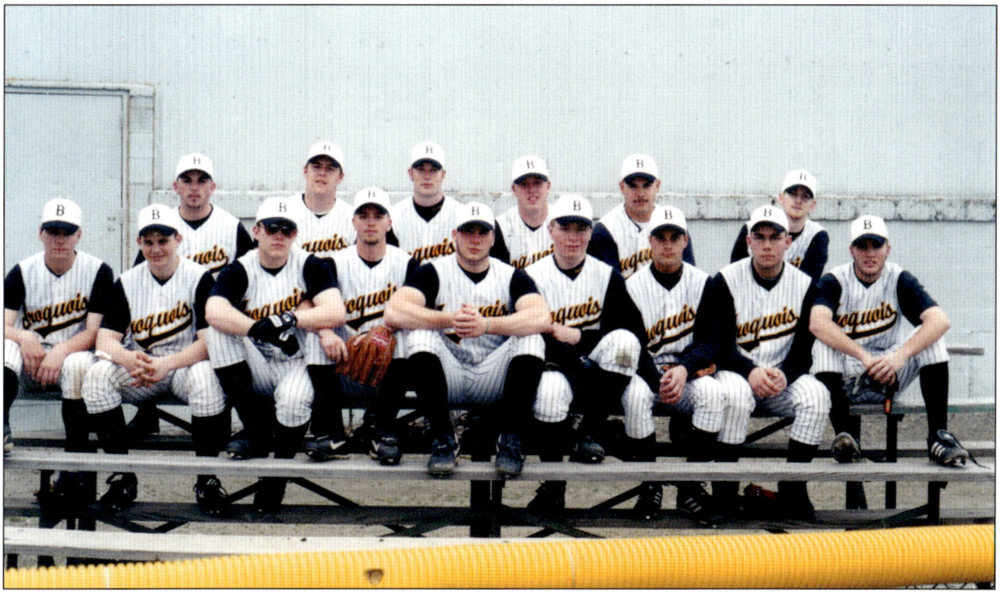

Members of the 2002 baseball team pictured here are, from left to right, (first row) R. Parker, J. Bartlett, K. Rogala, A. Jarosik, Grochulski, N. Troop, K. Mullaney, T. Bell, and J. Yurcak; (second row) J. Miller, M. Whitney, P. Murzynski, G. Snyder, D. Vrenna, and M. Kyle. In 2010, the team went all the way to the District 10 semifinal game. (Courtesy of Gerard Drozdowski.)

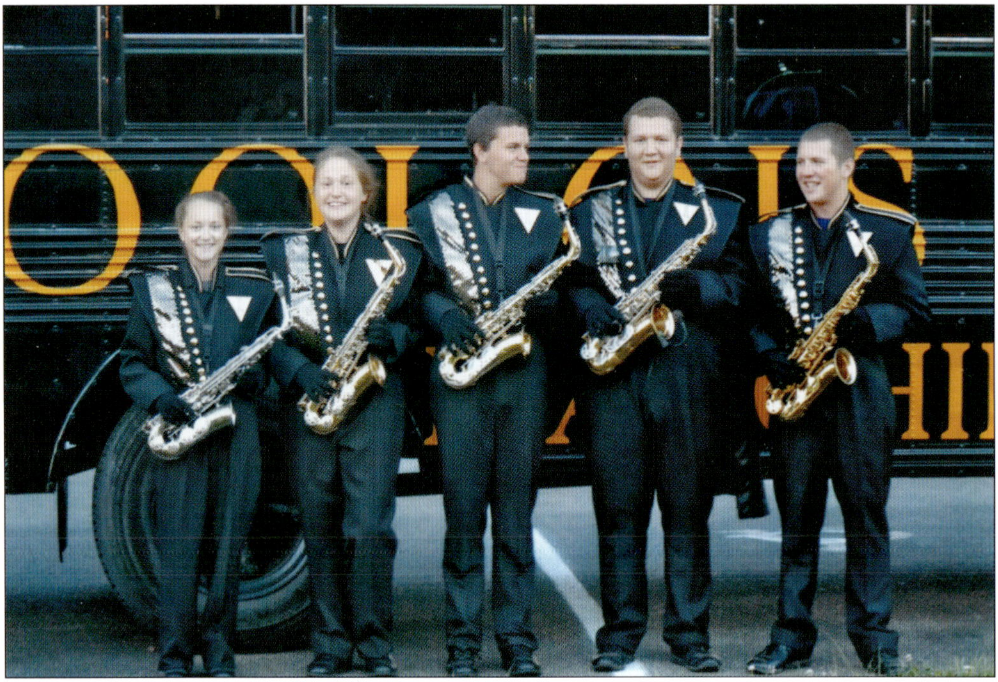

In 2014, the saxophone players look sharp in their new black uniforms. They are, from left to right, Nicole Loomis, Aislin Shannon, Kyle Kaliszewski, Zech Castillo, and Caleb Armstrong. In addition to the marching band, there is also a concert band that performs at Christmas and in the spring. Young musicians begin to learn the fundamentals of music in elementary school. (Courtesy of Diana Zejavic.)

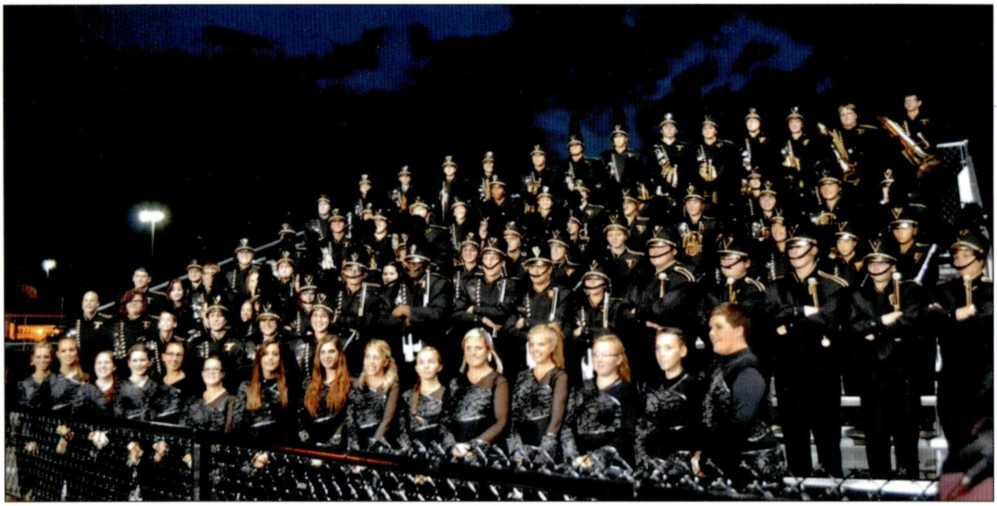

The Iroquois Marching Band, under the direction of Rob Chase, has participated in many Lakeshore Marching Band Association competitions and have the trophies to prove how well they have done. Twirlers and flags have added to the band's spectacular routines that are practiced long and hard to achieve excellence in performing. For a small school to produce such a large and excellent band is a tribute to good leadership and hard work. (Courtesy of Diana Zejavic.)

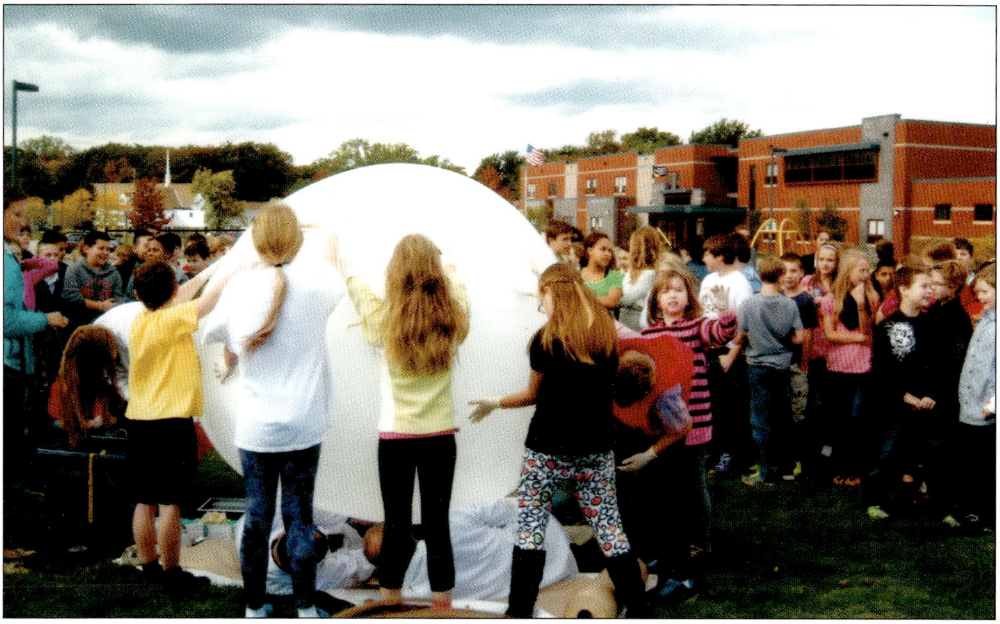

On October 8, 2014, the elementary school turned out to watch the weather-balloon launch, a project of the elementary gifted program in connection with the staff at the Tom Ridge Environmental Center. This balloon recorded an altitude of 73,000 feet, temperature, and solar radiation. It transmitted its landing location as near Addison, New York.

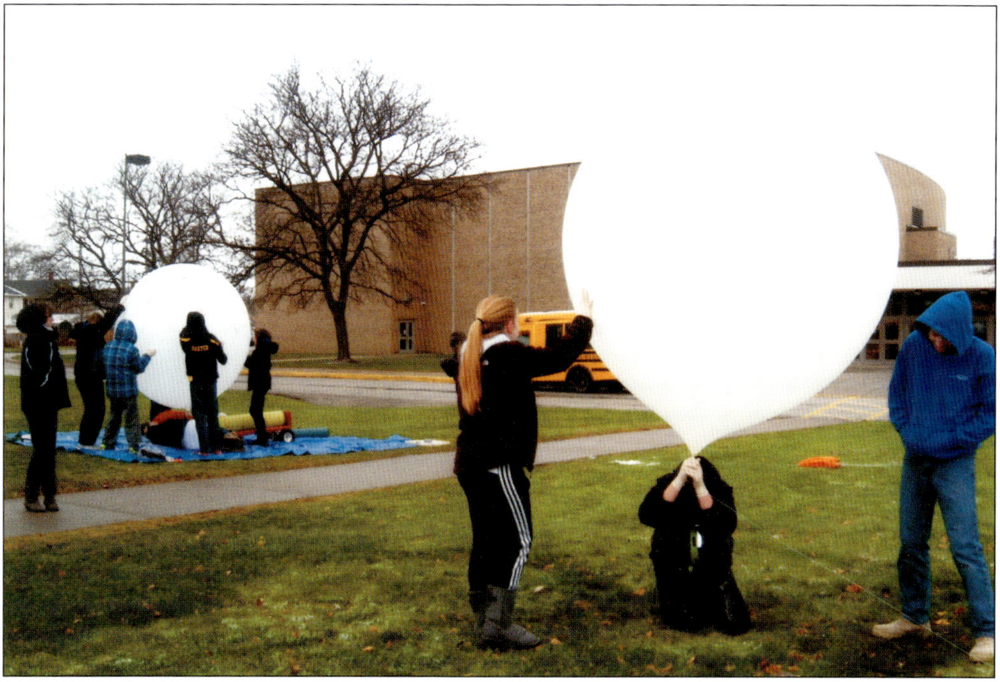

Several weeks after the elementary school weather-balloon launch, another try was made by the high school gifted group. This time all went well, and with the assistance of the personnel from the Tom Ridge Environmental Center, data was sent back to the students so they could record and analyze the information.

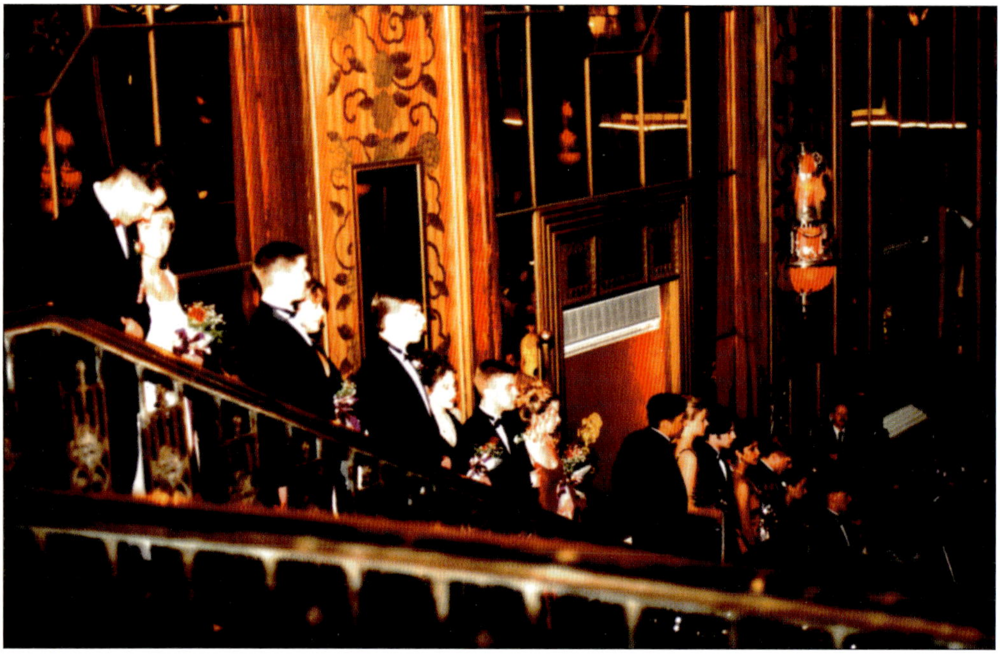

The 1993 prom court, presided over by King Todd Matlak and Queen Kim Hagle, is pictured here on the staircase of the elegant Warner Theater. The theme was "Never Say Goodbye," which indicated the wish to keep in touch through reunions. Proms are sponsored by the junior class to honor the seniors, and they have been held at many different locations, including the one in 2015 that was held at the Erie Art Museum. (Courtesy of Gerard Drozdowski.)

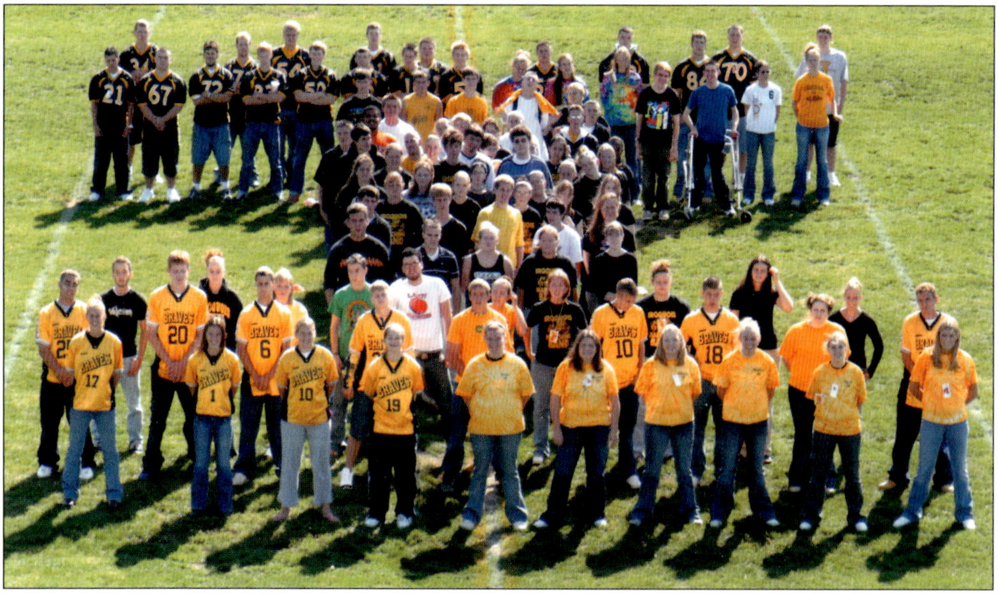

The class of 2004 created a living Big I as they prepared to go out into the world. Senior class officers were Adam Welch, Jason Bartlett, Megan Hammers, and John Armbruster. Every one of the more than 5,000 graduates in the 50 classes since 1965–1966 has different memories of teachers, subjects, sports, clubs, and activities. However, there is no more identification as Wesleyville or Lawrence Park, there is just one Big I. (Courtesy of Gerard Drozdowski.)

Four

BUSINESSES

The business districts of Wesleyville and Lawrence Park are very different. More than 500 businesses have come and gone in the 200 years Wesleyville has existed. Some of the more recent ones that are no more are the Penn Theater, Wesleyville Bakery, Plubell's Hardware, Schaffners Esso, Nickel Plate Mills, Tarzan's Barber Shop, George V. Thomas Jewelry, William Wright Jewelers, Hull Jewelers, Kehr's Grocery, Martin Shoe Repair, Toby's Shoes, Bon Bon, Bury's Drugs, Catrabones, Forty's Cleaners, and Hill Mill. Some of these business establishments met their demise as competition came from the malls that arose east of Wesleyville on Buffalo Road. Your Home Town Pharmacy, owned by B.J. Moon, Iroquois class of 1993, is located on the site that had been occupied by the Old Half Way House, the Hotel Wesleyville, the American Legion, the First National Bank, and the post office. Terry Etzel has been at 2914 Buffalo Road for 38 years and before that was at a different location for five years. Sal Alessie retired in 2010 after barbering for over 50 years. Eating establishments in Wesleyville include Barbatos, Coney Island Lunch, and Russ' Dinor. Dusckas Funeral Home has recently opened a handsome second location as Dusckas-Taylor Funeral Home just east of Wesleyville on Buffalo Road.

Although the business district of Lawrence Park was never as large as Wesleyville's, it did have Batchelor's Hardware, Demetters, and Sohl's Grocery Stores, a post office, Bootes gas station, Kellogg's Drug Store, Chatham 5 and 10, and Greenlee's. Mary's Dairy Bar and Soudan's were favorite hangouts for teenagers.

My Daddy's Barber Shop is still nestled next to the Park Dinor, and several beauty shops are in the three-block business district. The Lawrence Park Apothecary Shop is located where there once was a gas station. The Dairy Queen has been at the same location on Iroquois Avenue since 1952, when Reid Wood first established it. The convenience store now known as Circle K has been known as Dairy Mart and Lawsons. Bailey Funeral Home is nearby, and the familiar name of Beute is still seen on the Beute and Bliley building.

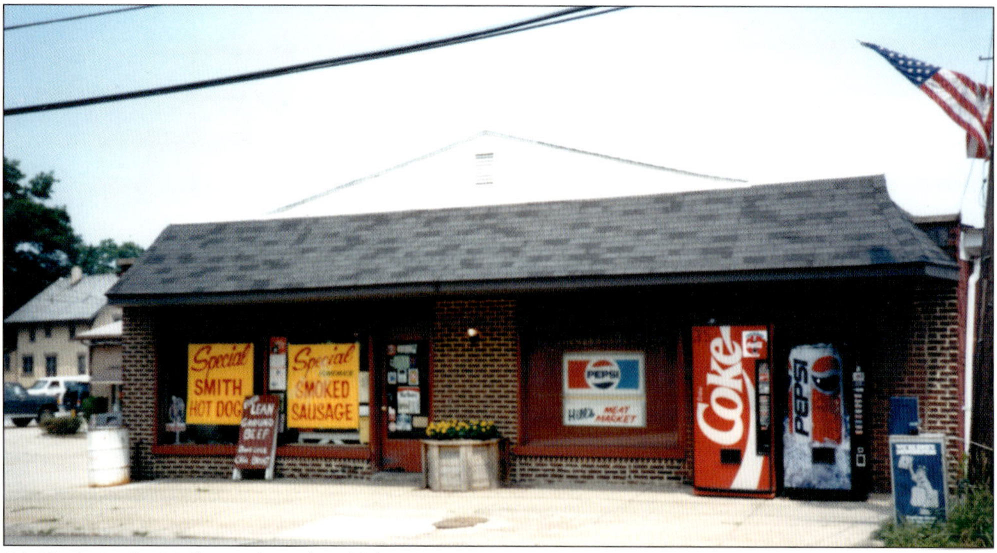

Clifford "Jack" Hill purchased Dibbles Dairy Bar on Station Road in 1943 and began the Hills Market. When it opened, Hills sold ice cream for 5¢. Prices did go up, but Hills was known for its excellent meats. Hills Market closed in 2014, leaving its many customers saddened. (Courtesy of the Lawrence Park Historical Society.)

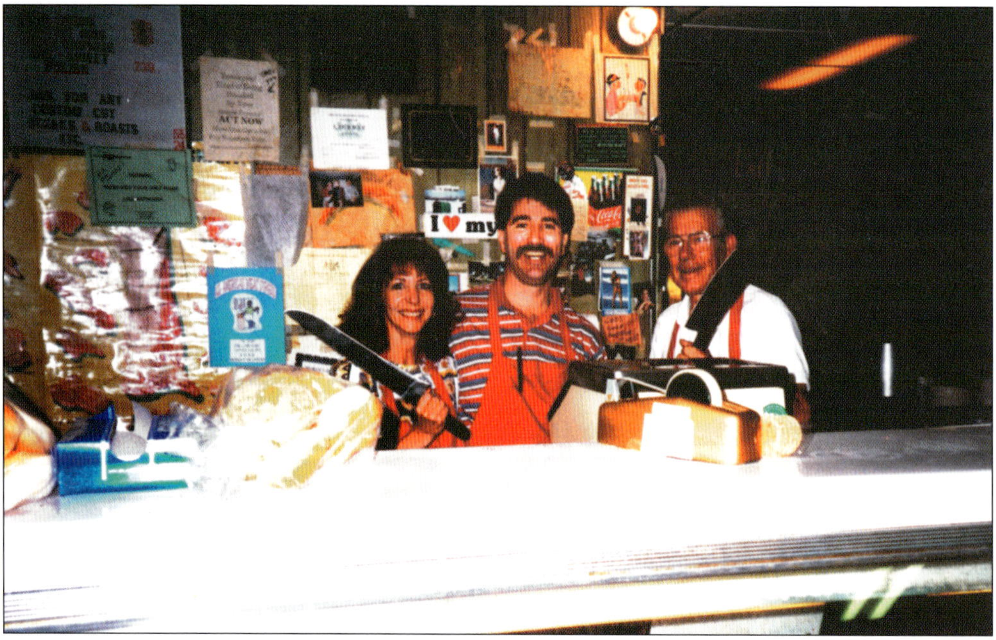

From left to right, Cindy, Don, and Jack Hill are shown here in a 1996 photograph of Hill's Market. Hill's Market passed from Clifford to son Jack in 1967 (Wesleyville graduate, class of 1942) to grandson Don (Iroquois graduate, class of 1970). Several generations of the Hill family were known for their good service and friendly smiles. (Courtesy of the Lawrence Park Historical Society.)

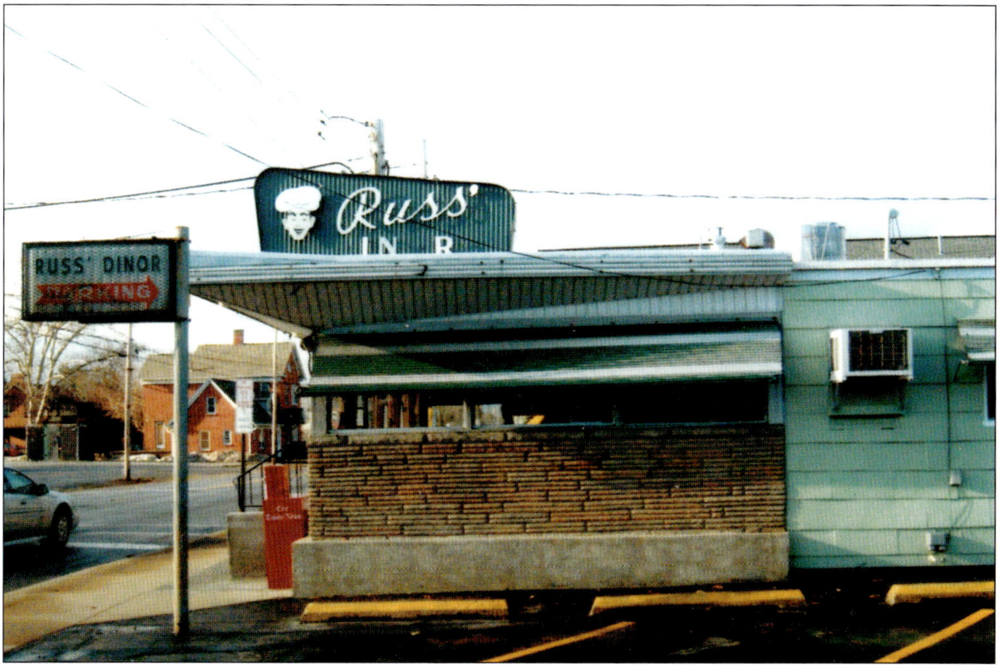

Wendell Russ purchased a diner in Wesleyville in 1946. He operated Russ' Dinor for many years before turning it over to his nephew Ron and Diane (Freeman) Russ. Russ' Dinor has long been a favorite spot for good food and a comfortable place to meet friends and neighbors.

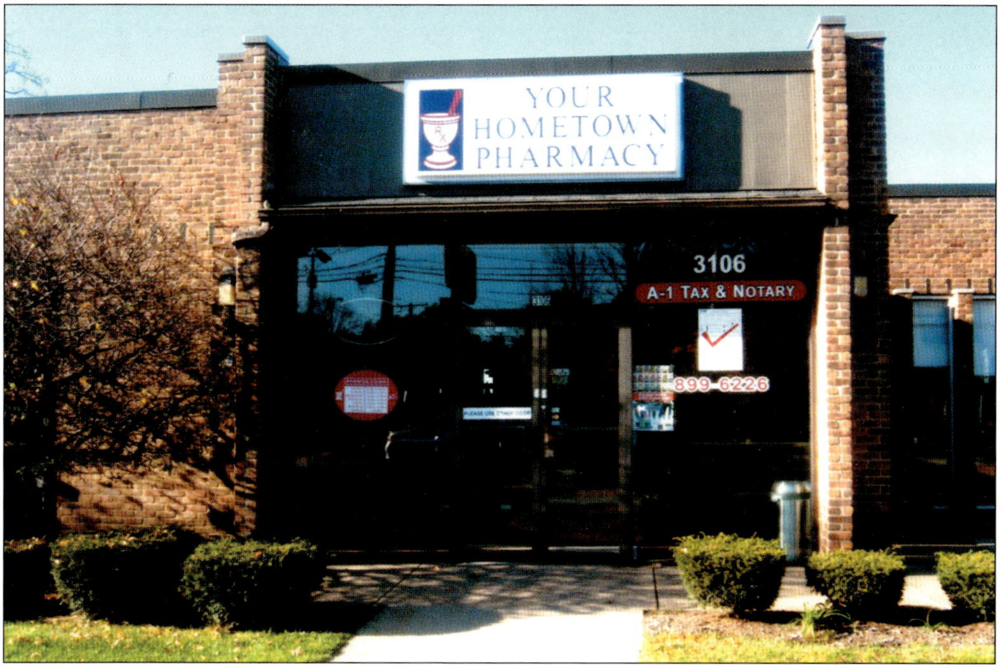

The site of the Your Hometown Pharmacy, 3106 Buffalo Road, has hosted a variety of businesses: the Old Half Way House, Niagara Hotel, Wesleyville Hotel, American Legion, First National Bank, and the post office. It has been remodeled by B.J. Moon (Iroquois graduate, class of 1993) and serves as a full-service pharmacy.

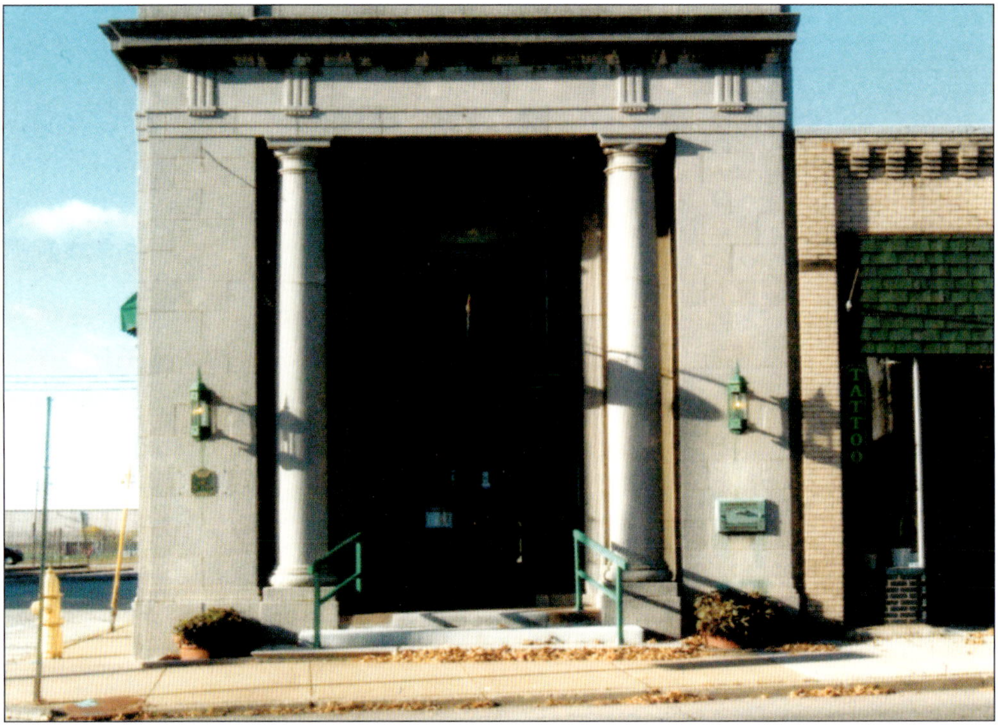

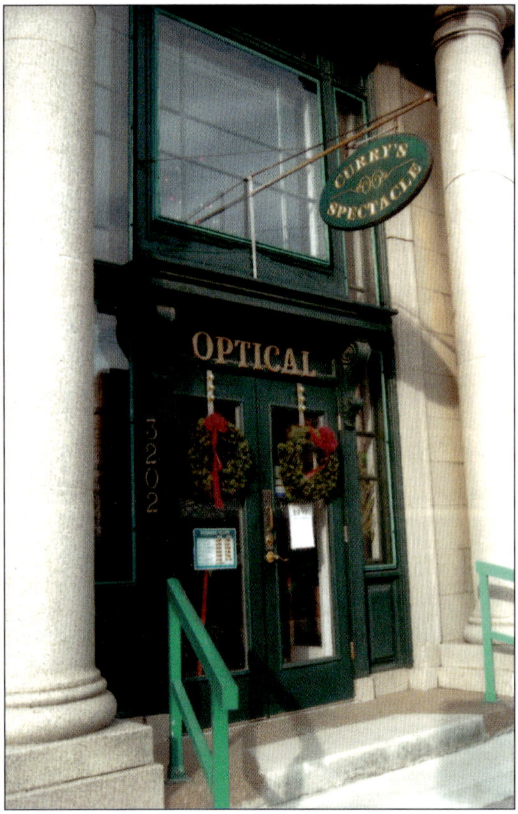

This handsome building, constructed in 1921, housed the Bank of Wesleyville for many years. In 1945, the First National Bank acquired the Bank of Wesleyville as well as the First National Bank of Lawrence Park. The old bank building is located at 3202 Buffalo Road.

Curry's Spectacle Shop has occupied the old bank building since 1990, when they moved from across Buffalo Road where Howard and Mary Ann Curry began Curry's in 1979. The interior of Curry's has been kept much like it was when the bank occupied the building, with tile flooring, dark counters, and a second-floor balcony.

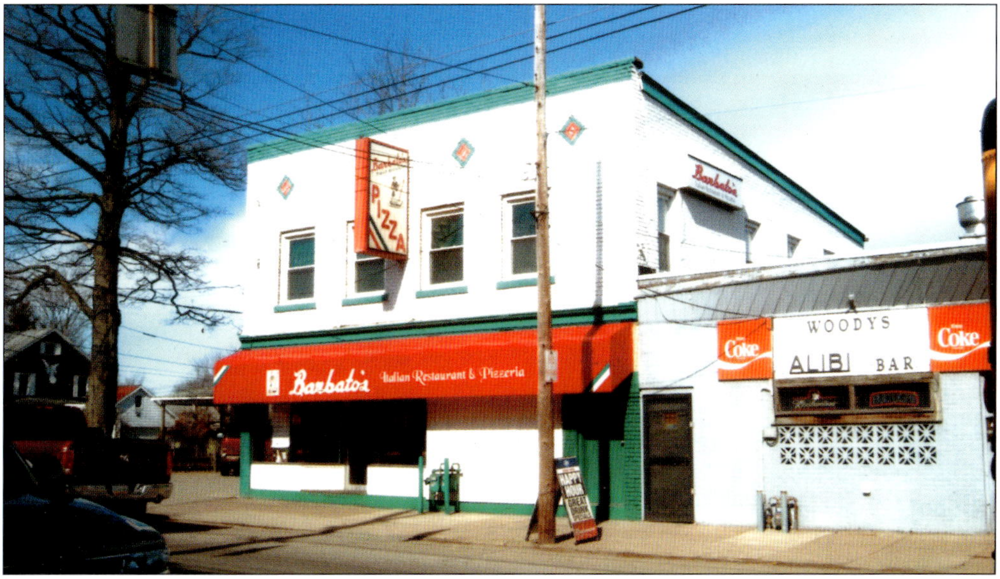

Barbato's Italian Restaurant has occupied the building at the corner of Water Street and Buffalo Road since 1955. The restaurant was begun by John and Amelia Barbato and is still in the family, as Robert Barbato is now the owner. The colorful red, white, and green sign indicates that here one will find savory Italian cuisine.

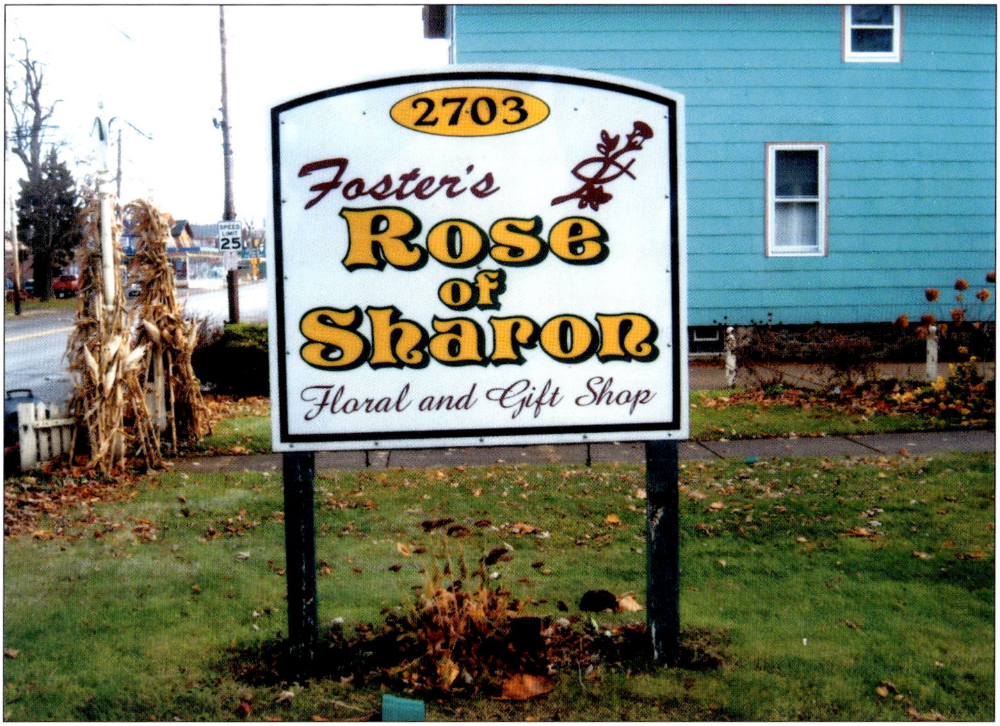

The Rose of Sharon floral shop was established on Bird Drive in 1979. Proprietor Gary Foster, an Iroquois graduate, class of 1970, has been very active in the community. He has also been involved in the Iroquois School District as a board member and as an officer in the Iroquois School District Foundation, which was established in 2003.

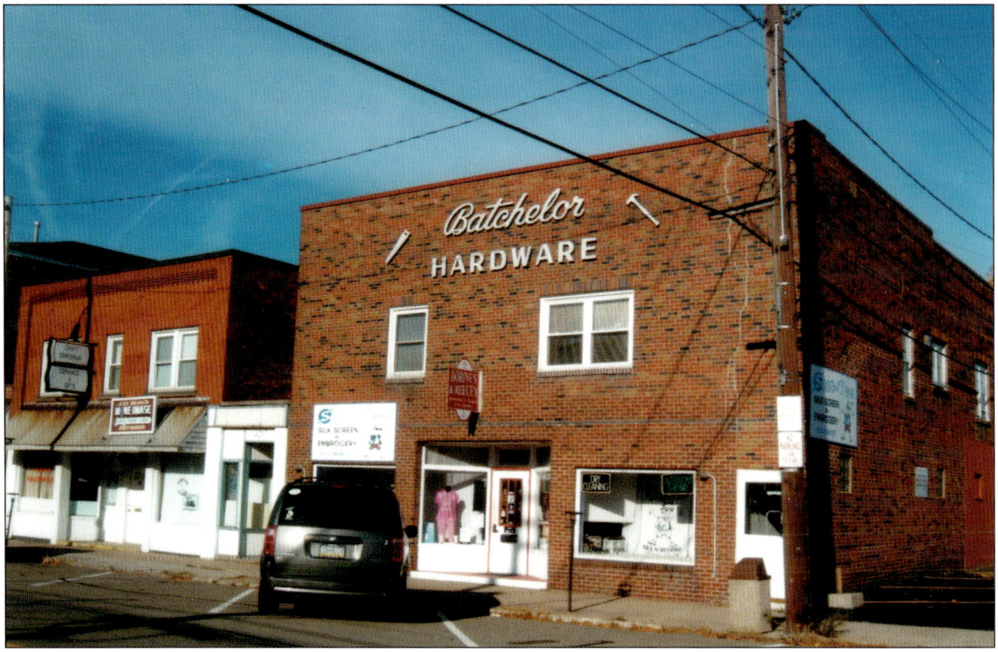

The big Batchelor Hardware sign is from a bygone day when in 1946, Marlow Batchelor opened his hardware store here. Although that store is long gone, since 1985 Dorine and Reese Cadwalader have operated their store here, providing much-needed services such as clothing repairs, alterations, and rentals. (Courtesy of the Lawrence Park Historical Society.)

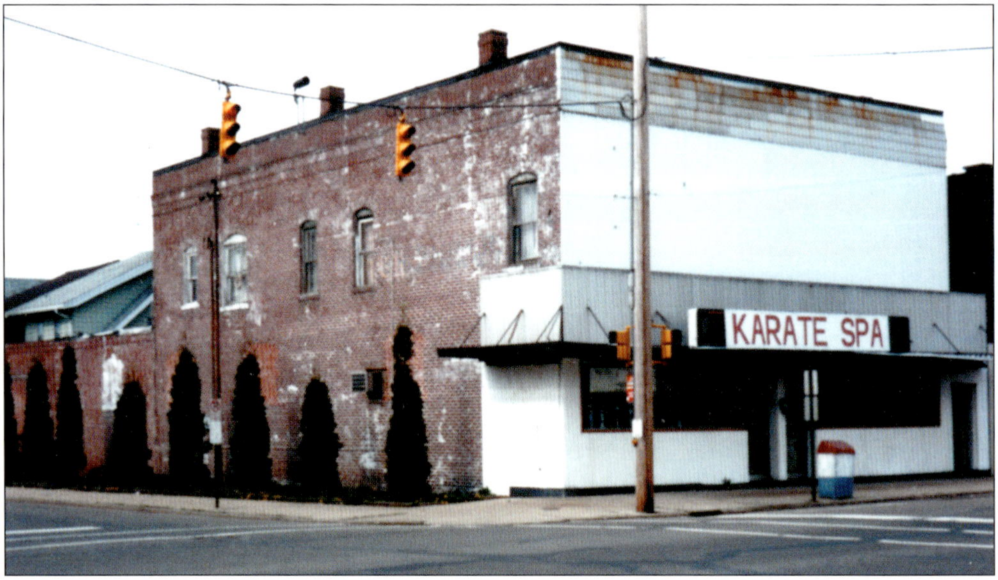

At one time, the Karate Spa was located on the northeast corner of Main Street and Rankine Avenue in one of the oldest buildings in Lawrence Park. It originally was Keim's Market. The very first school classes were held on the second floor from 1910 to 1913. It was also headquarters for the Pennsylvania State Police in the 1930s. (Courtesy of the Lawrence Park Historical Society.)

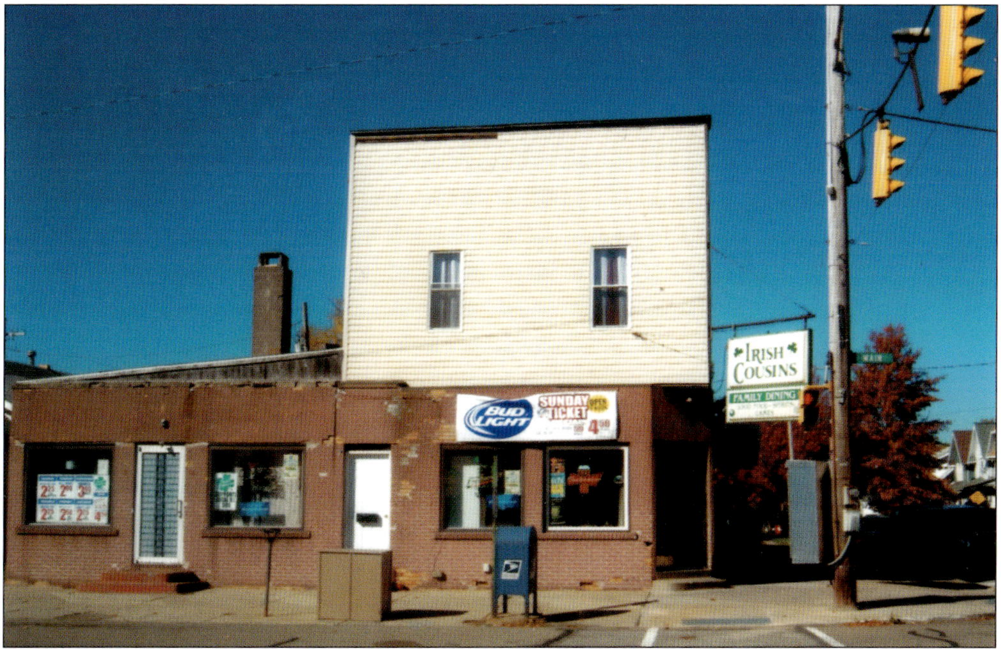

On the northwest corner of Main Street and Rankine Avenue is a popular watering hole known as Irish Cousins since 1970, when Ed Damico changed its name. The building was constructed in 1912 and housed one of the first stores. Irish Cousins is always one of the destinations of St. Patrick's Day revelers. (Courtesy of the Lawrence Park Historical Society.)

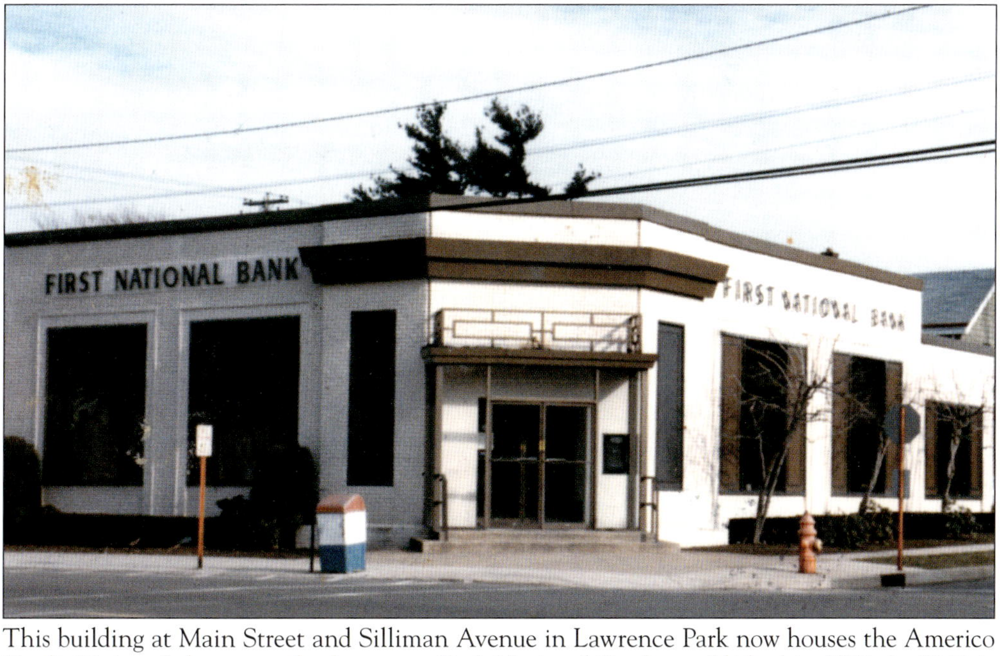

This building at Main Street and Silliman Avenue in Lawrence Park now houses the Americo Credit Union. It began as the Lawrence Park National Bank, established in 1930. In 1945, it became the First National Bank and later the PNC. In 1999, when the PNC Bank was moved to Wesleyville, the Americo Credit Union moved from across the street. (Courtesy of the Lawrence Park Historical Society.)

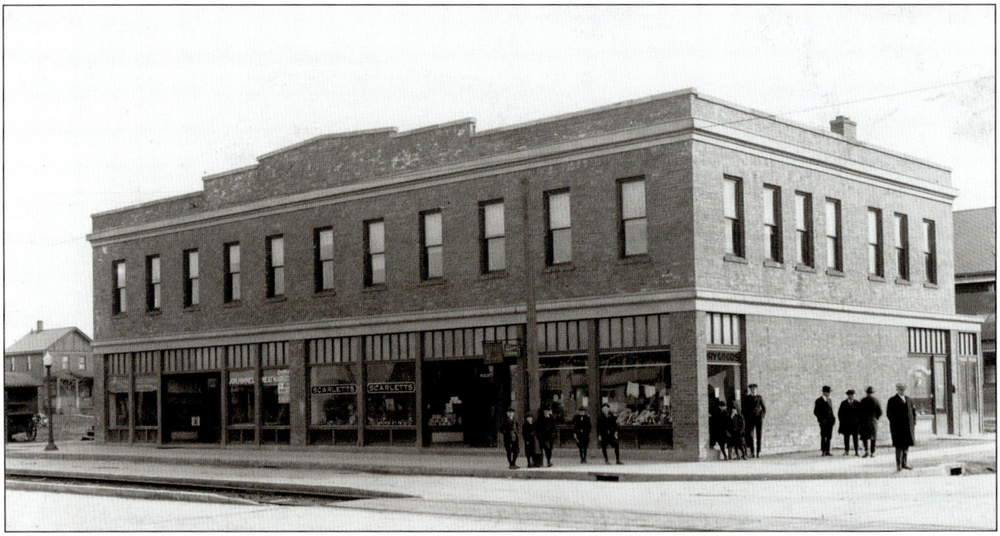

The large building on the south east corner of Main Street and Rankine Avenue in Lawrence Park had at one time housed Campbell's Drug Store and then Kellogg's Pharmacy. The Park Terrace and Campbell's bowling alleys were located on the second floor. This photograph from the 1930s shows boys in knickers and a store named Scarletts. The corner store appears to have sold dry goods. (Courtesy of the Lawrence Park Historical Society.)

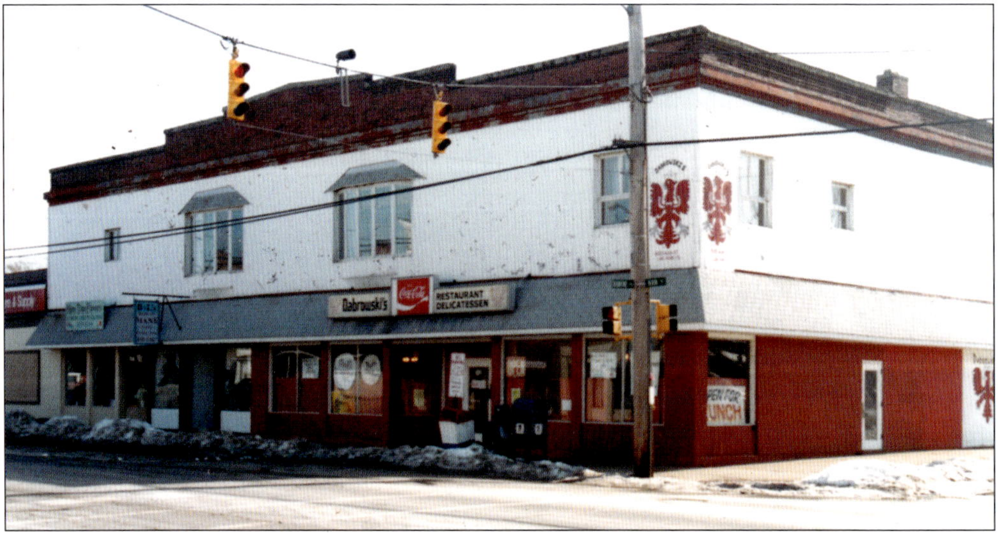

In 1983, Wieslaw Dabrowski began Dabrowski's Restaurant and Delicatessen in Lawrence Park at Main Street and Rankine Avenue. He and his wife had four sons and four daughters, some of whom have worked in the restaurant. The family has been serving Polish food such as pierogies, *golombki* (cabbage rolls), *czarnina* (duck-blood soup), and Polish donuts for over 30 years. (Courtesy of the Lawrence Park Historical Society.)

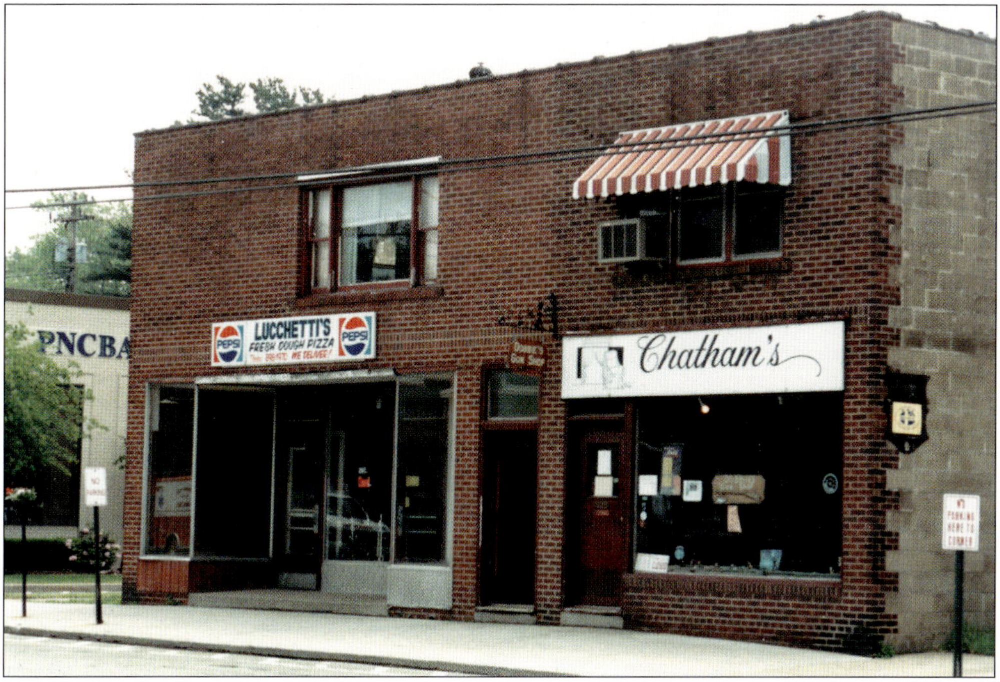

Chatham's Five and Ten was the favorite store of young and old in Lawrence Park for many years. The building has housed a variety of enterprises. Currently, Dave and Cherie Harger own the Dime Store Apartments and Guest Suites at this location, and the name refers back to Chatham's five-and-dime. (Courtesy of the Lawrence Park Historical Society.)

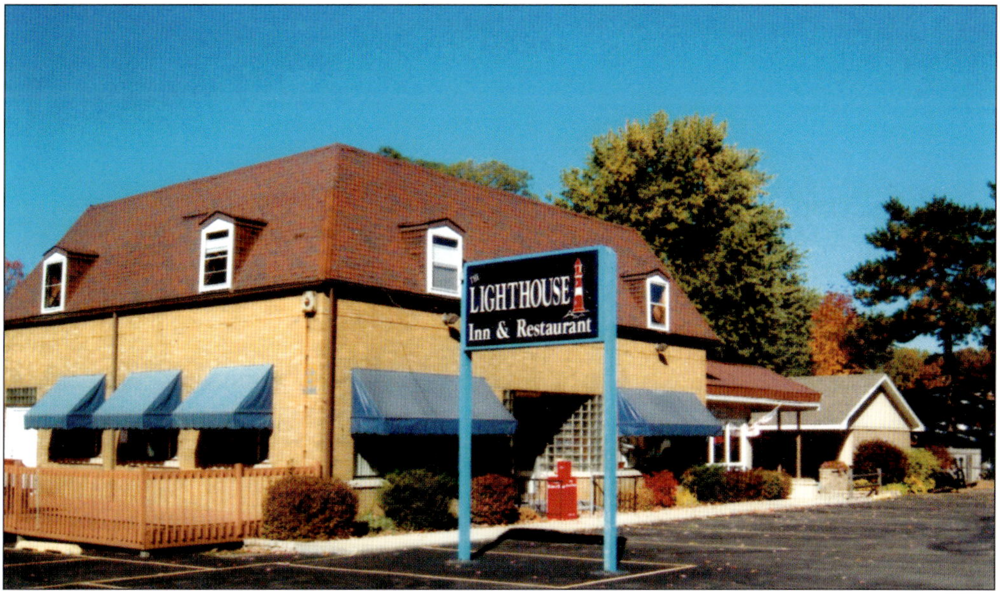

The delightful Lighthouse Restaurant on East Lake Road, owned by Adam and Jackie Lobenthal, was for many years known as Soudans, a favorite haunt of the young and not so young. Bernie Soudan built Soudans in 1947. In 1971, Bernie sold Soudans to Bill Underhill, his nephew, who retained the name Soudans. (Courtesy of the Lawrence Park Historical Society.)

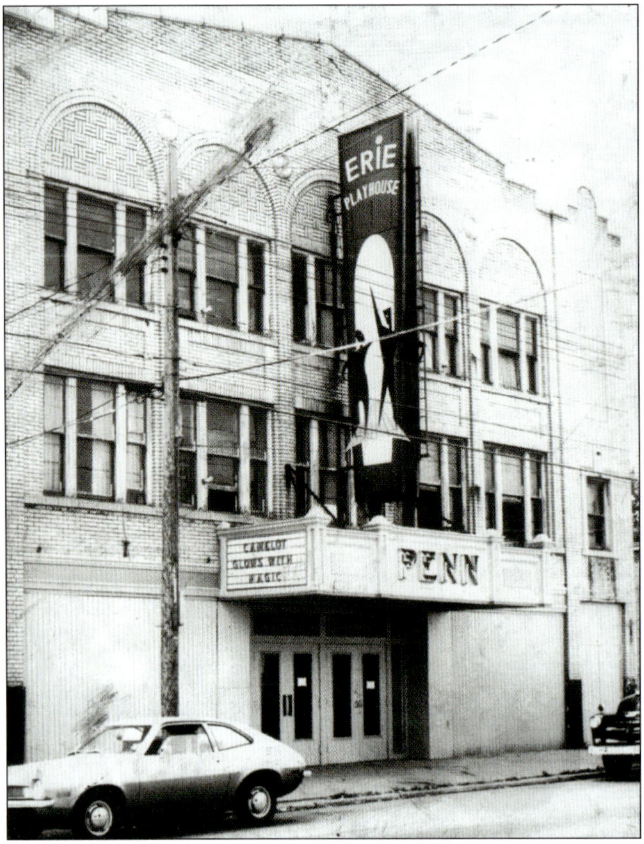

Movies were enjoyed at the Penn Theater from 1933 when Ed Brown bought the theater until it closed in the 1960s. From 1965 to 1974, the Erie Playhouse presented live theater at this location. After that, playhouse performances were presented in various school auditoriums, including the one at Iroquois High School. This 1972 photograph shows that *Camelot* was playing at the old Penn Theater. (Courtesy of Almie Clerkin.)

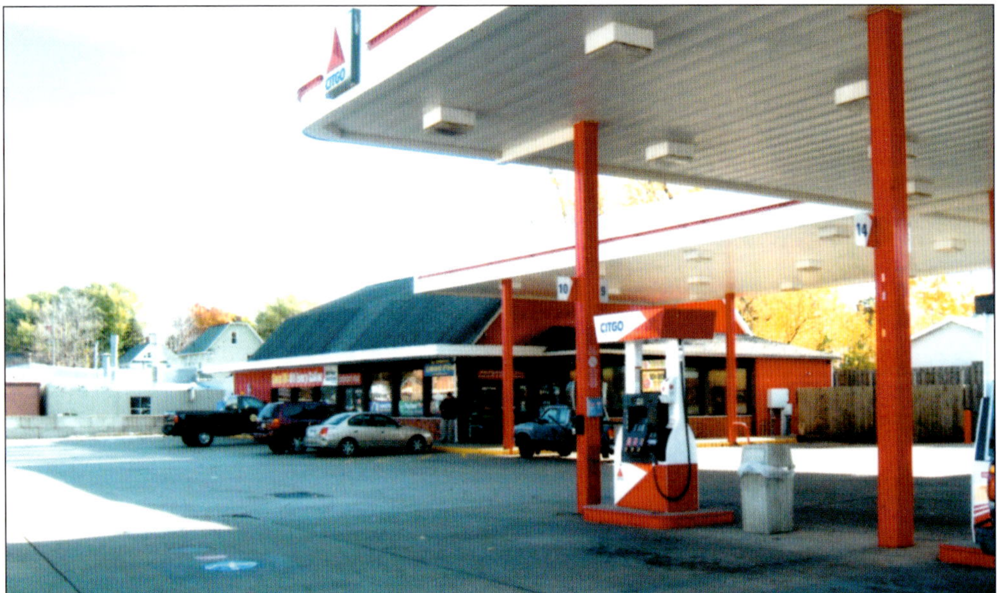

The old Penn Theater building deteriorated to such a degree that residents were relieved to see it torn down in 1993. The look of that block on Buffalo Road changed considerably when the Country Fair and the Citgo gas station were built at this location.

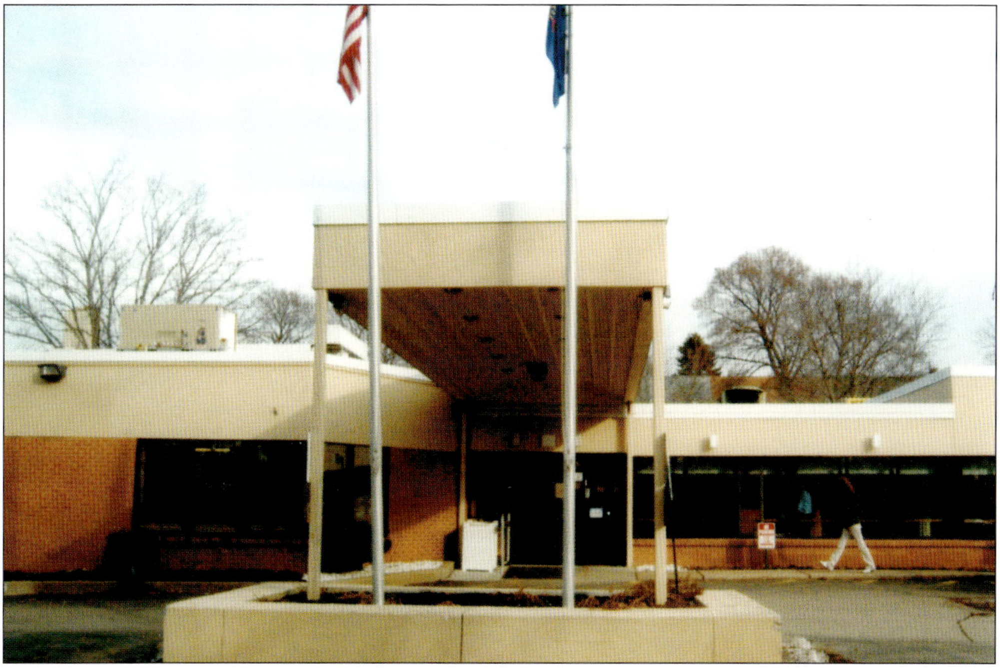

The Twinbrook Medical Center on Field Street in Lawrence Park has been providing needed services since 1984. It originally was known as Kalkhof Hospital when Tom Kalkhof built it in 1951. Its mission changed somewhat, and it then became the Twinbrook Nursing Home.

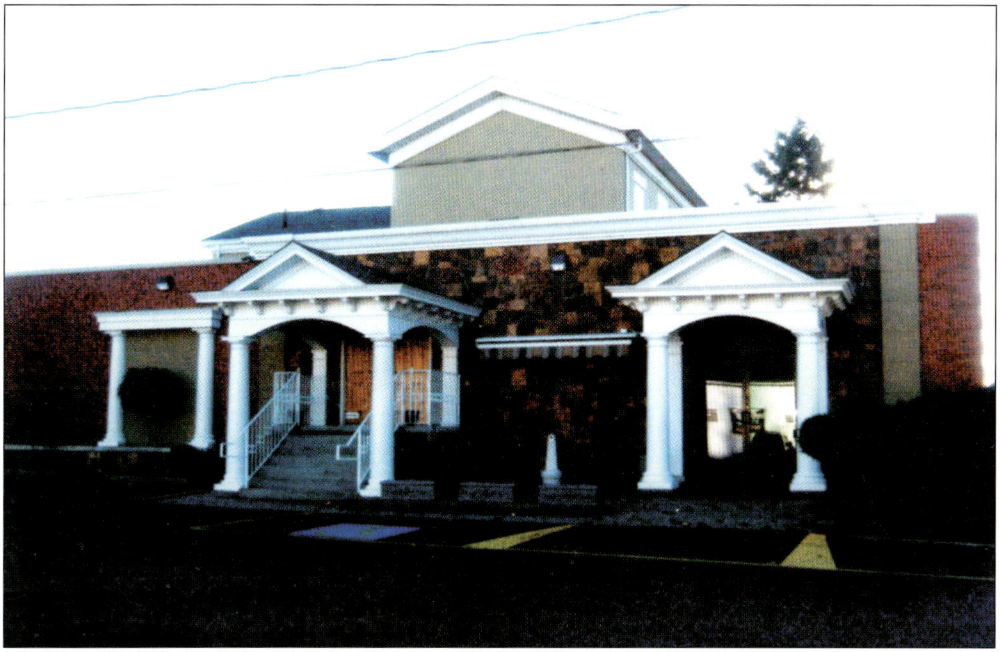

Although Dusckas Funeral Home is just outside the Wesleyville boundary, Gus Dusckas and presently his daughter Nancy have played vital roles in the communities of Wesleyville and Lawrence Park. Recently opened is the Dusckas-Taylor Funeral Home, a beautiful spacious establishment a few miles east of Wesleyville on Buffalo Road.

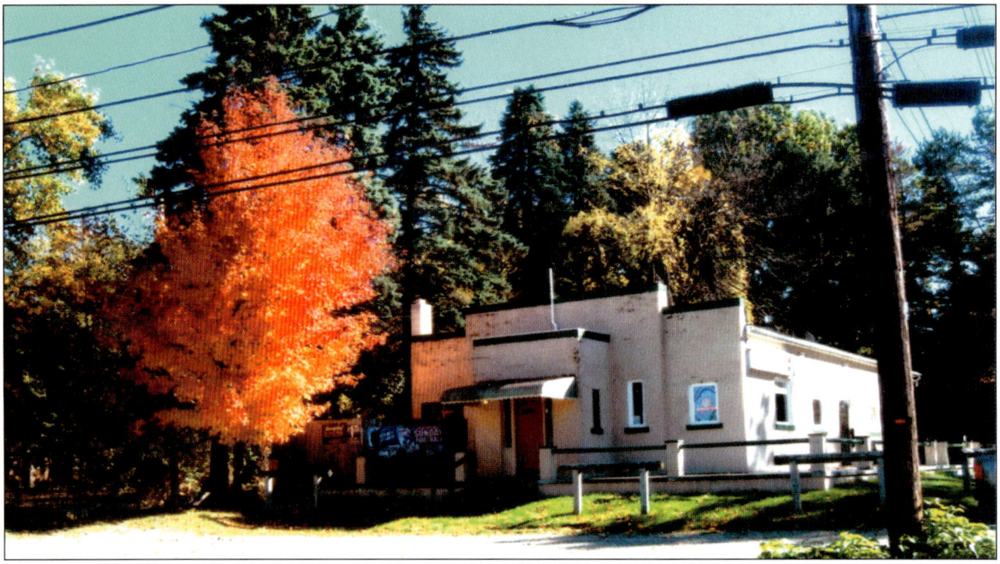

The Park Tavern on East Lake Road is a favorite "after the ball game" spot and for family dinners. The tavern has had several names but since Bob Leszek took over in 1978, it has been known as the Park Tavern. Chris Leszek, Bob's son, now manages the Park Tavern.

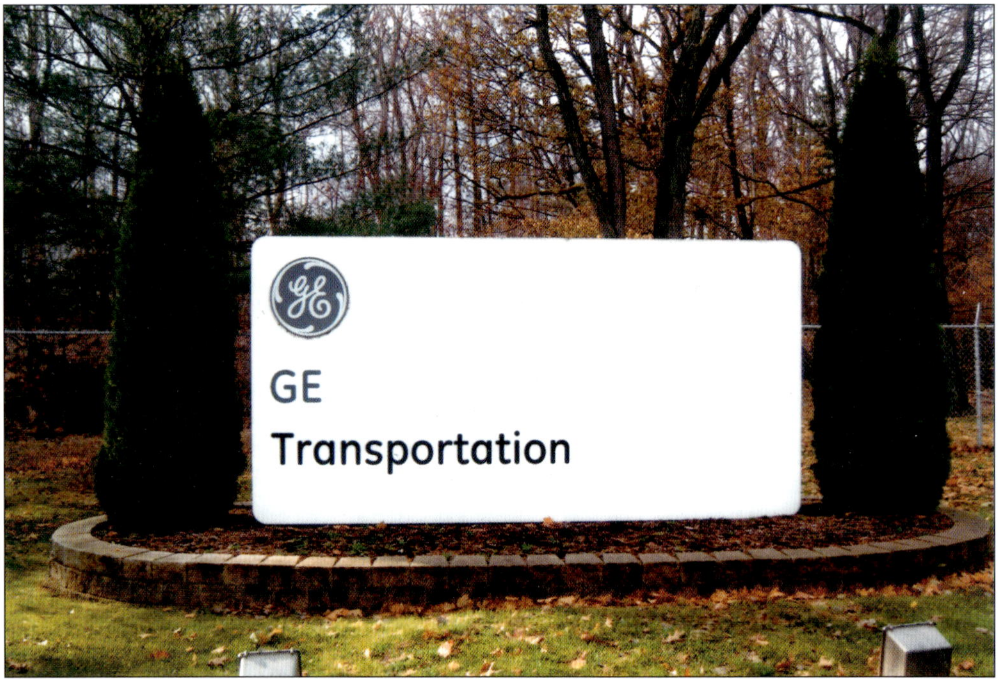

The General Electric Company was known as the Erie Works in the years that the plant manufactured refrigerators, DC motors, and locomotives. As the sign indicates, the Erie plant is now known as GE Transportation, which indicates its commitment to global transportation needs.

Five

Organizations and Events

The elements that create a vibrant community are its people and the organizations they support. Both Lawrence Park and Wesleyville are fortunate to have dedicated volunteer fire departments whose highly trained members respond to fire calls and emergencies. They also take part in events such as parades, Christmas celebrations, and Fourth of July fireworks. Safety is also the concern of police departments, with home-safety checks, bicycle safety, crime-watch efforts, crossing guards, and Safety Town. The East Lake and Lawrence Park Lions Club sponsors Safety Town and Christmas Tree Night. The Lawrence Park Rifle Club sponsors a hunter safety program for youth. Wesleyville Neighborhood Watch promotes safety and contributes to community events. The local churches are involved in many outreach efforts such as the food bank and "Eat Alone" diners. The Lawrence Park Recreation Board coordinates recreational activities, and in Wesleyville the Rotary Club contributes to the beautiful Christmas lights along Buffalo Road and many other activities. There are many organizations that bring together individuals that have common interests, including coin club, quilters guild, garden club, and Wesleyville Rotary.

Specific events mark milestones in the communities. A few of the many are the Wesleyville celebration of the bicentennial of the United States in 1976 with a parade, a quilt, a buried vault, and a Wesleyville history book. Also, there were happenings in Lawrence Park such as the Olympic torch passage in 1996, the dedication of the Harbor Park Bridge in 2003, and in 2011, the celebration of 100 years since the founding.

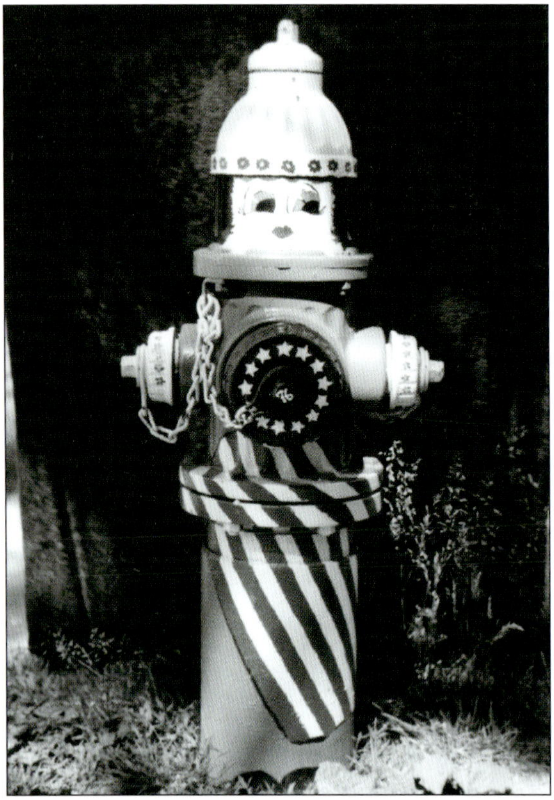

One of the unique ways Wesleyville celebrated the 1976 bicentennial was by holding a fire plug–painting contest. *Betsy Ross* was painted by the Norma and Russell Johnson family with the help of Rusty, Jack, and Barbara. Other families painted equally clever motifs on fireplugs. A centennial booklet that outlined the history of Wesleyville from 1795 to 1976 was produced by Richard Cheney, Wesley Gray, and Maurice Kolpien. (Courtesy of the Lawrence Park Historical Society.)

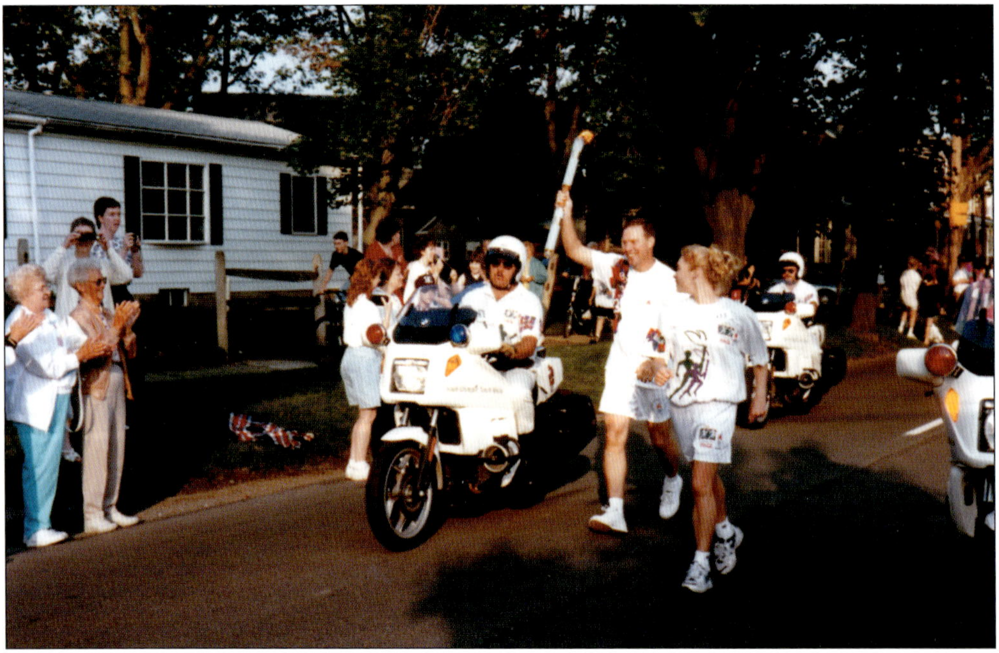

It was a thrill to have the Olympic torch pass through Lawrence Park on June 11, 1996. Attorney Robert G. Dwyer was the torchbearer who carried the torch as it traveled down Iroquois Avenue to the applause of bystanders. (Courtesy of the Lawrence Park Historical Society.)

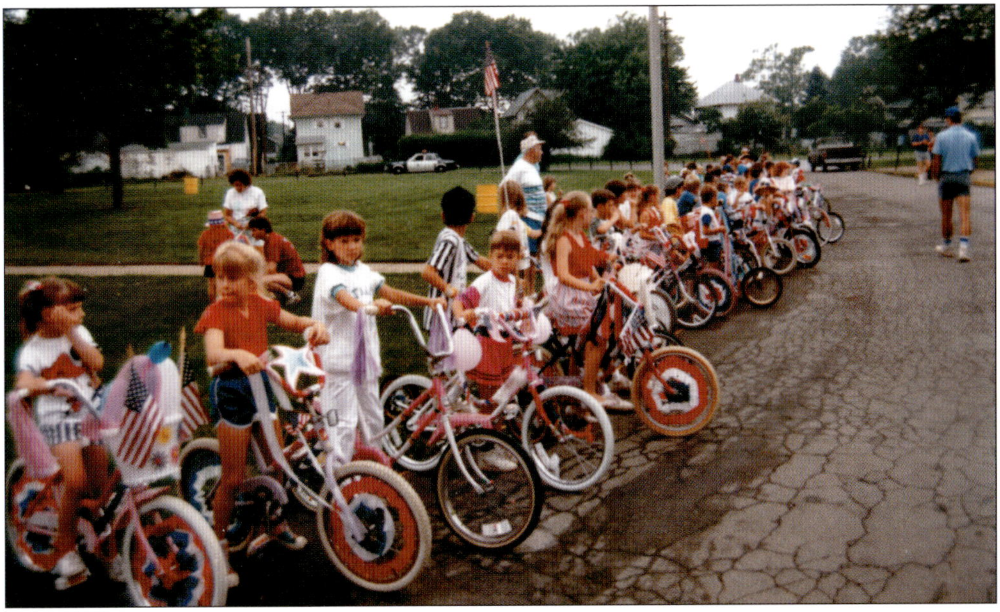

An event that precedes the Fourth of July parade in Lawrence Park is the bicycle parade. Youngsters spend hours decorating their bikes so that they can parade down Main Street in the morning before the big parade begins. (Courtesy of the Lawrence Park Historical Society.)

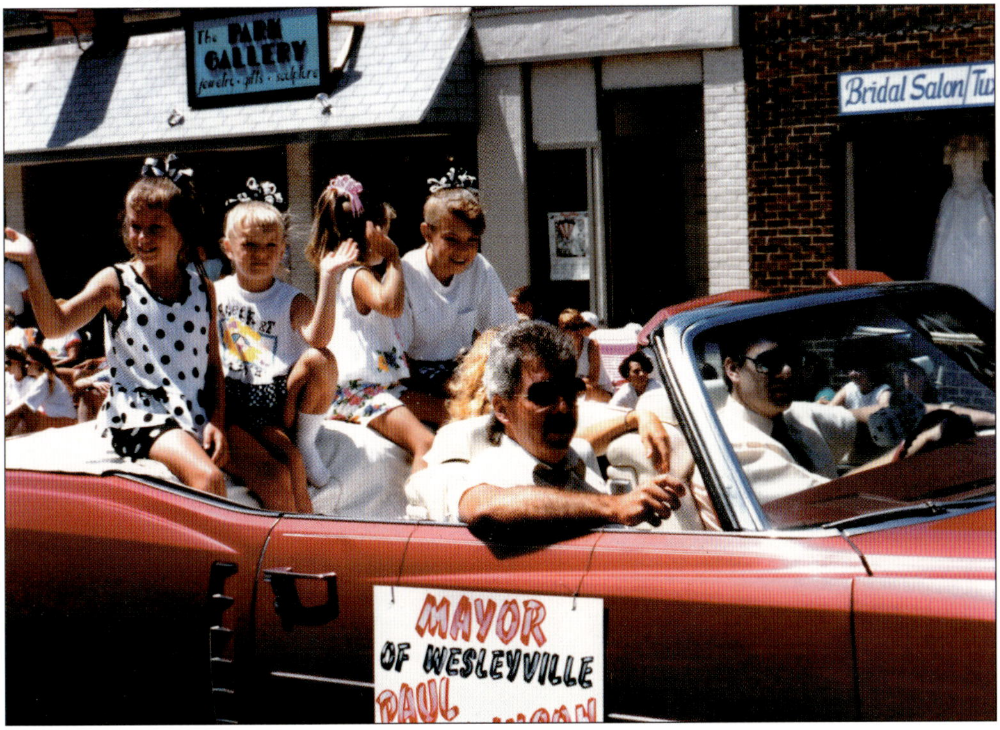

At a Lawrence Park Fourth of July parade in the 1990s, Wesleyville mayor Paul Johnson, who served as mayor from 1991 to 2013, joins in the festivities. The Iroquois Band, marching units, and fire trucks delight the crowd, and the children scramble to scoop up the wrapped candies thrown by the marchers. (Courtesy of the Lawrence Park Historical Society.)

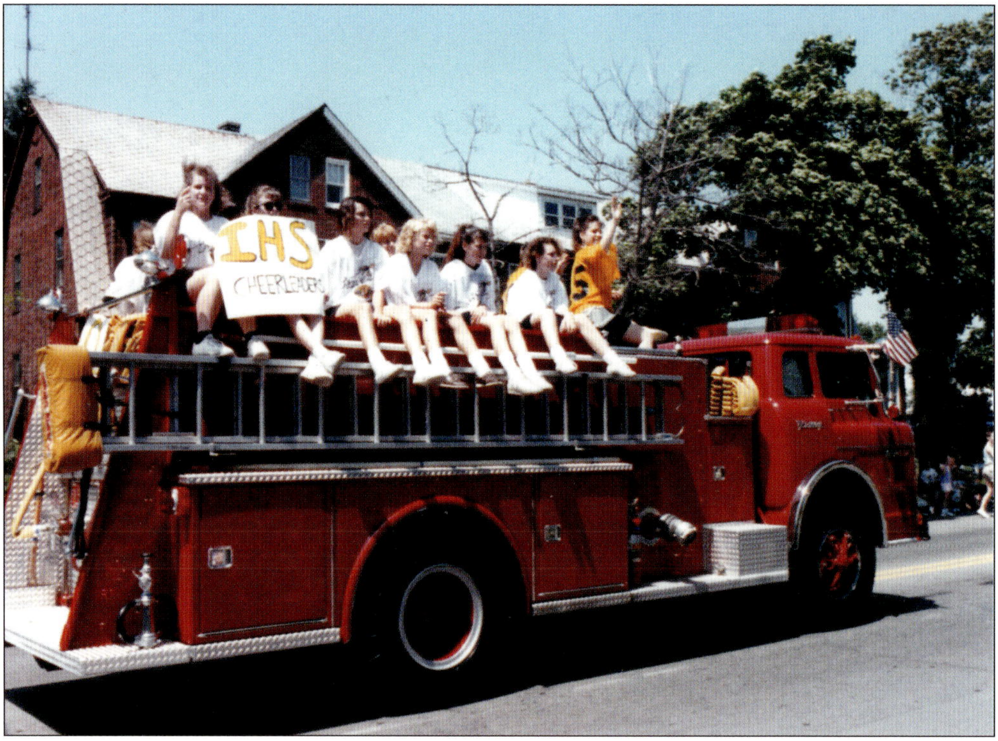

The Iroquois cheerleaders add to the festivities of the Fourth of July parade. Residents and visitors enjoy the daytime activities and look forward to the nighttime fireworks. In 2014, Lawrence Park was the only community in this corner of Pennsylvania to have fireworks. (Courtesy of the Lawrence Park Historical Society.)

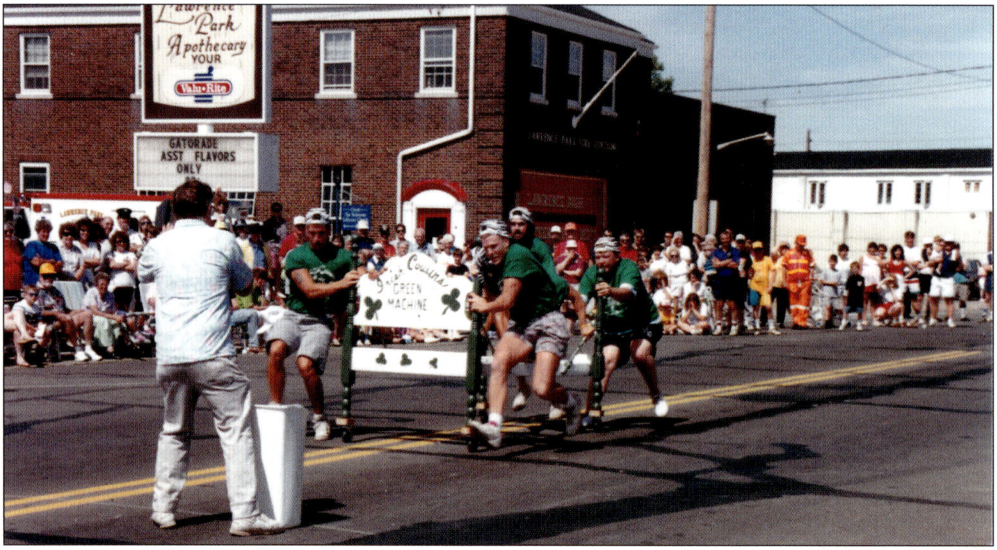

In 1990, a bed race was held to add to the humor of the Fourth of July activities. Teams competed as they raced down Main Street to the delight of the crowd. For several years, the football team participated as a "lawn mower brigade" that performed maneuvers with lawn mowers under the direction of coach Mike Mischler. (Courtesy of the Lawrence Park Historical Society.)

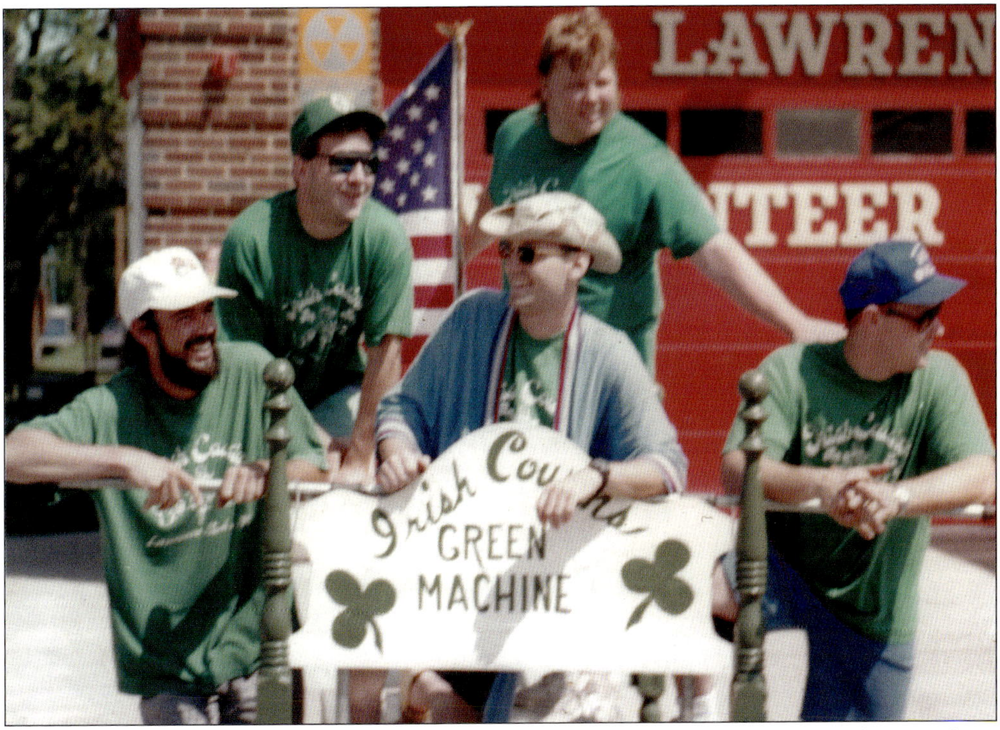

The crew of the Irish Cousin's Green Machine bed race are taking a well-deserved rest in front of the Lawrence Park Fire Hall. The crew is unidentified except for Eric Wingrove (class of 1984), who is at the top of the pyramid. (Courtesy of the Lawrence Park Historical Society.)

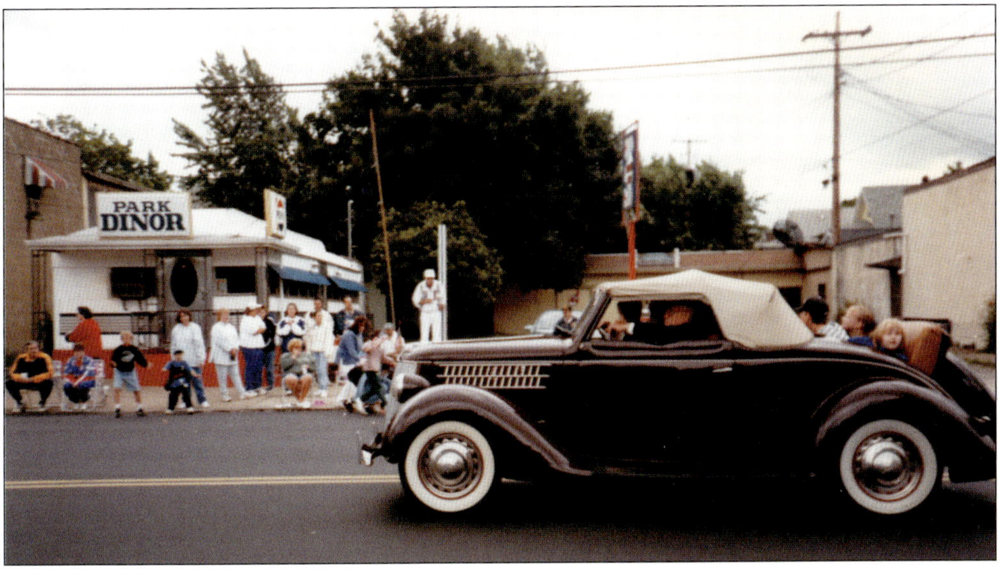

Ted Mohnkern drove his pride and joy, a 1936 Ford, in the Fourth of July parade in 1997. Mohnkern's twin grandchildren Mark and Amanda Medwid are enjoying their ride in the rumble seat. Mohnkern was a Lawrence Park commissioner for 16 years. Antique cars are always part of the parade on the Fourth of July. (Courtesy of the Lawrence Park Historical Society.)

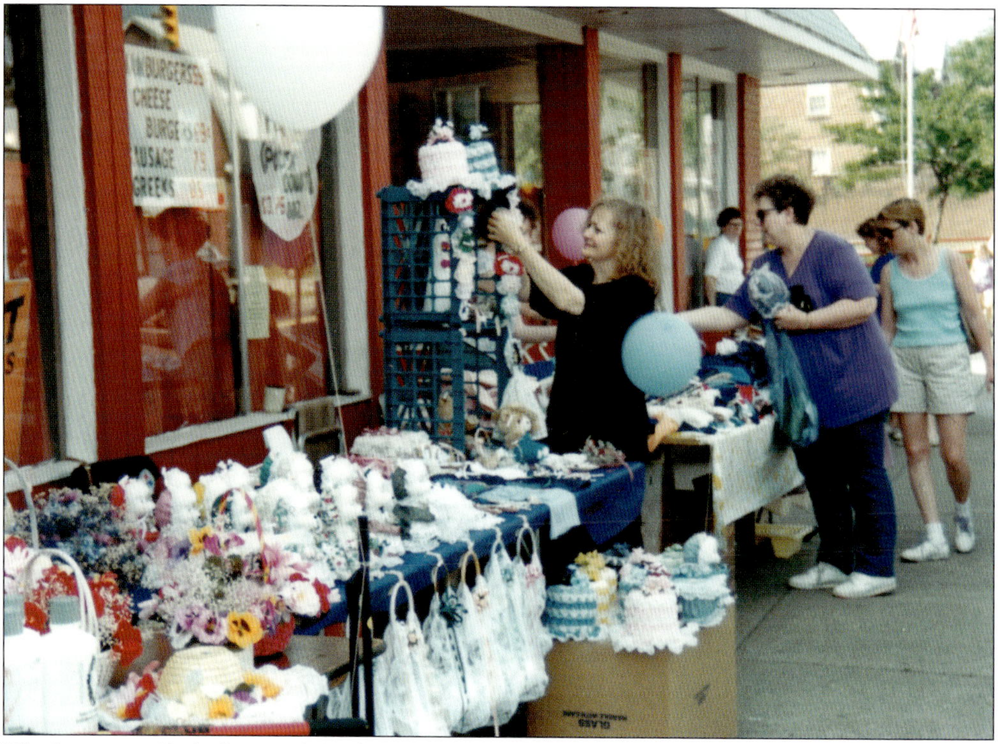

The Lawrence Park Arts and Crafts Festivals brought forth the talents of many area residents. It was fun to browse for unique treasures on Main Street. Donna Knight, with the help of Lee and Tom Sanner, organized these events from 1975 to 1995. (Courtesy of the Lawrence Park Historical Society.)

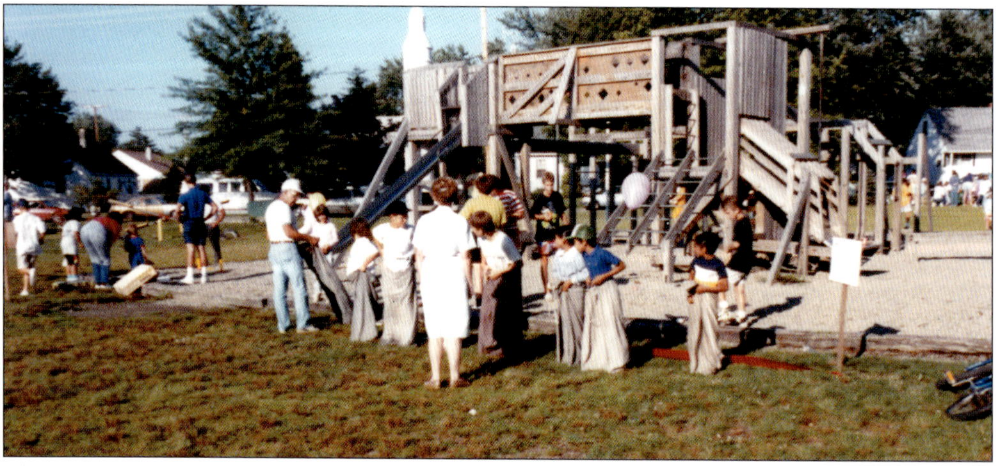

The 1990 Lawrence Park Days included an old-fashioned sack race for youngsters. Contestants were lined up in front of the wooden jungle gym at Barringer Playground at Morse Street and Tyndall Avenue. Colorful balloons and plenty of good snacks were part of the fun. (Courtesy of the Lawrence Park Historical Society.)

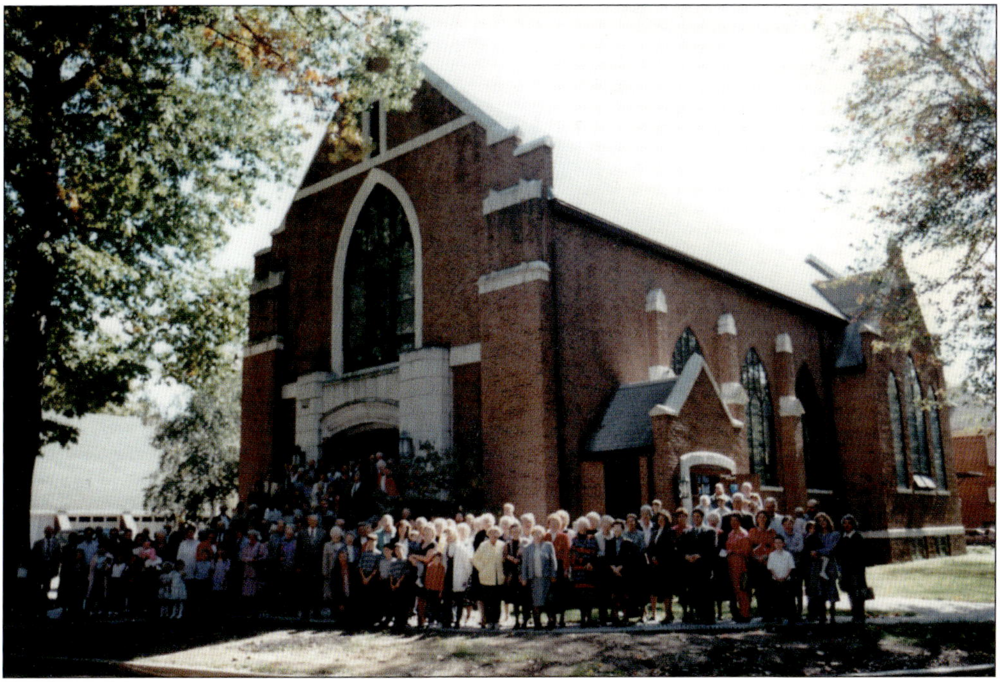

On November 24, 1996, the Lawrence Park United Methodist Church congregation gathered to celebrate its 75th anniversary. The sanctuary was built in 1921, and an addition, Welker Hall, was constructed in 1958. Welker Hall was named in honor of Georgiana Welker, the founder of the Lawrence Park church. (Courtesy of the Lawrence Park United Methodist Church.)

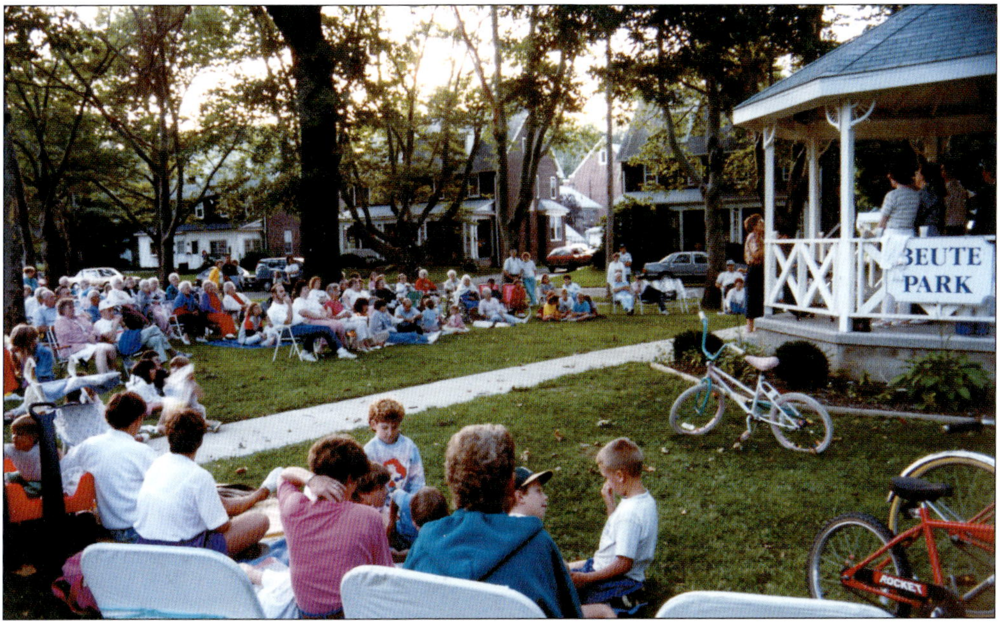

The gazebo in Beute Park makes an ideal bandstand for summer concerts. Various bands play every few weeks for the enjoyment of the community. The order of the day is to bring lawn chairs and blankets for an evening of musical entertainment. (Courtesy of the Lawrence Park Historical Society.)

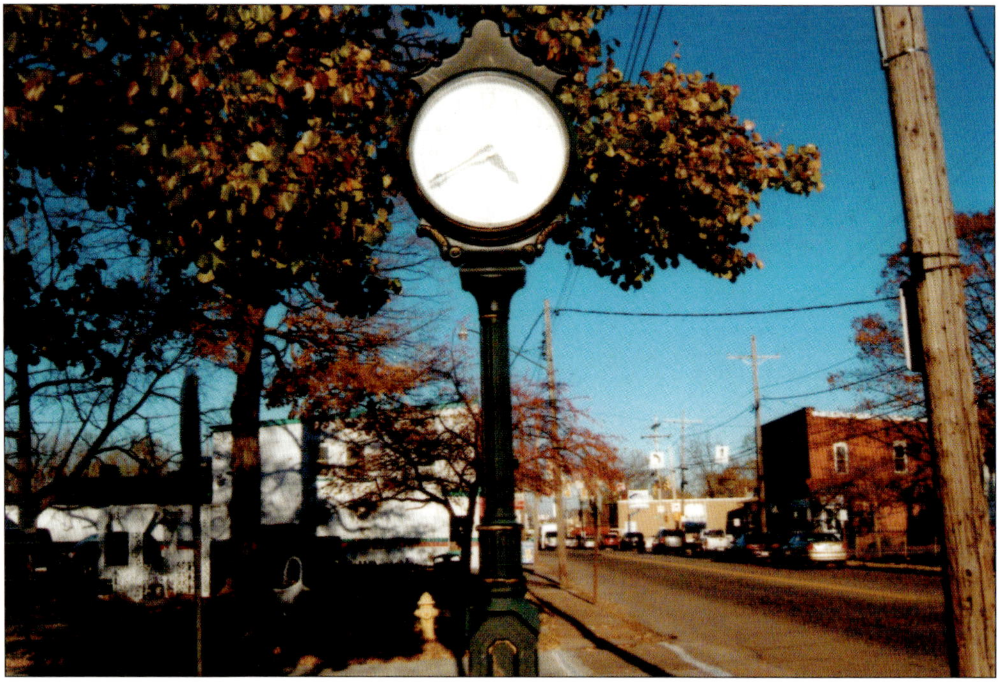

On May 25, 2002, the new gazebo and clock were installed in the C.J. "Gus" Dusckas Park in Wesleyville, at the corner of Market Street and Buffalo Road. The rededication ceremony was attended by county and borough officials who paid tribute to the giving and unselfish life of Gus, who was a friend to all.

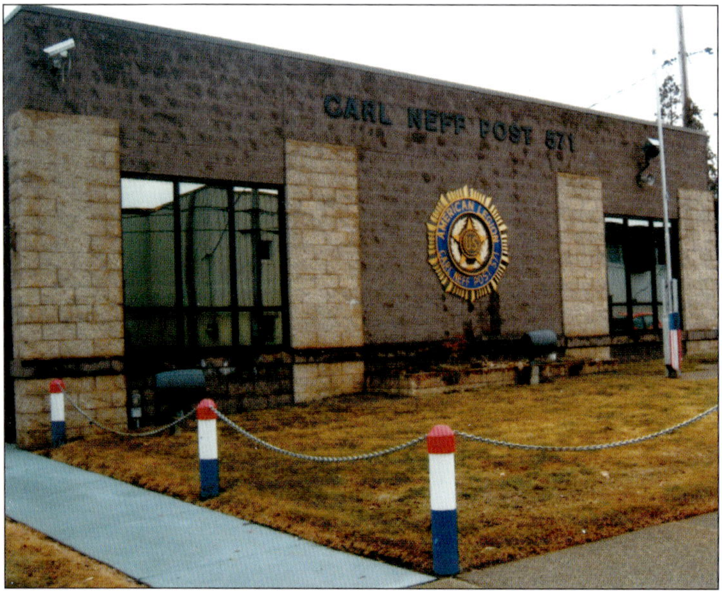

The Carl Neff Post 571 American Legion seen here at the new location at 1917 Eastern Avenue has had a long history in this area. In 1935, it was located in Lawrence Park. In 1952, they had a grand opening in the old brick hotel in Wesleyville on the corner of Buffalo Road and Wesley Avenue. How appropriate it is now to have it located across from the Wesleyville Veterans Memorial Park.

In 1999, some 38 members of the Iroquois Senior High Chorus and the Iroquois Show Choir, under the direction of Roberta Stoughton, were invited to participate in America Sings in Washington, DC. They joined 9,000 students from 175 schools to sing in the shadow of the Washington Monument. (Courtesy of Roberta Stoughton.)

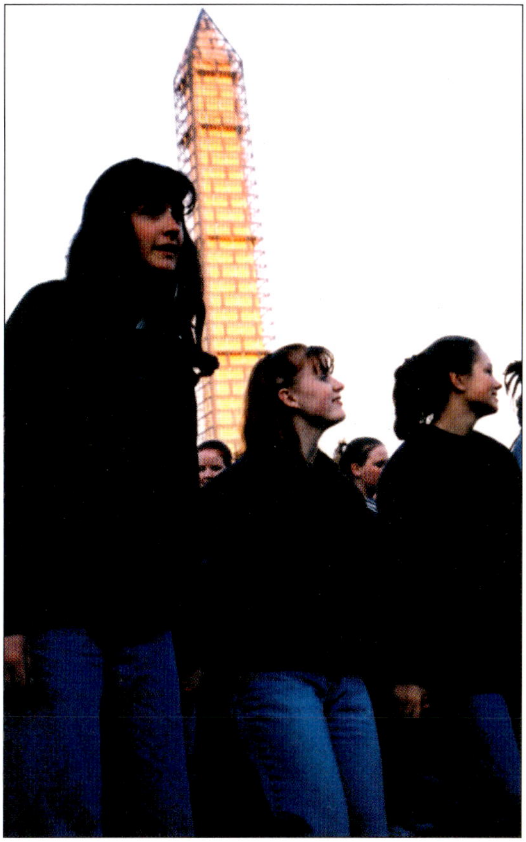

On January 2, 2002, the Olympic torch briefly passed through Erie on its way to Salt Lake City, Utah. The Iroquois Show Choir, under the direction of Roberta Stoughton, participated in the celebration at Perry Square on a cold winter's day. (Courtesy of Roberta Stoughton.)

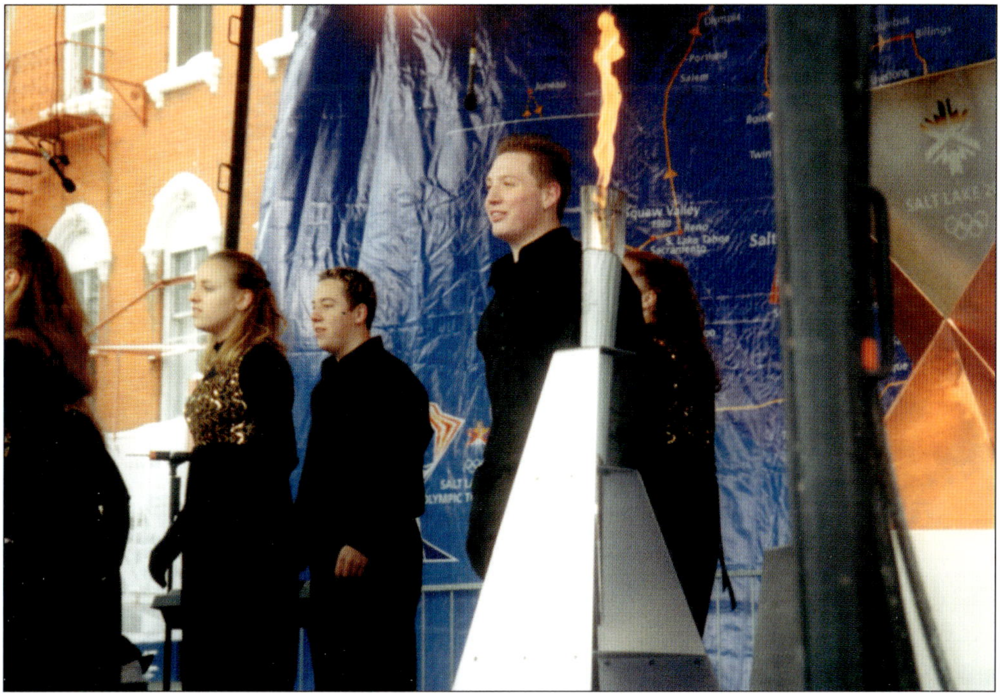

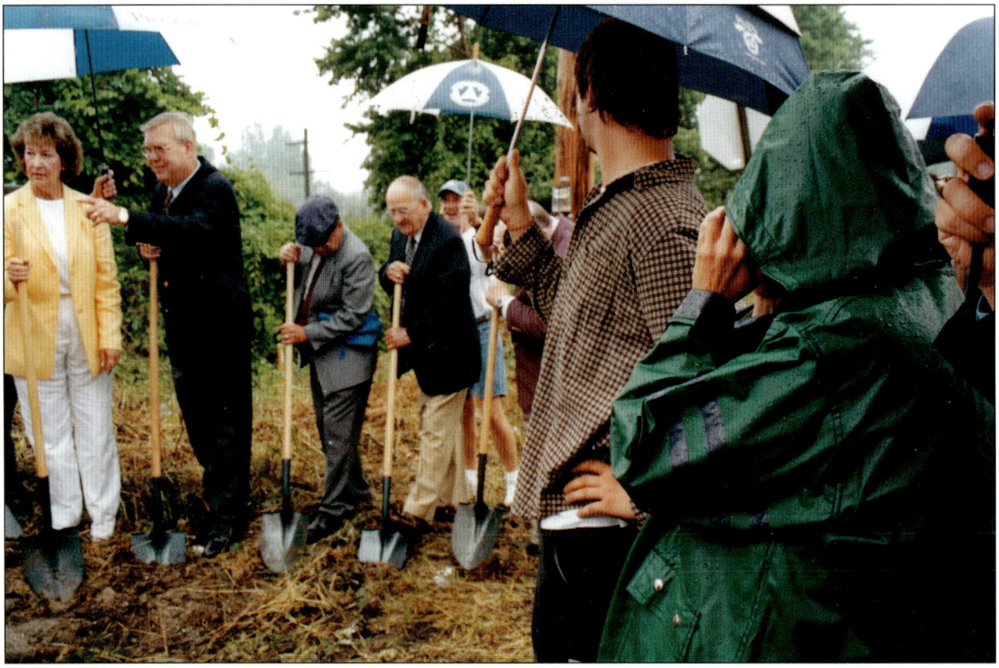

The ground-breaking for the Harbor Park Bridge took place on a rainy day, July 2, 2002, but that did not dampen the spirits of officials from Lawrence Park and Harborcreek as the long-awaited bridge would finally become a reality. The Nagle Road crossing had been closed since 1957. (Courtesy of Art Bennett.)

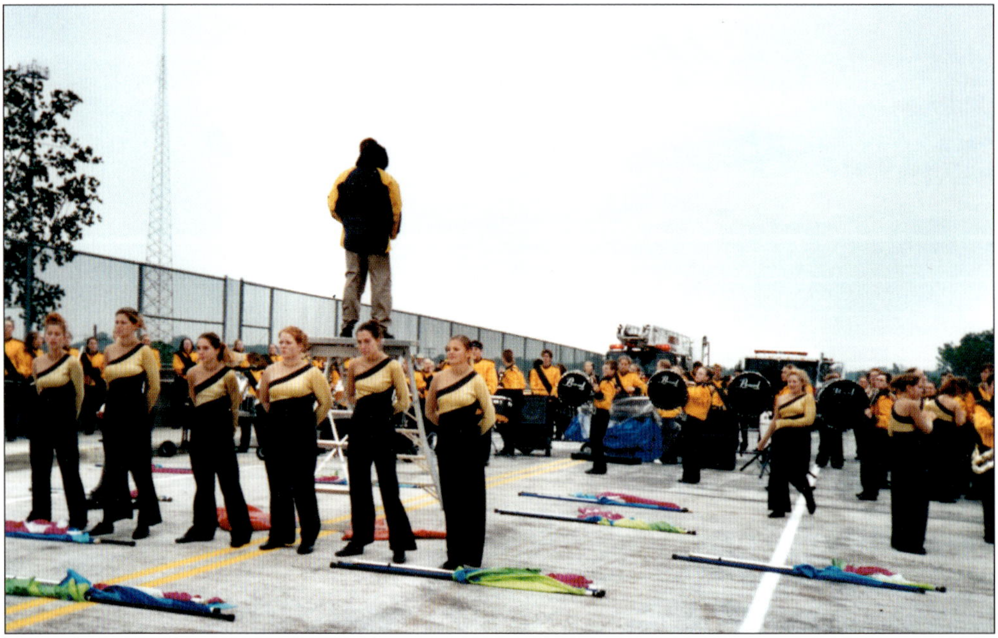

The dedication of the Nagle Road bridge was on September 22, 2003. This bridge carries Nagle Road over four sets of tracks and connects Iroquois Avenue and Buffalo Road. Bands and flags from Iroquois High School and Harborcreek High School took part in the ceremony. This photograph shows the group from Iroquois High School. (Courtesy of F. Catherine.)

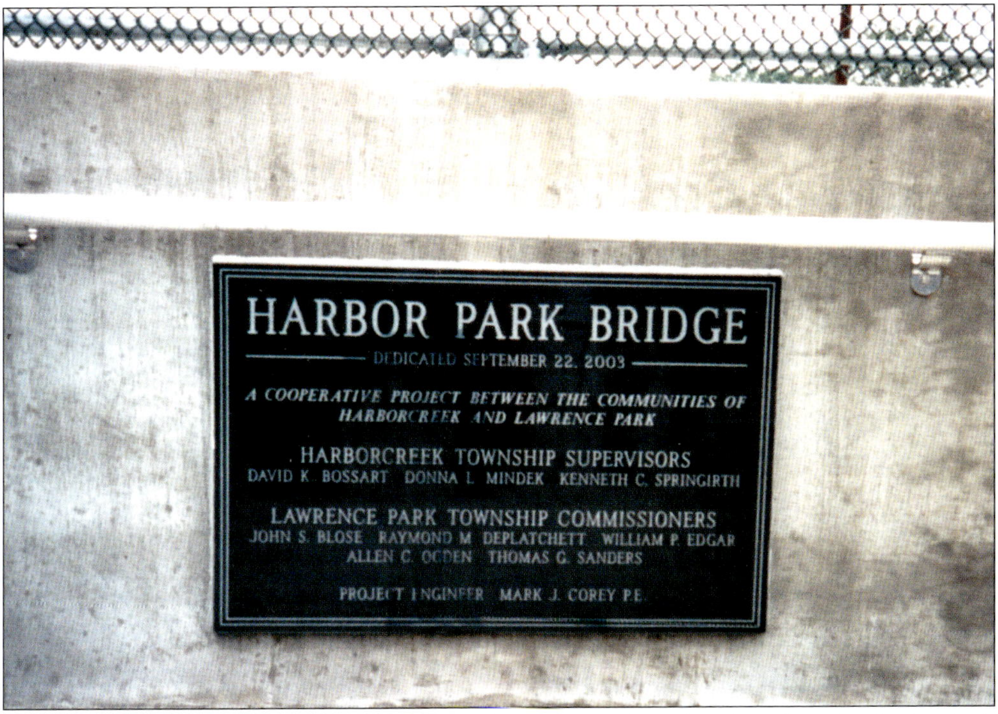

The official name of the bridge that carries Nagle Road over the railroad tracks is the Harbor Park Bridge, "a cooperative project between the communities of Harborcreek and Lawrence Park." Since the opening of the bridge, a spirited preseason football game has been played between Iroquois School and Harborcreek School called the "Battle of the Bridge." (Courtesy of the Lawrence Park Historical Society.)

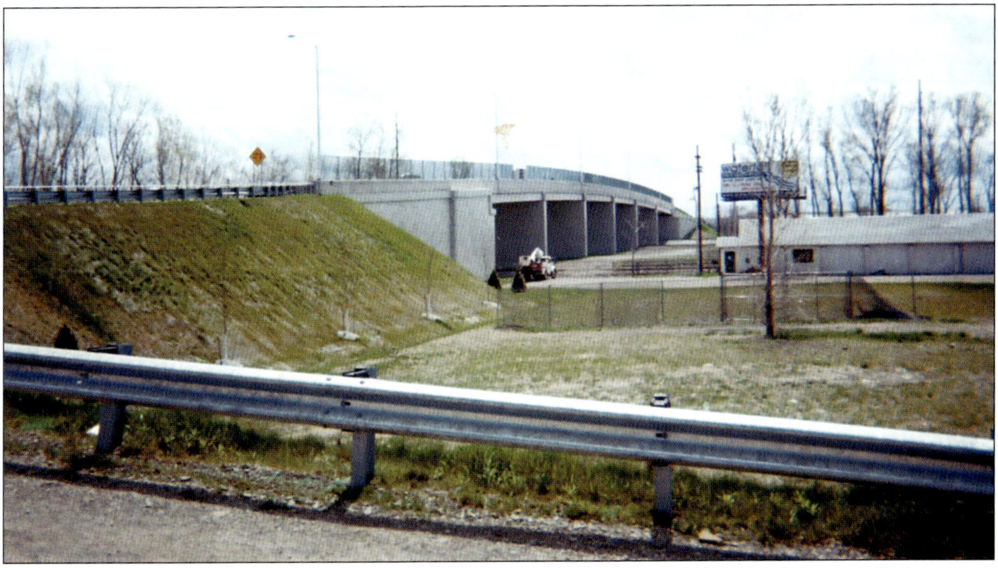

The new Lawrence Park Rifle Clubhouse is located on the west side of the new Harbor Park Bridge. The rifle club has a long history in Lawrence Park, having moved to several different locations. The rifle club provides hunter safety courses for youth. (Courtesy of the Lawrence Park Historical Society.)

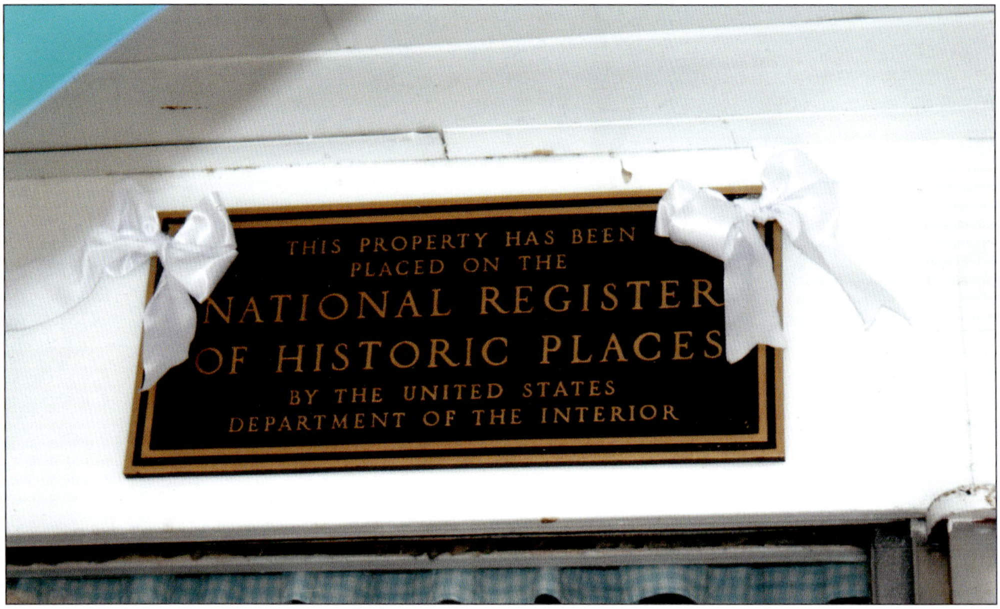

The sign indicating "This property has been placed on the National Register of Historic Places by the United States Department of the Interior" is a source of pride to a community. The honor was obtained by members of the Lawrence Park Historical Society for the Park Dinor. (Courtesy of Art Bennett.)

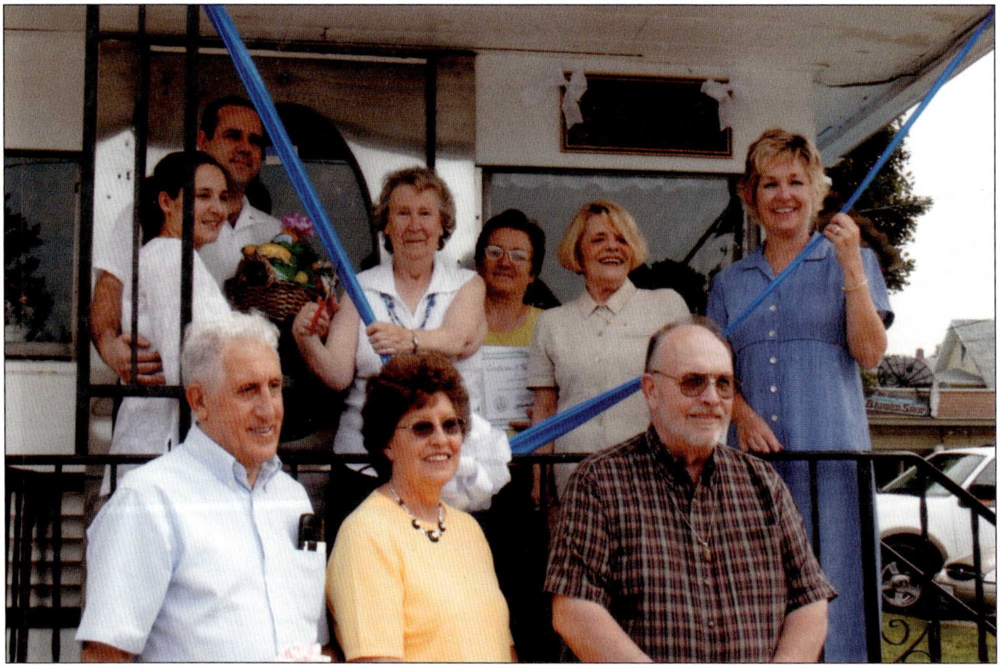

The Park Dinor in Lawrence Park in August 2004 received the honor of being listed in the National Register of Historic Places. Helping to celebrate this event are, from left to right, (first row) Mr. and Mrs. DeAngelo (sign maker) and Tom Sanders; (second row) George Gourlias and his wife, Virginia Andersen; George Gourlias's mother-in-law, Linda Bebko Jones; Jane Earll; and two unidentified. (Courtesy of Art Bennett.)

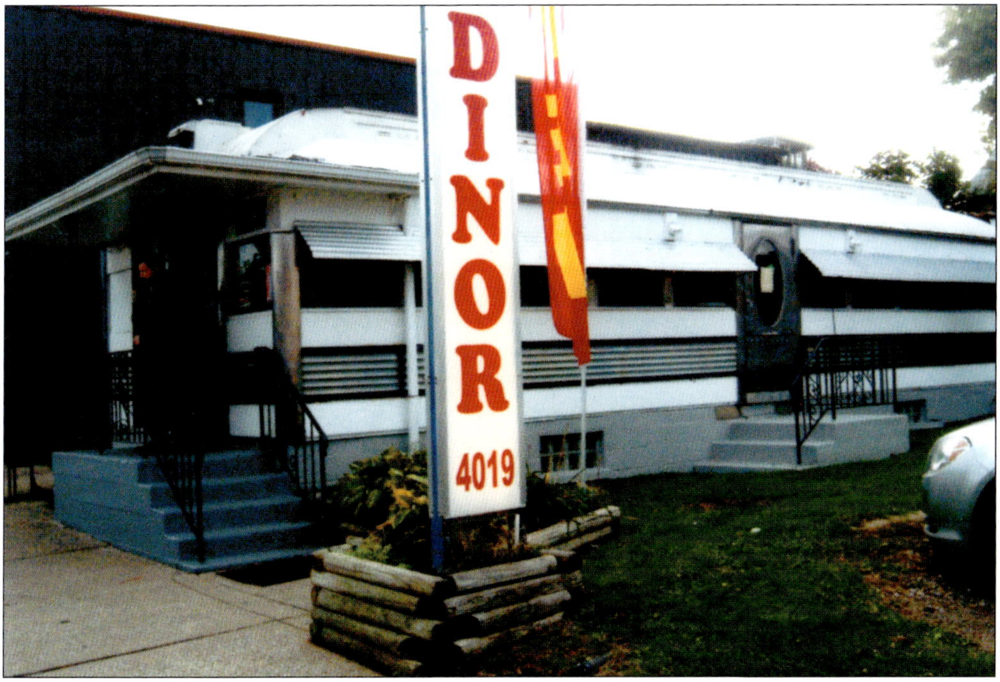

The Park Dinor has been a landmark in Lawrence Park since its beginning in 1949 when Harold Curtis was the owner. Other owners were Dorothy and Charles Spiegel and George Gourlias, who owned the dinor from 1991 to 2009. Presently, Becky and Rick Standley and their friendly staff create delicious food and a down-home atmosphere in this popular diner.

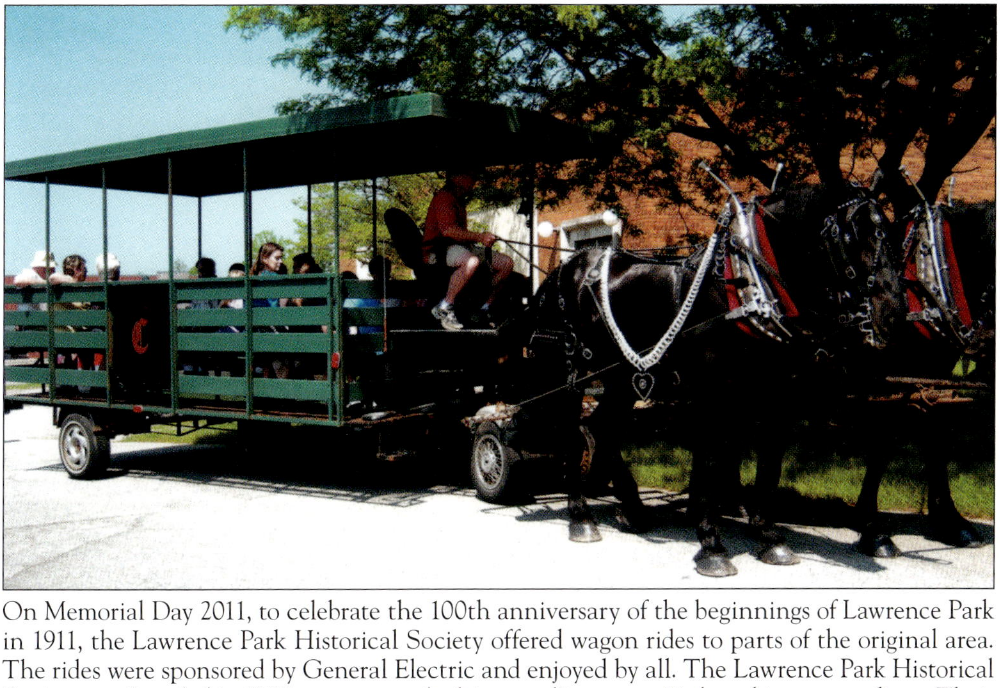

On Memorial Day 2011, to celebrate the 100th anniversary of the beginnings of Lawrence Park in 1911, the Lawrence Park Historical Society offered wagon rides to parts of the original area. The rides were sponsored by General Electric and enjoyed by all. The Lawrence Park Historical Society was founded in 1979 to preserve the history of Lawrence Park and its surroundings. Their offices are in the Lawrence Park Community Center.

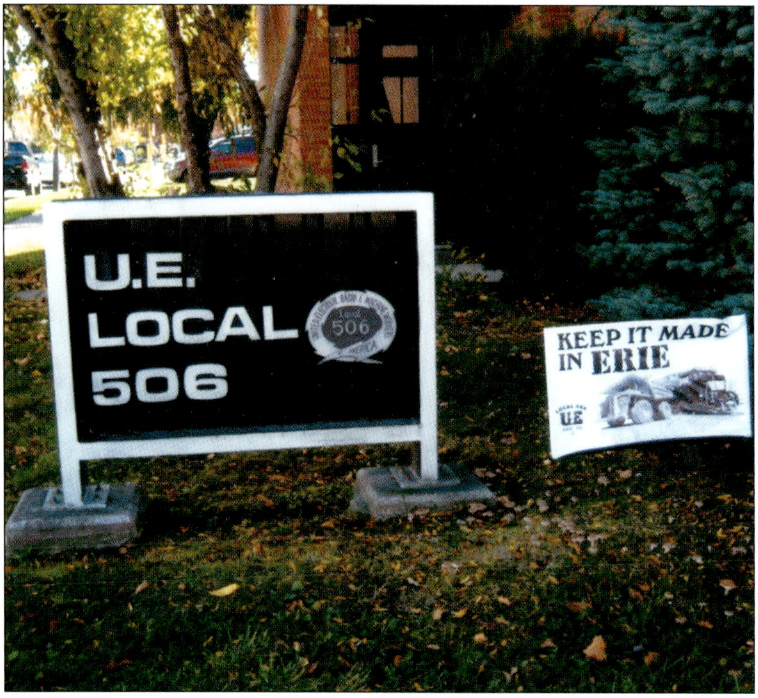

The headquarters of UE Local 506 has been in Lawrence Park since its founding, when the offices were located in the Lawrence, a hotel on the corner of Main Street and Rankine Avenue. The UE later remodeled the building. Youth from Lawrence Park and Wesleyville have fond memories of meeting on the steps of the UE hall. More recently, the UE has constructed a new building at the same location.

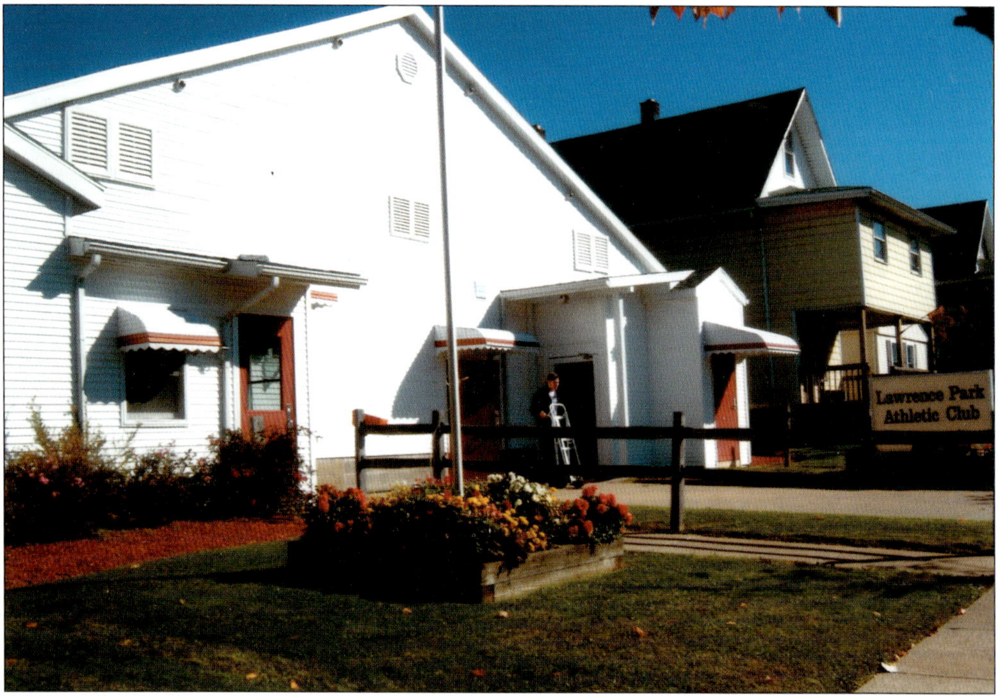

The Lawrence Park Athletic Club on Rankine Avenue was organized in 1945 and chartered to support community projects. In addition to being a local gathering place, LPAC has given generously to community events, fire and police departments, and in 1990 to the lighting fund for the Iroquois football field. It also provides scholarships for students.

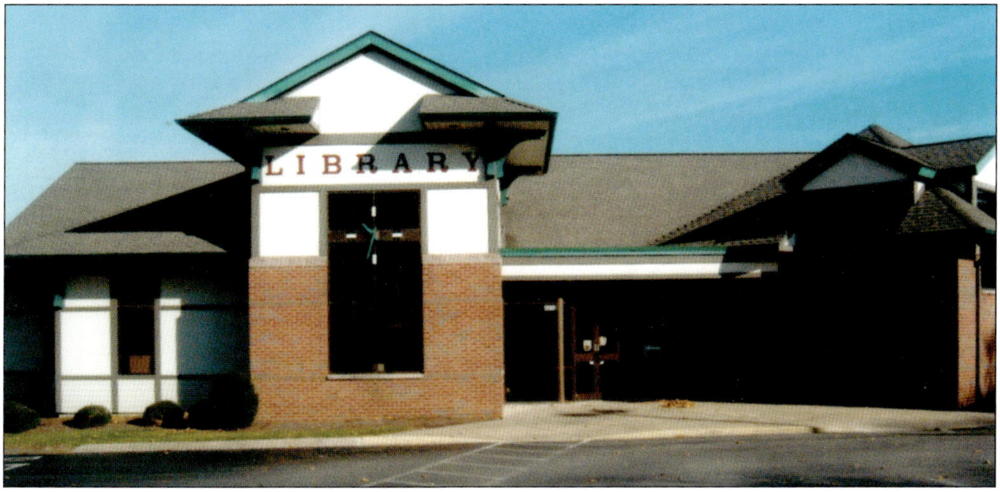

The Iroquois Avenue County Library serves the needs of residents in the eastern part of Erie County. The new library was constructed in 2002 on the same site as the old library, which since 1967 was located in the structure that had been the Lawrence Park Industrial Arts building. Jessie Schilken served as librarian for many years.

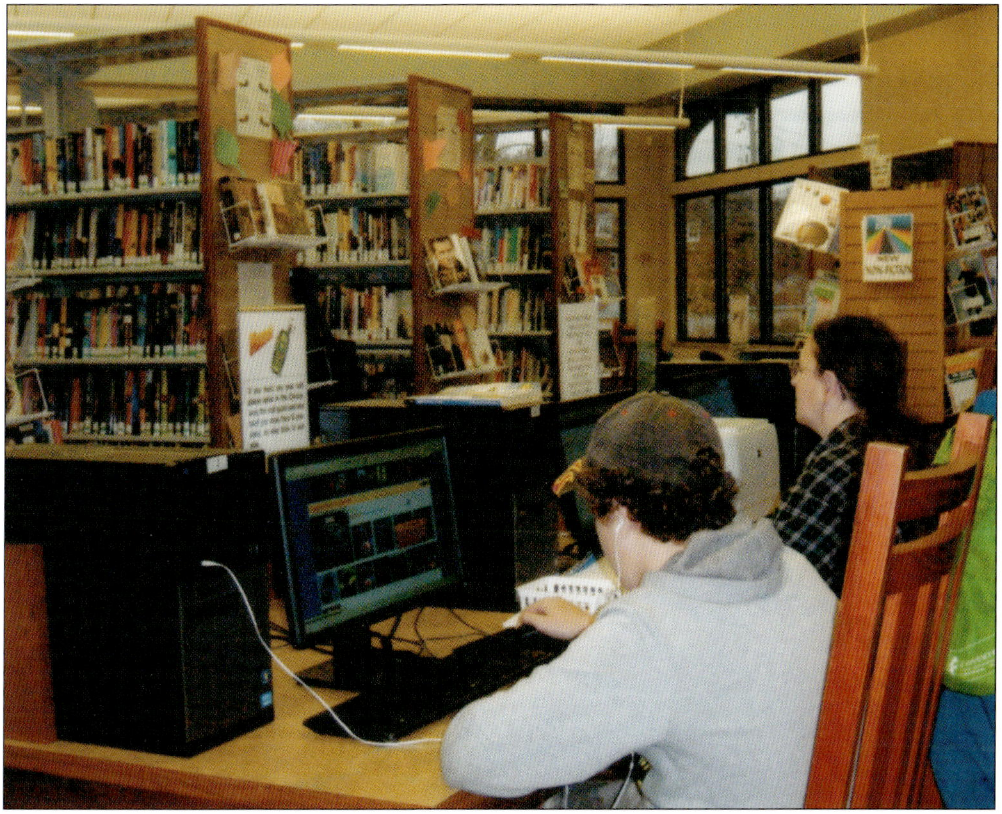

Today, libraries are much more that just books, as evidenced by the row of computers that are constantly in use by students and community members. The Iroquois Avenue County Library also includes a children's room where story time is held every week. Various interesting local collections can be viewed in the display case.

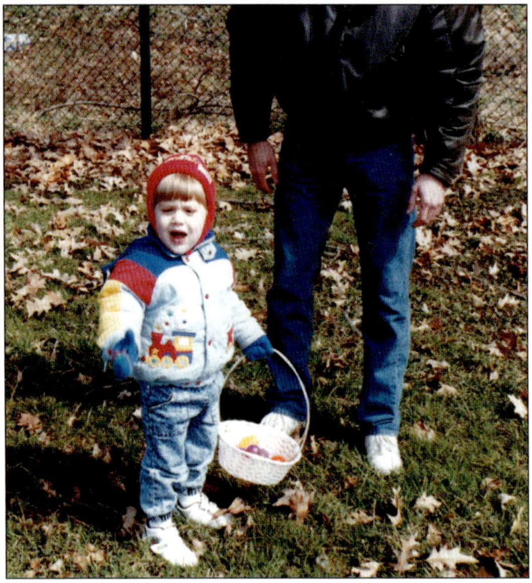

For many years, youngsters in Lawrence Park have looked forward to an Easter egg hunt on the Saturday before Easter. It is sponsored by the East Lake Shore Lions Club, an organization that is also involved in Safety Town, Christmas Tree Night, Save an Eye football game, and White Cane days. The Lions Club also provides eye care for students. (Courtesy of the Lawrence Park Historical Society.)

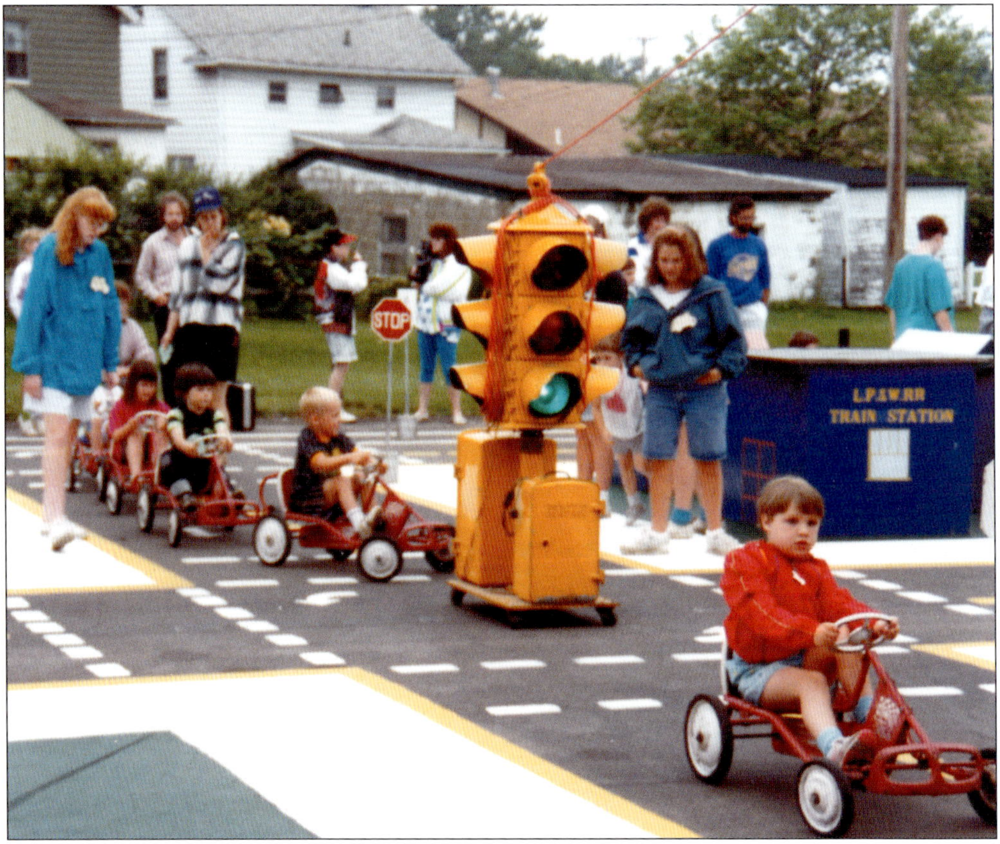

Safety Town is a program sponsored by the Lions Club to teach youngsters who are about to enter kindergarten how to safely cross streets and the meaning of traffic lights. The cars in this 1990 photograph have been updated and the course moved to the new Iroquois Elementary School parking lot. (Courtesy of the Lawrence Park Historical Society.)

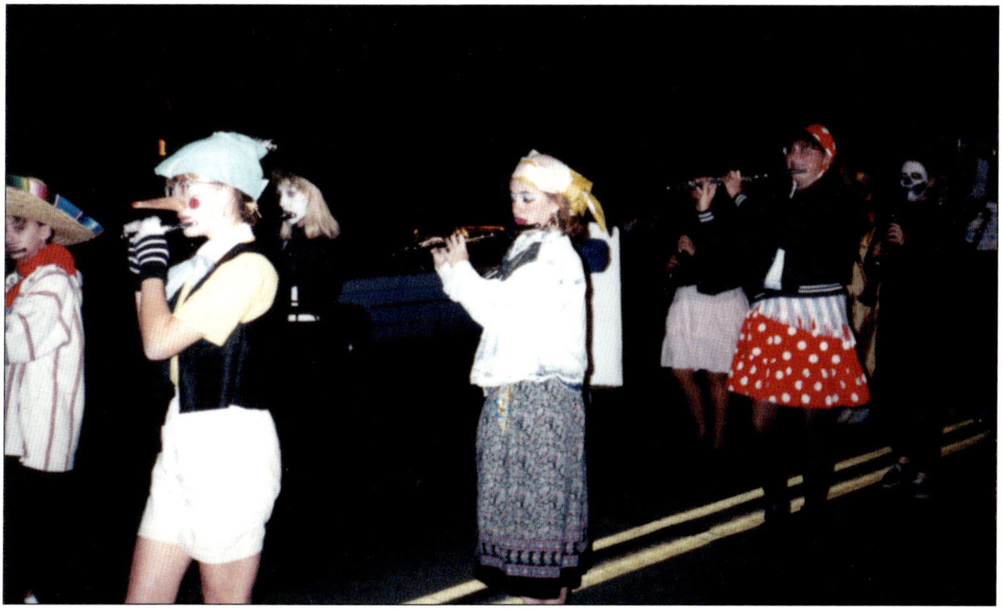

The Iroquois Band, dressed in costumes, leads the Halloween parade. This festive time precedes trick-or-treat night when youngsters go door to door with their sacks to be filled with goodies. The streets are patrolled by fire trucks and police cars. (Courtesy of the Lawrence Park Historical Society.)

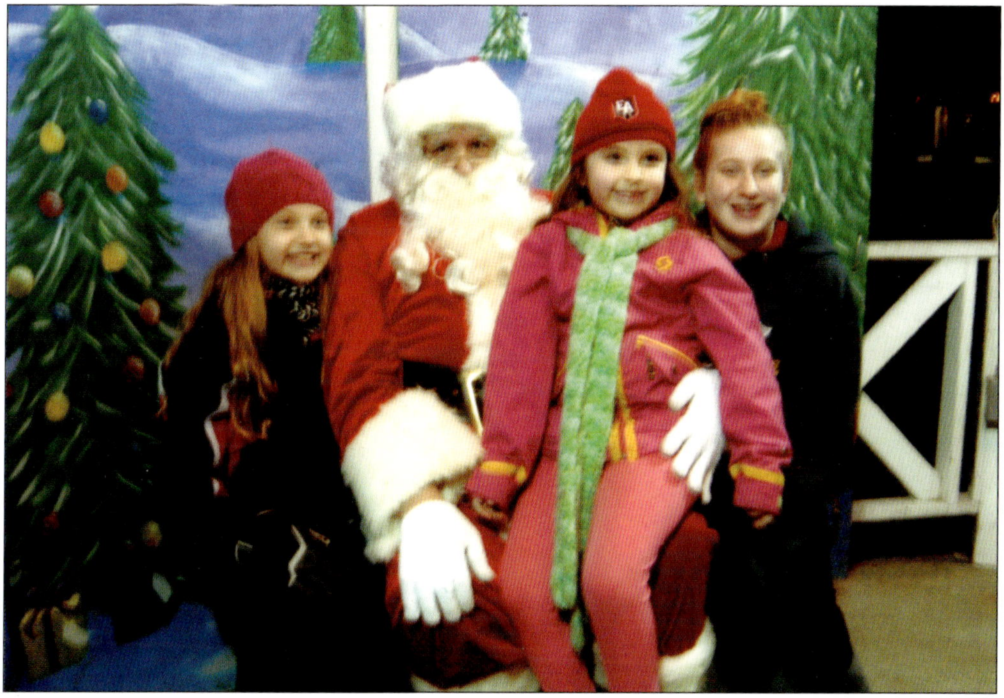

There is excitement in the air when on Christmas Tree Night, children and their parents listen for the fire truck that will bring Santa with his bag of goodies to the gazebo in Beute Park. This event is held two nights before Christmas and is sponsored by the Lions Club and the fire department. Smiles like the ones on the faces of the Schnars girls are repeated many times, as children take this opportunity to tell Santa their wish list.